INCARNATION IN HINDUISM AND CHRISTIANITY

Incarnation in Hinduism and Christianity

The Myth of the God-Man

Daniel E. Bassuk

Head Librarian, Gardner A. Sage Library
New Brunswick Theological Seminary, New Brunswick,
New Jersey

Foreword by
Robert S. Ellwood

Bishop James W. Bashford, Professor of Oriental Studies
University of Southern California

HUMANITIES PRESS INTERNATIONAL, INC.
ATLANTIC HIGHLANDS, NJ

First published in 1987 in the United States of America by
HUMANITIES PRESS INTERNATIONAL, INC., Atlantic Highlands, NJ 07716

Library of Congress Cataloging-in-Publication Data
Bassuk, Daniel E., 1938–
Incarnation in Hinduism and Christianity.
Bibliography: p.
Includes index.
1. Incarnation—Comparative studies. 2. Avatars—
Comparative studies. 3. Christianity and other
religions—Hinduism. 4. Hinduism—Relations—
Christianity. I. Title.
BL510.B37 1987   291.2'13   86–10475
ISBN 0–391–03452–9

PRINTED IN HONG KONG

This book is dedicated to my loving parents, the faculty and students of the University of South Florida, and those British theologians and scholars who participated in 'The Myth of God Incarnate' debate.

Contents

Contents

Foreword

God walking the earth among men and women . . . the Divine in human form, teaching us the highest things through human words on human lips, showering us with blessings from Eternity mediated through human hands.

That this has occurred, once or many times, is even happening today, has been the dream, or rather deeply-felt belief, of countless millions since before the dawn of history. Avatars (descents) of a god in the sacred Sanskrit tongue of India, an Incarnation in the language of Western theology, men who are really God incognito, though recognized by those of unsullied faith, are figures of pivotal importance in the history of religion.

The doctrine of avatar and incarnation may, humanly speaking, have ultimate roots in the paleolithic shaman in divine-possession trance, giving human voice to the gods. But its classic expression seems to be rooted in what the philosopher Karl Jaspers has called the Axial Age. This flexibly-defined era of several centuries beginning around the 6th century BCE marks the crucial transition of the human way of being in the world from the prehistoric or that of the archaic agricultural empires to a fresh way in which the individual human, and awareness of human history, comes into focus. It is a time of gradual, and of course uneven and only half-conscious, movement in many parts of the world from submersion of the individual in society and its stereotyped roles, whether of king, hero, priest, or peasant, and of society into the ahistorical cycles of the cosmos, to a time characterized by the emergence of individual thinkers with distinct personalities and distinct ideas bearing the stamp of originality. It was close upon each other's heels, around the sixth century BCE, that there appeared in China Confucius and Lao-tzu, in India the Buddha and Mahavira, in Iran Zoroaster, in Judaea Isaiah and Jeremiah (a little earlier, for the ancient Israelites were in the forefront of the change), in Greece a little later Socrates and Plato.

Several factors lay behind this era: the discovery or increased use of writing, increased division of labour within society, the stimulus of new intercultural contacts, and on a deeper level, the discovery of history, a slowly-dawning awareness that human time is linear, that things change and do not change back, and the future is a mystery. But this realization gives rise almost before it is articulated to what Mircea Eliade has called the 'terror of history' demanding to be countered by paradigms and controls. Thus the religions of this era made their histories into epics in which God or the gods were acting meaningfully in human affairs. They pointed to eschatological consummations of history, they compensated for change with, in S. G. F. Brandon's phrase, 'ritual perpetuations of the past', they devised immense cycles overriding the linear movement of experienced time, they sought the high ground of mystical oneness with an Absolute before which all time is contingent or illusory.

Finally, the Axial Age need to stabilize history combined with its emergence of the spiritual individual to produce that most élite group of all human élites, the half-dozen or so men who have been founders of great religions, or ascribed such a role, from the largely mythical Krishna to the historical Confucius, Buddha, Jesus, and Muhammad. These are men seen as bearers of unique and ultimate revelations of sacred truth, and so pivots of history, the points of reference for meaning in its onward flow, where 'the hopes and fears of all the years are met'. Inevitably, some have been regarded in faith as avatars or incarnations of the Divine upon earth, embodiments of unparalleled power, presence, and wisdom.

Once fixed, the idea of avatar and incarnation has shown a remarkable persistence and adaptability. Probably on the model of Axial Age belief, persons down to the present have been reckoned God among us; it is an idea whose time came long ago, but has not yet passed. Faith in more than one ancient divine descent still sways millions, giving them hope for this world and the world to come in the transcendent realms whence He came to earth and whither He returned as invisible king of believing hearts.

Daniel Bassuk has written a unique book which admirably displays the worldwide and multi-eraed character of this belief. *Incarnation in Hinduism and Christianity* shows its provenance east and west, ancient and modern. It is for all who hunger and thirst after traces of the divine in this dark world, who wrestle with religion as, in Peter Berger's words, 'man's audacious attempt to see the whole universe as humanly significant', for the avatar or incarnation is supremely the assurance of that significant. It is also for those who are merely fascinated by the

panorama of human religion. For both, this book's scope will be a
challenge and a reward.

Professor of Oriental Studies   ROBERT S. ELLWOOD
School of Religion
University of Southern California
Los Angeles

Acknowledgements

As all new ideas are the result of the Zeitgeist, so this book is based upon a few seminal works. After World War II the renowned New Testament scholar Rudolf Bultmann showed that the worldview of the New Testament was mythical and proposed a 'demythologizing' of the New Testament and of Jesus. Bultmann's methodology inspired a spate of studies, one example being *Christ without Myth: a Study Based on the Theology of Rudolf Bultmann* (1961), by Shubert Ogden. Bultmann's methodology of demythologizing finally focused upon Jesus as the Incarnation of God, and a theological debate ensued. 1977 saw the publication of two books, *The Myth of God Incarnate* (edited by John Hick) and *The Truth of God Incarnate* (edited by E. M. B. Green). These were followed two years later by *Incarnation and Myth: the Debate Continued* (edited by Michael Goulder). In 1980, Aidan Nichols, a Dominican priest and theologian, responded with an 'aesthetic theology' in *The Art of God Incarnate*.

Meanwhile, from another perspective, that of comparative religion, Geoffrey Parrinder delivered the Wilde lectures in Comparative Religion at the University of Oxford on 'Avatar and Incarnation' from 1966 to 1969. And in 1977 John Moffitt published *Incarnation and Avatara: an Imaginary Conversation*. These two works compared the Christian God-man with the Hindu Godmen. Clearly, no work stands alone. Each is the outgrowth of what has come before. I owe much to many. I wish to thank the many scholars who read the manuscript and offered criticism and support: Robert Ellwood, Ray DeHainaut, Judith Ochshorn, James Strange, William Shea, Joan Keller, George Artola, Peter Murray, Chris Buck, Harry Buck, Robert McDermott, Clara Cooper, Patricia Thomas, Sape Zylstra, and my graduate and undergraduate students in Religions of India classes at the University of South Florida.

In the course of writing this book I have been quite fortunate to have had the opportunity to teach all of the major world religions many times at the University of South Florida. In addition it has been a most rewarding experience for me to have portrayed Avatar Ramakrishna in dialogue with Dean James Strange who portrayed St Paul a dozen times for church, school and television audiences.

Especially do I wish to express my gratitute to Professor Norvin Hein for the guidance that he offered in his courses on Indian religions at Yale University. I am forever indebted to three fine scholars for their support of my efforts through the many years, Harold French, John W. White and John Hick. I wish to thank my sister Felice Bassuk for her fine editorial work, Jill Lones for her fine typing, my children, Andrew, David, and Anne, for playing the avatar guessing game, and my wife, Nancy, for her supernatural patience.

The author and publishers wish to thank the following who have kindly given permission for the use of copyright material: Princeton University Press, for 'Shri-Yantra' by Sir John Woodroffe which appeared in Heinrich Zimmer's *Myths and Symbols in Indian Art and Civilization*, edited by Joseph Campbell, Bollingen Series 6, © 1946, © renewed 1973 by Princeton University Press; and the Ahmadiyya Muslim Foreign Missions Department, for the map 'Probable Route of Jesus during his travel to India' from *Jesus in India* by Hazrat Mirza Ghulam Ahmad (Rabwah, Pakistan, 1962).

Introduction: Religions and Their God-Men

Almost no theologian of stature, however, has yet evinced a serious awareness of, let alone has delineated intellectually, the Christian perspective as seen within the context of, and from the perspective of, other faith: human faith at large, in its polymorphic continuities. Now I am contending that this needs doing; but also that a doing of it will prove dramatically rewarding, enriching – will bring the human mind (including the Christian mind) closer to the truth.[1]

(Wilfred Cantwell Smith, Former Director, Centre for the Study of World Religions, Harvard University)

Religion has always supplied mankind with a way of aspiring toward the most profound possibilities of life. Starting from a deeply felt division between human limitations and God's omnipotence and impelled by the desire to annul that division, religion attempts to form a bond between God and mankind which will bring them closer to each other. People know that they are finite and mortal yet they yearn for transcendence and infinitude, to eat from the trees of life and knowledge and be like the gods. The Nietzschean lament can still be heard upon the lips of the divinely intoxicated, that 'if there were gods, how could I bear not to be one!'[2] Perhaps Bertrand Russell said it best: 'Every man would like to be God, if it were possible; some few find it difficult to admit the impossibility.'[3]

All of the world religions have offered some means of bridging the distance between God and mankind, some by admitting various celestial beings such as demi-gods, angels, and saints, and others through scripture. But in at least two world religions, Christianity and Hinduism, there is a common belief that there has been a divine descent through which God has sent his surrogate to the earth and graced us with His presence in a Being known as the God-man. The God-man is an extraordinary Being, compelling us to stretch our minds to the limit in order to grasp

1

His presence. It is believed that the Christian and Hindu God-men have all the power and capacity of God, and share a portion of that omnipotence with us so that we may be able to gain a glimpse of that glorious power, brilliance, and splendour.

This study traces the origins and development of the divine descent and inquires into incarnational theory and practice in Hinduism and Christianity and their influence upon the East and the West. The question raised here is not whether the God-man is real or unreal. The question is, in what sense is He *real*, that is, from within what perspective of divine–human relationships does the belief in the God-man originate and operate?

In Christianity the form that the divine descent has taken is known as the Incarnation, which is synonymous with Jesus Christ, prophet, messiah, saviour, and especially, God-man. Jesus Christ as God-man means that beginning with the Father in heaven, Jesus, perceived as the Son of God, is sent as an expression of grace and salvation, and He becomes the revelatory medium of God's intentions and purposes. The Christian doctrine of the Incarnation is based upon the belief that the Son of God took upon Himself human nature and that Jesus Christ is both human and divine. Only He is *Deus-Homo*.

In the Hindu religion it is believed that the divine descent has occurred not once but many times. Unlike Christians, many Hindus believe that there has been more than one God-man, but, like Christians, they acknowledge Jesus Christ as a God-man. God-men, whether in Hinduism or in Christianity, are recognized as incarnations of the deity, i.e. God taking on human form and coming to our world to offer mankind a concrete example of the ultimate Being so that we may relate to the divine in a form apprehended as human and mould our lives according to the ideals which He embodies.

A common feature of both the Hindu God-man and the Christian Incarnation is the imagery of the descent of the divine. This image occurs in all of the Gospels of the New Testament. The first two Gospels report that the heavens opened and the Spirit of God descended like a dove upon Jesus while he was being baptised by John (Matt. 3:16; Mark 1:10). The Gospel of Luke further indicates that 'the Holy Spirit descended upon him *in bodily form*, as a dove . . .' (Luke 3:22), and in the Gospel of John, Jesus says 'I am the living bread which came down from Heaven' (John 6:51). This image of divine descent is prominent in Hinduism as well. There the deity is reported to descend from the heavenly realm to the earthly, where He is embodied in His surrogate, the God-man.

One of the earliest attempts to portray the human embodiment of the divine was made by the ancient Hindus a few centuries before the Christian era. In the ancient Hindu scriptures, the sacred hymns called the Vedas, the god Indra wandered about in many forms, sometimes as a bull and sometimes as a ram, and the god Varuna is said to have come out of the point of an arrow and appeared as a bull. The phenomenon of God's multiformity, metamorphosis, and incarnation was part of the mentality of *homo religiosus*. Ancient religious man in India connected God with animals which he revered and feared, so he attributed God-like qualities to these animals, creating theriomorphic deities. The Sanskrit terms used to express the manifestation of God coming into this world evolved from *rūpa*, *vapus*, and *tanu*, to *pradurbhava* (appearance), and gradually there came about the Sanskirt word *avatara*, composed of two parts, the verb root *tr*, meaning pass or cross, and the prefix *ava*, signifying down. The finite verb form *avatarati* means 'he descends'. This passing, crossing, or coming down is symbolic of the passage of God from eternity into the temporal realm, from unconditioned to conditioned, from infinitude to finitude – the descent of the divine to our world. A variant of the word *avatara* is the Sanskrit word *avatarana*, a term used to describe the entry of an actor upon the stage making his appearance from behind a curtain, just as the God-man manifests himself upon the world-stage coming down from heaven. The Anglicization of the Sanskrit term avatara is the word avatar, the word designated to describe the advent of the divine, God appearing on earth.

There is no explicit mention of the avatar concept in the Vedas. Neither the word 'avatar' nor the idea of one occurs in the classical Upanishads, India's later scriptures, although there are a few references to the Avatar in the minor Upanishads. Within a few hundred years before the Christian era, during the time when two Indian epics, the *Mahabharata* and the *Ramayana* were forming, a popular Hindu belief was that God could appear on earth. The seminal concept of the Avatar is found within the *Mahabharata* in that section known as the *Bhagavad-Gita*, *The Lord's Song*, composed c. 100 B.C.

The *Gita* is essentially a dialogue between a man and a God. The man, Arjuna, is a prince and a warrior, and the God, Krishna, is his charioteer. Krishna, who until this point has appeared to Arjuna only in human guise, reveals his divine form, and indicates the nature of his incarnation. The essential passage in the *Bhagavad-Gita* is chapter 4 verses 6 and 7:

> 6. ajo 'pk sann avyayātmā
>   bhūtānām īśvaro 'pi san
>   prakṛtim svam adhiṣṭhāya
>   sambhavāmy ātmamāyaya
> 7. yadā-yadā hi dharmasya
>   glānir bhavati bhārata
>   abhyutthānam adharmasya
>   tadā 'tmānam sṛjāmy aham

English translations of this passage indicate how, when, and why the divine descends. One translator expresses it in the following way:

> Tho unborn, tho My self is eternal,
>   Tho Lord of Beings,
> Resorting to My own material nature
>   I come into being by My own mysterious power.
> For whenever of the right
>   A languishing appears, son of Bharata,
> A rising up of unright,
>   Then I send Myself forth.[4]

Another translator interprets it thus:

> Though (I am) unborn, and My self (is) imperishable,
> though (I am) the lord of all creatures, yet establishing
> Myself in My own nature, I come into (empiric) being
> through My power (maya).
> Whenever there is a decline of righteousness and rise of
>   unrighteousness,
> O Bharata (Arjuna), then I send forth (create incarnate)
>   Myself.[5]

Still another translator offers the following:

> Although I am unborn, everlasting, and I am the Lord
>   of all,
> I come to my realm of nature and through my wondrous power
>   I am born.
> When righteousness is weak and faints and unrighteousness
>   exults in pride, then my Spirit arises on earth.
> For the salvation of those who are good, for the destruction
>   of evil in men, for the fulfilment of the kingdom of
>   righteousness, I come to this world in the ages that pass.[6]

A careful reading of this passage from the *Gita* reveals an intended paradox. The Lord is unborn and unchanging, yet He enters into the world of becoming and is born. While this seems to contradict His nature, God has the ability to render the impossible possible. Furthermore, this passage from the *Gita* describes what may be taken as a miracle occurring by 'wondrous power' (*yoga-maya*). It is not an illusion, and it is not an illusory or unreal incarnation, as in Docetism. It is by the free will of God that the supernatural presence of the Lord manifests. The vision of God, which occurs when Krishna reveals His divine form to Arjuna, is a vision of a Being who is immeasurable.

The word 'avatar' does not appear in these verses nor in any section of the *Gita*. However, this passage is the earliest formulation of the avatar doctrine in India and it states the doctrine clearly and unambiguously. It is this significant passage, expressing the avatar concept, that has been the most influential passage in promulgating the God-man idea in the East. Its counterpart in the West is found in the New Testament at the opening of the Gospel of John that 'The Word became flesh and dwelt among us, full of grace and truth' (John 1:14). From scriptural statements such as this there developed in the West the standard for the God-man which was established and set down at the Council of Chalcedon in A.D. 451. The comparable standard in the East is established by the few short verses in the *Bhagavad-Gita*, but no set criteria for the Avatar has ever been established.

Major religious systems within Hinduism place mankind and God on a sliding scale where there are ascending levels of spirituality attainable by human beings and descending degrees of divinity for God. Hinduism deifies man and humanizes God, thus allowing man and God to converge, creating what is known as the man-God and the God-man. Prominent traditions of Hinduism tend to view mankind and God isomorphically and thus offer human beings a ladder by which to ascend to a supra-human level. Just as the hierarchical caste system is indigenous to Hindu society, so, too, is there a hierarchical structure to Hindu spirituality. This hierarchy is comprised of various levels of spiritual attainment: *rishi* (seer), *sadhu* (holy man), *yogi* (practitioner of yoga), *guru* (spiritual teacher), *satguru* (great spiritual master), *mahatma* (highly evolved soul), *jivanmukti* (living liberated soul), and *paramukti* (liberated soul with power over life and death). In general, the goal of the spiritually directed Hindu is to attain the state of liberation and become God-realized. The man-God (*jivanmukti* or *paramukti*) has attained that state, for he has liberated his soul through an ascending spiritual path whereby he has reunited himself with the divine soul, and in accomplishing this, will no longer require to reincarnate.

As there is an ascending hierarchy in Hinduism for the spiritual aspirant, so, too, is there a descending hierarchy for God. For example, the supreme God and progenitor from whom all God-men (Avatars) originate is called the Avatarin. Directly below him is the full, complete, or integral Avatar known as the *purnavatara*, and below him is the *amsavatara* who embodies only a portion or aspect of the power of the divine. Still a lesser type of Avatar is the *avesavatara* in whom God possesses the individual partially and temporarily. Thus in Hinduism there are degrees of avatarology. Schools of Hindu metaphysics later elaborated upon this scheme and developed various types of heterodox Avatars such as *arcavataras* (image-forms of God), *purushavataras* (spirit Avatars), and *lilavataras* (playful Avatars), etc. But no matter what the degree of avatarhood, the Avatar is regarded as markedly different from the ordinary man and the man-God. For the Hindu, while it may be humanly possible to become a man-God, it is not humanly possible to become a God-man, for when matter is spiritualized it is through the will and actions of man, but when spirit materializes as in the case of the Avatar, it is by the will of God alone. Avatars are perfect beings, not perfected beings; ichor flows through their veins, not blood.

Within Hinduism there exists the belief that the Avatar has special characteristics which distinguish him from mere mortals. The Avatar is supposed to be born in a supernatural way

(*Ayonija*),[7] to have no karma to expiate,[8] to remember previous lives,[9] and to be conscious of his mission throughout life.[10] Although many special physical and spiritual characteristics are attributed to the Avatar, no authoritative standard has been established. The designation of attributes, therefore, is quite arbitrary and lacks consistency. Traditionally, however, there is unanimous agreement that the Avatar originates in heaven and not on earth, which makes the God-man qualitatively different from the man-God and all human beings.

Various traditions within Hinduism have acknowledged certain individuals who broke the cycle of birth and death, attained liberation, and became man-gods. There have also been rulers and heroes, such as kings, pharaohs, emperors and chiefs, in sundry times and places who have been deified, or who glorified themselves and made themselves into man-gods. These, however, are not our concern, for they were first and foremost human and gradually became divinized. The focus in this book shall be those rare beings in whom God is recognized as disclosing His divine presence, the God-man, originating in heaven and manifesting his glory here on earth.

In the Hindu religion there are really two categories of incarnation: general and special. General incarnation is the Hindu doctrine of God *in* man, in which the divine soul is embodied in human beings. The doctrine of special incarnation is that in which God is *made* man. The two types are quite different. According to the Hindu religion all human beings participate in the general incarnation, but those who participate in special incarnation are the God-men. In the former all humans are divinely endowed, whereas in the latter only very special beings can claim divinity. The same categories apply to Christianity.

In Christianity, the God-man is Jesus Christ, the Incarnation. The word 'incarnation' is the English translation of the Latin term for 'enfleshing', and the Greek *Sarkothenta*. In Christianity it means God's Word or *Logos* embodied in Jesus. However, incarnation is not synonymous with inspiration. Inspiration denotes God's breathing into a person, or the entry of the divine Spirit into a person. Inspiration is similar to the Hindu doctrine of general incarnation, for in inspiration the divine enters the prophet, seer, poet, or artist, as Spirit, Wisdom, or Logos. But in Jesus we can observe a special incarnation, for Christianity understands it as the Logos *becoming* a man of flesh and blood. In John 1:14 we have 'the Word became flesh', and this has traditionally been interpreted as describing something distinct and unique. It may be true that etymologically incarnation and inspiration could mean much the same thing, they could denote the entry of the divine into the human as in any or all inspired people. But incarnation has the added dimension of God *becoming* flesh and blood, rather than God merely entering a man of flesh and blood.

The incarnational doctrine agreed upon in Christianity was the formula of *homoousios*, that Christ is 'of the same substance' as the Heavenly Father. The Council of Nicaea declared that

> . . . in one Lord Jesus Christ, the only-begotten Son of God, Begotten of the Father before all the ages, Light of Light, true God of true God, begotten not made, of one substance with the Father, through whom all things were made, both the things in heaven and the things in the earth: who for us men and for our salvation came down, and was incarnate, and was made man.

The Council of Chalcedon stated that the two natures of Christ, divine and human, were perfectly blended

> . . . one and the same Christ, Son, Lord, Only-begotten, recognized in two natures without confusion, without change, without division, without separation; the distinction of natures being in no way annulled by the union, but rather the characteristics of each nature being preserved and coming together to form one person and subsistance, not as parted or separated into two persons, but one and the same Son and Only-begotten God the Word, Lord Jesus Christ . . .

Christianity declared that theological attempts to explain the phenomenon of Jesus' incarnation, such as those offered by Arius, Eutyches, Apollinarius, and Nestorius, lead to false and heretical interpretations. Absolutely all theological attempts to explain the Incarnation were deemed false, said the Church, because Jesus Christ's incarnation is a 'divine mystery', beyond rational thought and explanation. In both Hinduism and Christianity special incarnation is pre-eminent over general incarnation and designates God becoming man, not merely found in man or entering man. In the words of Emil Brunner, the quintessential mystery of Christianity is 'that the son of God took upon himself our humanity and not that the man Jesus acquired divinity'.[11] The God-man is a most exceptional, extraordinary, preternatural being.

Is there incarnational belief in other world religions? In his book *The Perennial Philosophy*, Aldous Huxley said that 'the doctrine that God can be incarnated in human form is found in most of the principal historic expositions of the Perennial Philosophy – in Hinduism, in Mahayana Buddhism, in Christianity and in the Mohammedanism of the Sufis'. He added that 'every human being can thus become an Avatar by adoption'.[12] But Huxley's statement is rather loose and imprecise, and deals more with general incarnation than with special incarnation.

Incarnation is virtually unthinkable in the religions of Judaism and Islam. In both of these, God is monotheistic and transcendent, and the idea of His sending a divine surrogate is anathema. However, at the very inception of Israelite religion intermediaries between God and man appear quite often. In the book of Genesis, for example, it is said that at that time 'the Nephilim were on the earth' (Gen. 6:4) and Nephilim, which is usually translated as giants, literally means 'those who come down'. The book of Genesis, furthermore, reveals that Abraham is approached by three heavenly visitors (Gen. 18:1–8), Jacob wrestles with an angel (Gen. 32:22–32), and the Sons of God have intercourse with the daughters of men and make them pregnant (Gen. 6:1–4). Just a few centuries later, King Solomon declares 'But will God indeed dwell on the earth? Behold, heaven and the highest heaven cannot contain thee; how much less this house which I have built' (I Kings 8:27). By this time the idea of intermediate beings between the divine and the human had all but disappeared.

The religion of Islam, founded by Muhammad 1400 years ago, insists upon the Oneness of God and condemns the concept of divine incarnation (hulul), finding it totally unacceptable and repugnant. However, the human desire to reduce the gulf between God and man gradually evolved a modified incarnational belief among heterodox Muslims in which Imams and Manifestations of God are regarded as more than human and in some sense divine. One of the most sacred books of a sect of Shiite Muslims known as the Khojahs, is Sadr-ud-Din's *Das Avatar*, written in the 15th century.[13] This work endeavours to demonstrate that Ali, Muhammad's son-in-law, was the long expected final Avatar. There are also more recent esoteric interpretations of Muhammad in which he is viewed as Allah's Incarnation, or where the 'Spirit of Muhammad' is the Logos, even statements referring to the 'avataric nature of the Prophet' Muhammad.[14]

The Sikh religion of India is a syncretism blending Hinduism and Islam, and the Sikh God-man combines elements of both faiths. According to the Sikh religion the God-man comes down from the kingdom of *Sat Lok*, crosses the intermediary planes and reaches *Bhu Lok* or the physical world. A leading interpreter of the Sikh religion explains that

> Brahma cannot speak of Brahma alone. He too needs a human agency for His self-expression (among human beings). We, as human entities encased in flesh and bones, cannot have an idea of that attributeless Formless One, unless he assumes a likeness to our own, on this material plane, and becomes for us a living God capable of being seen, heard and understood. He is at once both God and man, and may be called Godman. He works as a means to an end, a link between man and God. He is Word personified so that He may impart instructions about God and guidance toward God.[15]

The Sikh God-man is physically, mentally, morally, and spiritually perfect.

While incarnational belief occurs in varying degrees in some religions, Christianity and Hinduism are the only two religions in which salvation is actually dependent upon belief in incarnation. In these two religions the idea of divine descent has engaged the minds of millions of people for thousands of years. For the past seven hundred years, Catholics the world over have recited the Angelus three times a day in commemoration of Christ's Incarnation. And among the largest sect of Hinduism, the worshippers of Vishnu (Vaishnavites), the descent of the deity has been a dominant theme for nearly two millennia. For most Christians and Hindus God's incarnation is special, strategic, and salvific.

This study of incarnationism is comprised of two parts. Part One spans the history of the Avatar in India from ancient to modern times. Part Two covers the treatment of the God-man in the Western world and ultimately relates it to the Christian God-man, Jesus Christ. Without making any value judgments on the intrinsic merit or reality of the God-man's existence or achievements, this book elucidates how the God-men of Hinduism and Christianity are similar and yet demonstrably different.

Chapter 1 demonstrates how the ancient ways of conceiving of the descent of God in India were mythic. Chapter 2 reveals how the personification and apotheosis of the Avatar developed. By describing the lives of six Avatars chronologically, the gradual evolution of incarnationism in India will become evident. The epilogue to Part One establishes the criteria for Indian Avatars drawing upon the mythic themes from the lives of the Avatars in the first two chapters. Chapter 3 shows how the Hindu concept of the Avatar was transplanted and transmogrified upon Western soil, especially in America, England, and Ireland during the past 200 years. Chapter 4 traces the growth of incarnationism in the ancient Near East and in Palestine culminating in the Christian Incarnation.

This book is a comparative study of the phenomenon of divine incarnation in Hinduism and Christianity. The theme of the entire work is incarnationism with a study of its two forms, avatarhood and incarnation. Thus each chapter concludes with a section comparing Avatars with Christ until finally in Chapter 4 the focus is on Christ as both an Incarnation and an Avatar. In the conclusion the similarities and distinctions between the two types of God-men unfold. The final epilogue explains how the process of divine incarnation is an aspect of the mythopoeic and religious propensities in the East and West. This study begins in ancient India where there arose the earliest examples of the divine descent to earth in the form of Avatars.

> The Great One comes,
> sending shivers across the dust of the earth.
> In the heavens sounds the trumpet,
> in the world of man drums of victory are heard,
> the Hour has arrived of the Great Birth.[16]
>
> (Rabindranath Tagore)

Part One
The God-Man in the East

1

Classical Avatars of India

INTRODUCTION: THE RELIGIOUS UNIVERSE OF ANCIENT INDIA

The way in which a reality came into existence is revealed by its myth.[1]

(Mircea Eliade)

In ancient India, religious man dwelt in a cosmos vibrantly energized by gods close-by. It was generally acknowledged that there was an overall struggle being waged between the gods and the demons, and good and evil were evenly balanced. At certain times the balance was destroyed and evil gained the upper hand. This situation was deemed unfair, and at such times the God Vishnu intervened by descending to earth in the form of a manifestation of himself known as an Avatar.

At the beginning of the cosmos the waters from the cataclysmic flood cover the earth. Vishnu-Narayana is lying upon the primal waters, floating on a banyan leaf while picking his toe, a position symbolic of unity, eternity, and the *uroboros*.[2] When he decides to create the universe, speech is born from his mouth, the Vedas from the tumours of his body, nectar (the elixir of the gods) from his tongue, earth from his nose, heaven and the sun from the pupils of his eyes, clouds and rain from his hair, flashes of lightning from his beard, rocks from his nails, and mountains from his bones. The golden cosmic egg or embryo, (*Hiranyagarbha*) has been floating on the water for a thousand years. There occurs a crack in the cosmic egg and it bursts to reveal the Lord of the universe, Vishnu. He takes the form of the primal man, Narayana, whose soul is identical with that of the universal spirit. Narayana feels alone and desires another, so he divides into half male and half female. Feeling disunited he joins the two

15

halves together and bears offspring which become the human race.

For the mythic imagination of India, the universe is tripartite, composed of heaven, sky, and earth. Each of the three main regions of the universe is subdivided into three parts. One of the three heavens is Vishnu's abode, located atop Mount Meru, called Vaikuntha. Vaikuntha is made of gold and precious jewels, and through it flows the Ganges River, originating from Vishnu's toe. Vaikuntha contains five pools abounding with lotuses where Vishnu and his wife Lakshmi shine radiantly. The earth is thought to be supported either by four elephants, or by four giants who cause earthquakes when they shift their burden from one shoulder to the other. The shape of the earth is thought to be like a wheel with its centre at Mount Meru.

As myth reflects man's first awareness of time,[3] so mythic time in India is a never-ending cycle of creation, preservation, and destruction, each complete cycle being one hundred years in the life of Brahma. At the end of each period, the entire universe – Brahma himself, gods, sages, demons, men, animals, and matter – is dissolved in the cataclysm known as the great dissolution (*Mahapralaya*). This is followed by one hundred years of darkness, after which another Brahma is born and the cycle begins anew. When Brahma wakes, the three worlds, heaven, sky, and earth are created, and when he sleeps they are reduced to abysmal darkness. Within this system are many divisions and sub-cycles, the most important of which is the Kalpa, equivalent to 4320 million years on earth or one day in the life of Brahma. The Kalpa is divided into one thousand periods (*Mahayugas*), each of which is further divided into four ages or yugas called Krita, Treta, Dwapara, and Kali.

All four yugas are represented by the image of a cow, and each yuga differs from the others in the number of legs that the cow can stand on. The Krita yuga is the perfect or golden age, also called Satya yuga (Satya meaning truth) for this is a time when the truth is wholly accessible to all. This age lasts 1 728 000 years, and the cow has all four legs. People are contented, healthy, virtuous, and prosperous, and the colour of the deity they worship is white. The Treta yuga lasts 1 296 000 years and is an age in which virtue falls short by one-quarter, and now the cow has only three legs. In the Treta yuga men are quarrelsome and often act from ulterior motives. Work, suffering, and death are the common features of this age, and the deity is red. In the Dwapara yuga, virtue is only half present and now the cow stands on two legs. Some tread the right path, but lying and quarrelling abound and vice and evil increase. During this age, which lasts for 864 000 years, the deity is yellow. The Kali yuga, or age of degeneration, is the one that many Hindus believe we are currently in. The cow is one-legged and helpless, and all but one-quarter of virtue has vanished. In this age, lasting 432 000 years, the deity is black. Man and society reach an extreme point of disintegration. The majority of people are wicked, quarrelsome, and beggar-like. They value what is degraded, eat voraciously and indiscriminately, and live in cities filled with thieves. They are oppressed by their rulers and by the ravages of famine and war. Their miseries can only end with the coming of a final saviour and Avatar. The complete cycle ends with a dissolution called a *pralaya*. The final destruction is preceded by the most terrible portents. After a drought lasting one hundred years, seven suns appear in the skies and dry up all remaining water. Fire, swept by wind, consumes the earth. Clouds, looking like elephants garlanded with lightning, release rain continuously for twelve years submerging the whole world. Then Brahma, contained within a lotus floating on the waters, absorbs the winds and goes to sleep until the time comes for his awakening and renewed creation. During this time gods and men are temporarily reabsorbed into the Universal Spirit (*Brahman*). The renewal of creation consists of a redeployment of the same elements.

The restoration of the balance between good and evil is felt by Vishnu to be desirable, and he sends an incarnation of himself four times in Krita yuga, three in Treta yuga, two in Dwapara yuga, and one in Kali yuga, in opposition to what might be expected, based upon the characteristics of the four ages. However, the diminishing number of Avatars in the successive yugas corresponds with the diminishing length of their time. In no sense do the Avatars appear at regular intervals, as some modern Avatars (discussed in Chapter 2) have suggested.

A pattern develops in the myths discussed in the remainder of this chapter, in which God enters the world in times of cosmic imbalance and manifests Himself in visible form. For the religious consciousness of ancient India, the relation between mankind and God is one of participation and eventual reintegration. A special relationship is established in which God is understood to be homologous with man. The 'foremost function of myth is to reveal the exemplary models for all human rites and all significant human activities',[4] for as the Hindu literary works called the Brahmanas, say, 'we must do what the gods did in the beginning'.[5]

1. VISHNU – THE NAVEL OF THE WORLD

I will declare the mighty deeds of Vishnu, of him who
    measured out the earthly regions,
Who propped the highest place of congregation,
    thrice setting down his footstep, widely striding.

For this his mighty deed is Vishnu lauded, like some wild
    beast, dread, prowling, mountain roaming;
He within whose three wide-extended paces all living
    creatures have their habitation.

Let the hymn lift itself as strength to Vishnu, the bull,
    far-striding, dwelling on the mountains,
Him who alone with triple step hath measured this common
    dwelling-place, long, far extended,

Him whose three places that are filled with sweetness,
    imperishable, joy as it may list them,
Who verily alone upholds the threefold, the earth, the
    heaven, and all living creatures.

                                      (*Rig Veda* I.154.1–4)

In the ancient Indian writings called the Vedas, two sets of divine 'trinities' emerge – a cosmological and a functional. The cosmological trinity is based on the conception of three worlds: the celestial sphere whose principal image is the sun, the realm of the sky, and the terrestrial realm. Each of these is under the authority of a god: the celestial realm is under the dominion of Surya or Savitri; the sky region is under Indra or Vayu; and the terrestrial region is under the deity Agni (fire). There later developed the more familiar Hindu trinity based on conceptions of divine functions rather than divine loci: Brahma, the creator, Vishnu, the preserver, and Shiva, the destroyer. These three gods are known collectively as *Ishvara*, a word referring to the power of God. From this divine trinity Vishnu emerges as the supreme God, the one who subsumes Brahma and Shiva, and the only one who sends divine representations of Himself to the terrestrial realm where they are known as Avatars.

The name 'Vishnu' means immanent, all-pervasive principle, and is a cognate of the Sanskrit root 'vish', to pervade. The holy men (*rishis*), to whom the authorship of the Vedas are attributed, prescribed meditation on the gods, and the name Vishnu led the meditator to recognize world-maintenance and preservation in him. Vishnu is referred to as thousand-named (Sahasra-nama), and many of the names are descriptions of his physical characteristics or references to his specific deeds and accomplishments. Some of the names of Vishnu are *Ananta*, endless; *Ananta-sayana*, he who sleeps upon the endless serpent; *Mukunda*, deliverer; *Narayana*, who moves in the waters; *Pitambara*, yellow-clad; *Purushottama*, highest spirit; *Vaikuntanatha*, lord of paradise; and *Janardana*, awe-inspirer. Vishnu, the all-pervasive, is known and worshipped in many ways.

'In the beginning, everything was like a sea without a light',[6] and upon the cosmic waters Vishnu sleeps. From earliest times in India, water has been regarded as a residence or seat of the god, a tangible manifestation of the divine essence.[7] Vishnu's bed is the cosmic waters, and the Hindu symbol for water is the serpent. Vishnu reposes upon the coils of a gigantic serpent on the water. In fact, the cosmic serpent, the cosmic waters, and Vishnu resting thereupon are all manifestations of a single essence which is Vishnu.[8]

At the end of every yuga Vishnu falls asleep upon the coils of the serpent Sesha and floats upon the cosmic waters called the Ocean of Milk, which form his bed. Within this Ocean of Milk lies the divine nectar of immortality (*amrita*), which Vishnu obtains for the gods. As Vishnu sleeps his creative function stirs and he awakens. Then, engaging in meditation for the re-creation of the universe, a lotus grows from his navel sprouting Brahma, the creator, and after each destruction of the universe by Shiva, Vishnu resumes his position upon the Ocean of Milk.

Vishnu's navel is the source of all. It is the omphalos of the universe and the connection between heaven and earth. Its shape is like that of an egg; thus it is a reflection of the cosmic egg, or golden embryo.[9] From Vishnu's navel grows a lotus that produces Brahma, and from Vishnu's forehead comes another lotus which results in the goddess Lakshmi (or Sri) his consort. The lotus is the generative organ of the cosmic waters, the womb of the universe, and a symbol of the first product of the creative principle.

In the mythopoeic imagination of ancient India, Vishnu stood for many things: sun god, fertility god, mountain god, and water god. His various names and epithets associate him with the sun, the wind, the rain, lightning, trees, plants, and precious stones. One of his names, *Hari*, associates him with sun, lightning, fire, and the colour gold. That he was a solar deity also accounts for some of his names that are associated with gold (*suvarnavarna*).[10]

Vishnu's fertility was the life-force in animals, plants, and human beings. His giving of rain was thought to be his conjugal relations with the goddess Earth. He was thought to be a beneficent and liberal god, willing and able to bestow abundant riches upon his devotees. The granting of wealth and possessions (Vasu) later associated him with the god Vasudeva-Krishna.

Vishnu is represented in a variety of prominent positions. Often he is reclining in the coils of the cobra Sesha, the cosmic serpent, and at other times he is riding upon his vehicle, the garuda, a creature of gold that is half man and half bird. The golden-winged garuda is the master of the sky and the annihilator of serpents, and the cobra who winds its way upon the ground looking like a river is regarded as the source of all water. Vishnu embodies both the cobra and the garuda, for he represents the absolute Being that becomes differentiated into polarized manifestations through which the vital tensions of the world-process are brought into existence and preserved. He is the reconciler of these opposites, the *conjunctio oppositorum*.

At the beginning of India's recorded history, which is found within the Vedas, Vishnu was a god of minor rank. Here the story of Vishnu is called the three strides (*Trivikrama*), in which Vishnu takes three long steps and measures out the seven worlds. By measuring the universe, Vishnu took part in its creation. Vishnu's benevolent aspect became prominent in the Vedas, where he was called 'the unconquerable preserver', a sign of his later prominent place in the Hindu trinity.

The myth of the three strides portrays Vishnu taking one stride that clears heaven, another that traverses the sky, and finally a third step that crosses the earth. These three strides explain the great reverence for, and worship of the footprints of Vishnu found throughout India, as well as the kissing and washing of the feet of his Avatars. Gradually Vishnu's role grew in prominence. His position became the sun at its zenith, higher than that of any other deity in the Hindu pantheon. He became the all-pervading solar deity with his beams enveloping all things. By the time of the *Mahabharata* epic he is equated with Prajapati, the supreme god. Vishnu becomes the second god of the Hindu trinity, being regarded as the preserver and sustainer, and encompasses Brahma the creator and Shiva the destroyer. As preserver he is the embodiment of the qualities of mercy and goodness, and he sustains and maintains the universe and the cosmic order (*dharma*).

A grand literature developed describing Lord Vishnu. In epic and puranic literature Vishnu is represented anthropomorphically as a handsome young man dressed in royal robes wearing a brilliant jewel (the kaustubha) upon his breast, and a curl of hair upon his chest. In each of his four hands he holds one of his symbols: a discus, a lotus, a mace, and a conch. The discus represents the sun and is associated with the thunderbolt (*vajra*) of the god Indra; the lotus is of golden colour; the mace has a phallic character; and the conch shell represents the female sexual organ. Vishnu is usually portrayed as blue and clothed in yellow. His blue colour indicates his infinite stature, for blue is associated with immeasurable entities such as sky and sea. Yellow represents the earth. The blue Vishnu clothed in yellow symbolizes the descent of the heavenly to the terrestrial realm.

The epics call Vishnu the protector of the gods and the universe. In the *Mahabharata* he becomes recognized as the invincible and unconquerable god. The Puranas call him the guardian of the world and the restorer of peace. Ancient poets sing of his generosity in coming from heaven to earth with readiness to protect humanity and assume a variety of forms to preserve the world. All these sentiments contribute to making Vishnu the deity to whom worship (*bhakti*) is most appropriately addressed.

Vishnu is an androgynous deity consisting of half male (Vishnu), and half female (Lakshmi or Shiva).[11] According to a Hindu text, Shiva became an androgyne at Brahma's request, and by means of yoga, Shiva enjoyed the female half of himself and created Vishnu, who then split his body in two and created all creatures.[12] In so doing Vishnu became the father and mother of mankind, and in him can be observed a divine marriage between the god and the goddess, a hierogamy.

In summation, Vishnu represents the light, warmth, and energy of the sun. He is also the Lord of the waters. He can be both for he

represents the resolution of opposites. He permeates and pene-
trates all things, rules far and wide, and traverses the entire
universe. His three strides indicate his universality and perva-
siveness, i.e. all beings abide in his three steps. By striding,
Vishnu obtains for the gods their omnipotence and for mankind
ample living space.

Vishnu's navel is the place of birth and creation and the source
of all existence. It is also the world's navel, the *axis mundi*. Being at
the centre of the universe Vishnu can protect, preserve, and
sustain the forces of good. He is the waters, represented by the
cosmic serpent, and he is the sky, symbolized by the garuda bird.
He is a hierogamy, the divine mother and the heavenly father, the
parents of all living creatures. That the idea of Vishnu's descents
(Avatars) may have developed from within the circles of Vishnu's
own worshippers is not that surprising. In the Hindu religion the
divine descent in the form of an Avatar is thought to come from
the God Vishnu.

In Nepal, a country that is officially Hindu, the king has traditionally been regarded by his subjects as Vishnu incarnate.
Among the Indo-Nepalese of Southern Nepal, all young girls
marry Vishnu for eternity, and this symbolic marriage prevents
stigma from divorce or widowhood.

2. ANIMAL AVATARS OF THE KRITA YUGA

The Hindu procession of the ten Avatars is itself, as it were, a
parable of evolution.

(Aurobindo, the Supramental Avatar)

Matsya . . . . Fish! that didst outswim the flood;
Kurma . . . . Tortoise! whereon earth hath stood;
Varaha . . . . Boar! who with thy tusk hold'st high
                      That world that mortals might not die
Narasimha . . . . Lion! who hast giants torn,
Vamana . . . . Dwarf! who laugh'd a king to scorn,
Parasurama . . . . Sole subduer of the dreaded!
Rama . . . . Slayer of the many-headed!
Balarama . . . . Mighty ploughman!

Buddha . . . . Teacher tender!
Kalki . . . . Of thine own the sure defender!
Under all thy ten disguises
Endless praise to thee arises.

(*Gita Govinda* by Jayadeva)

The idea of the descent of God to the earth appears unambiguously for the first time in the *Bhagavad Gita*. In the fourth chapter of this Hindu scripture, Krishna, as an emissary of Vishnu, states that he has been born repeatedly in material form to renew his teachings, to destroy the wicked, and to restore righteousness to the world. The unnamed descents of Vishnu suggested by the *Gita* developed into various accounts of Avatars, as found in the Hindu epics, the Puranas and the Brahmanas. In the *Mahabharata* there are three lists of Vishnu's incarnations and these lists are not uniform. First, four Avatars are mentioned, then two more are added, and finally there is a list of ten Avatars consisting of (1) Swan, (2) Tortoise, (3) Fish, (4) Boar, (5) Man-lion, (6) Dwarf, (7) Bhargava Rama, (8) Dasaratha Rama, (9) Krishna, and (10) Kalki.

All of the Puranas deal at least in part with the exploits of Vishnu in his various avataric appearances. The *Garuda Purana* alludes to innumerable Avatars of Vishnu and lists 19. The *Bhagavata Purana* mentions Vishnu's Avatars on several occasions, but there is hardly any uniformity among the accounts. In one place there are 22 Avatars listed and in another there are 23. A third account in the same text lists the Avatars as fish, tortoise, boar, man-lion, dwarf, two Ramas, Buddha, Kalki, and Vasudeva. The Pancaratra school substituted Krishna for Vasudeva. Since the time of the *Bhagavata Purana* the number of Vishnu's Avatars has been uniformly recognized as ten. The number of Avatars seems to have been fixed at ten even before their identity was agreed upon. The traditional list of the ten Avatars which developed included (1) Matsya, the fish, (2) Kurma, the tortoise, (3) Varaha, the boar, (4) Narasimha, the man-lion, (5) Vamana, the dwarf, (6) Parasurama, Rama with the axe, (7) Rama, (8) Krishna, (9) Buddha, and (10) Kalki.

Avatar folklore counter-balanced the tendency within the sacred literature of the Upanishads to stress the remoteness of the Supreme Being. The Avatars sustained faith in divine support by bringing God down to earth where He could be known and seen.

The mythology of the Avatars developed into elaborate and varied forms without institutional regimentation. Substitutions in the list of the ten Avatars were common during the Puranic period of nearly a thousand years. The mythic narrative surrounding each of these ten Avatars follows.

(A) Matsya, the Fish Avatar

Creation takes shape from the undifferentiated source and primal element of existence, water. The mighty Vishnu is resting upon the primal waters, known as the Ocean of Milk. He creates out of an excess of power and an overflow of energy, and begins to incarnate first in the form of animals. In some of the Puranas the first descent of Vishnu is the swan Avatar (*Hamsa*). After the flood, Vishnu appeared in the form of a swan to ascertain whether the waters were fit for fish and other aquatic animals. It was believed that the swan could separate milk from water when they were mixed together as in the Ocean of Milk, that he could also live both upon water and under it, and that he could determine water's good and bad properties. Gradually this swan Avatar was replaced by the fish Avatar who became recognized as the first appearance of Vishnu.

The myth of Matsya is recounted in the *Mahabharata* and in the Puranas. The *Matsya Purana* assumed its present form during the classical period of medieval Hinduism around the 4th century A.D.[13] Although there the fish Avatar occupies a primary place on the list of Vishnu's Avatars, it was not the first Avatar to appear in Sanskrit literature, despite what contemporary Hindus (and modern Avatars) would lead us to believe.

Matsya, the fish Avatar, was originally part of the mythology of the god Brahma, and only gradually was it incorporated into the Vishnu myths. In the Vishnu version, toward the end of the Krita yuga, Manu (a primordial man) was performing his oblations in the river and caught a tiny fish. He placed his little fish in a bowl where it grew so large – 40 million miles long – that no man-made container could hold it, and Manu was forced to put it in the sea. Beholding such a wondrous fish, Manu was filled with awe and recognized that it was indeed an avataric form of Vishnu and prostrated himself before it. Then the fish said to Manu that in seven days there would be a flood because a demon had stolen the Vedas. Therefore Manu should build a large boat for himself and the seven sages and their wives, and in it Manu was to put a pair of everything that lived upon the earth and in the air. Using the serpent Vasuki as a cable, Manu would tie the boat to Matsya's horn and be guided over the waters. When the flood finally covered the earth Matsya appeared as a giant fish with golden scales, lifting his head which had a single horn, above the waters. He brought the boat to the mountains of the North and showed Manu how to let it slide down as the waters subsided. The demon was drowned, the Vedas were recovered, and Manu, saved from the flood, became the progenitor of the human race.

The purpose of the fish Avatar myth is to account for the recovery of the Vedas from the flood and for the preservation of the righteous people who replenished the earth. The fish Avatar is the transformation of Vishnu into Matsya when he is sorely needed and not at his birth.

Various aspects of the Matsya myth can be found in the mythology of other nations. The flood is a universal mythic theme, perhaps best known in the Old Testament account. Manu is the primordial man, equivalent to Noah, and his ship functions like the ark. In both accounts all species of animals are saved, and the few righteous human beings are saved from the corruption of the wicked, and from these righteous ones mankind gets a new start.

(B) Kurma, the Tortoise Avatar

The myth of Kurma, the tortoise Avatar, is most extensively found in the *Bhagavata Purana*. During the cosmic flood many treasures were lost. One of these treasures was the ambrosia or heavenly nectar (*amrita*) by which the gods renewed their youthfulness and avoided death. Vishnu, therefore, transformed himself into the gigantic tortoise, Kurma, whose upper shell is the sky and whose lower shell is the earth, and dived into the ocean's depths. The gods placed Mount Mandara on his back, and the search for the ambrosia would not have proceeded if Kurma had not used his curved back as a pivot. The gods twisted the serpent Vasuki around Mount Mandara and churned the Ocean of Milk by pulling on the serpent, hoping to bring to the surface everything in the Ocean, including the nectar. Fourteen treasures emerged from this churning including the moon, a black youth holding a cup in which the ambrosia foamed and sparkled. Vishnu's wife Lakshmi, and the Kaustubha jewel belonging to Vishnu. By drinking the nectar of immortality the gods gained superiority over the demons.

The main objective of the tortoise Avatar is to retrieve the nectar of immortality for the benefit of the gods. Like the fish Avatar, the tortoise Avatar is a transformation of Vishnu, and it turns back into Vishnu when its mission is completed.

(C) Varaha, the Boar Avatar

After his aquatic and reptilian manifestations, Vishnu appears next as a mammal, a boar with highly developed sense of smell, a creature more complex than fish or tortoise. Hindu literature recounts how the demon Hiranyaksha, the golden-eye, cast the earth into the ocean where it sank due to the weight of the demons who oppressed the gods. An appeal for the rescue of the earth is made by the gods to Brahma, who seeks Vishnu's aid. Vishnu chooses the shape of a gigantic wild boar, Varaha, and plunging into the water follows the earth by its smell. He kills the demon Hiranyaksha and succeeds in lifting the earth from the depths of the ocean, supporting it upon his tusks.

In the Indian view, the drama of creation is subject to sundry setbacks. It is punctuated by recurrent crises that require the intervention of Vishnu, who acts as world preserver. Like the fish and tortoise Avatars, the boar Avatar is also a case of Vishnu's transformation. Rescue of the afflicted, establishment of the general welfare, and destruction of the wicked appear to be the objects of this myth.

Hindu art presents a diversity of forms of the boar Avatar, some of which are based on various myths of rescuing the earth. Around A.D. 400 in Northern India, King Chandra Gupta II commissioned a gigantic sculpture with the head of the boar Avatar and the body of a mighty king in the act of lifting the earth. It is very likely that King Chandra Gupta II intended this huge relief as symbolic of his own victorious military campaign, in which he overthrew the dynasty of Western satraps and its Scythian rulers. Thus the Gupta king saved and upheld the earth in historical time just as Varaha saved it in mythical time. The strong association between the boar Avatar and the king in ancient India helped the Gupta kings to blur the distinction between mortal and immortal, king and God. In this manner they suggested that their authority to rule was drawn from Vishnu.

It is noteworthy that in this myth and those connected with the previous two Avatars, Vishnu is concerned with rescuing something from the waters. In mythic traditions water symbolizes the undifferentiated, the formless, the chaotic, from which creation, order, and form arise.

(D) Narasimha, the Man-Lion Avatar

Traditionally, the fourth Avatar of Vishnu is Narasimha, the man-lion. The myth surrounding Narasimha is as follows. Kasyapa Prajapati was performing a sacrifice. The costly gifts selected for the offerings included a golden seat for the sacrificial priest. While the sacrifice was being conducted, his wife gave birth to a son who immediately walked into the sacrificial room, sat on the golden seat, and chanted sacred texts. The priests were amazed, named him Hiranyakashipu, the golden-clad, and forecast that he would be very powerful. Hiranyakashipu was the older brother of Hiranyaksha of the previous Avatar, Varaha, the boar.

In the early years of Hiranyakashipu's life he adored Brahma, and obtained a promise from him that he would not be killed during day or night, nor by man, nor beast, nor God, and so he concluded that he was invincible. He strove to get revenge on Vishnu for the death of his brother Hiranyaksha, and as a result his behaviour became intolerable. He proceeded to persecute gods and men, including his own son Prahlada, who was a source of consternation to him because he preached the doctrine of the Vaishnava faith and the greatness of Vishnu. It became imperative that Hiranyakashipu perish, but at the same time the promise conferred by Brahma had to be respected. Thus, Vishnu assumed the form of a composite personality, half man and half lion, and burst forth from a pillar in the palace at twilight, when it was neither day nor night, and tore Hiranyakashipu in two with his claws. The man-lion's fury was ultimately pacified by Prahlada who had pleased Vishnu from the start. Therefore, not one of the promises conferred by Brahma was countermanded, as Vishnu as the man-lion was neither wholly divine, nor wholly man, nor wholly animal. After killing Hiranyakashipu, Vishnu resumed his original form and returned to his abode on the shore of the Ocean of Milk. The Narasimha Avatar myth depicts how evil, personified by the powerful Hiranyakashipu, is destroyed, and how devotion to Vishnu, such as that of Prahlada, will be rewarded.

Narasimha Avatar is portrayed in Indian iconography in either of two major renditions. The basic pattern portrays him with a lion's face and a human body seated on a throne in a yogic posture. This figure possesses two or four arms. When Narasimha has four arms and four hands they hold the symbols of Vishnu: conch, discus, mace, and lotus. A second version has Narasimha coming out of a pillar wearing the entrails of Hiranyakashipu as a garland. Here he has between four and thirty-two hands.

Some kings of ancient India took the epithet of Narasimha. These kings struck gold coins bearing the emblems of Narasimha, denoting the unity of the god with themselves. The third Gupta king, Mahendraditya (A.D. 415–55) was partial to Narasimha. Various inscriptions identify him with this Avatar, such as 'Narasimha as it were incarnate, (the King) Mahendra (as it were) among the lions, is ever-victorious.'[14] Thus, some Gupta kings added a timeless and cosmic dimension to their kingship by identifying with Avatars of Vishnu, and this helped to legitimate their temporal authority and conquests. They were considered to be larger and greater than ordinary mortals in physical form, god-like beings dwelling on earth, and at least partial embodiments of Vishnu, if not full Avatars.[15]

To recapitulate, until now Vishnu has incarnated into animal creatures only and the Indian mythic tradition has woven stories around these Avatars dealing with good and evil, cosmogony, and immortality. Indian rulers and kings adopted these animal Avatars as their symbols, thus giving themselves the divine right of kings. In the mythology of these earliest of Vishnu's Avatars, Vishnu has been transformed into these animal forms, there being no birth or death for these Avatars. When the achievements of Hamsa, Matsya, Kurma, Varaha, and Narasimha are completed, Vishnu either resumes his original form, becomes invisible, or returns to his original abode. The mythic mind of ancient India placed Vishnu in these animals in order for him to accomplish the necessary results. All of these animal Avataric descents took place in the Krita yuga, the first cosmic age.

3. HUMAN AVATARS OF THE TRETA YUGA

All three of the human Avatars discussed in this section descend during the second cosmic age, the Treta Yuga. With these human Avatars the God-man originates at birth and ends at death.

(A) The Dwarf Avatar, Vamana

The dwarf Avatar, Vamana, appears frequently in ancient Sanskrit literature, in the epics, the Puranas, and the Brahmanas. Brahma unwisely granted an inordinate amount of power to a king named Bali who lived an austere and ascetic life. Bali was permitted to rule not only upon the earth but also in the dwelling places of the gods in heaven. The gods saw their power being challenged and endangered and begged Vishnu to aid them. Vishnu, realizing that the power of Bali was threatening the proper balance, decided to descend to earth in the form of a dwarf, called Vamana, who was the son of Kasyapa and his wife Aditi. After praising Bali's generosity, Vamana asked that one request be granted. Bali told him to name the boon. Vamana then asked to possess as much space as he could cover in three steps. The king laughingly agreed. The dwarf suddenly became immense, and with the first step traversed the earth, and with the next, heaven. In so doing he won back for the gods most of Bali's kingdom. But he did not take the third step for it would have deprived Bali of all that he had acquired through his asceticism. Moreover, Vamana allowed Bali to visit his former kingdoms on earth and in heaven once a year.

The myth of the dwarf who covers the realms of the universe with his strides is first told in the ancient Vedas, where it is ascribed to Vishnu himself, who at that time was a minor deity. By the time Vishnu had evolved into a major god the Vamana Avatar was substituted for him.

(B) Rama with the Axe, Parasurama

There are two Ramas who are Avatars of Vishnu. The first is Parasu-Rama, Rama with the axe. The myth surrounding this Avatar tells that he was of the Brahmin caste, and from the Bhrigu race.

Vishnu descends to earth for the sixth time to restore the power of the priestly caste (Brahmin) from the warrior caste (Kshatriya).

The sixth Avatar is Parasurama, the youngest son of a Brahmin hermit, Jamadagni. One day Jamadagni's wife saw a young couple frolicking in a pool and was filled with lustful thoughts. When she returned home, Jamadagni intuited her thoughts and was incensed, deciding that she did not deserve to live. As each of their sons returned from the forest Jamadagni ordered him to kill his mother, but each refused. Finally Parasurama came back from the forest, and he alone of the sons did as his father instructed and struck off his mother's head with the axe, Parasu, that was given to him by Shiva and for which he was named. Jamadagni was pleased with his son's obedience, and offered to grant him a wish. Parasurama immediately requested that his mother be restored to life and that he be made invincible in combat and enjoy long life. These wishes were granted with Parasurama's mother restored to her former status.

One day a powerful warrior king called at the hermitage and was offered hospitality by Jamadagni's wife. While a guest of the house he caught sight of Jamadagni's wonderful cow that could grant wishes. The monarch decided that such a cow should be owned by a king rather than a hermit, so he departed with the cow despite the protests of his hostess. When Parasurama arrived home and heard what had happened, he set off immediately, overtook and killed the king in combat and returned with the cow. When the king's sons heard of his death they came marching with their troop to the hermitage, and finding Jamadagni alone slew him. Parasurama vowed vengeance for his father's death on the whole warrior caste. His vow was fulfilled in the course of twenty-one battles in which all their soldiers were exterminated, their blood filling five lakes.

While Parasurama is alive, Vishnu appears on earth for a seventh time as Ramachandra. Both Avatars figure in the two Indian epics, the *Ramayana* and the *Mahabharata*. In the *Ramayana*, Parasurama is annoyed with Ramachandra for having broken the bow of Shiva, and challenges him to a test of strength in which Parasurama is defeated. The rivalry also appears in the *Mahabharata* where Parasurama, armed with Shiva's bow, is knocked unconscious by Ramachandra, armed with Vishnu's bow.

The existence of two Avatars at the same time bearing the same name, Rama, does not present problematic ramifications for the mythic imagination, since Vishnu, being all-powerful, can have two or more simultaneous manifestations.

(C) Rama (Ramachandra)

The greater of the two Rama Avatars is Ramachandra, hero of the second great Indian epic, the *Ramayana*, or story of Rama. The *Ramayana* is one of the most popular stories of all Indian folklore. Its authorship is attributed to Valmiki, who may have written it just prior to the Christian era.

Vishnu's seventh Avatar was Rama whose purpose was to subdue the most dangerous and powerful demon king. This was Ravana, the ten-headed king of Lanka (Ceylon) who practiced austerities in order to propitiate Brahma and Shiva. Brahma had granted him immunity from being killed by gods and demons and thinking himself invincible, Ravana persecuted gods and men. The gods consulted on how they could dispose of Ravana and decided that the only way was for a god to take human form, for Ravana had been too proud to ask for immunity from men. Vishnu agreed to be the one to fulfil their wishes, and the gods said that they would lend him their powers. Thus Vishnu was born on earth to king Dasaratha by his union with Kausalya, and named Rama.

Rama heard that King Janaka's beautiful daughter Sita was to be married. A contest was to be held and the man who could bend a bow given by Shiva to Janaka would receive Sita in marriage. Rama bent the bow and even broke it, winning the contest. Shortly after Rama's marriage to Sita, his father, Dasaratha, decided to abdicate the throne in his favour. But one of Dasaratha's three wives asked a wish, and without thinking he consented. The wish was that her son, Bharata, should have the throne. Dasaratha was forced to comply, and furthermore he had to send Rama into exile in the forest for fourteen years. Sita accompanied Rama into exile along with Rama's brother, Lakshman. A week later Dasaratha died of grief.

Meanwhile Ravana abducted Sita and carried her away to the island of Lanka where he tried to seduce her, but she rejected his advances and stayed faithful to her husband Rama. Rama and Lakshman searched for Sita with the aid of a flying monkey and a garuda, and after finding her attempted her rescue. After many a bloody battle, Rama and Ravana fight to the finish in hand-to-hand combat. As all the gods looked on, these two engaged in a deadly battle, and eventually Rama struck off Ravana's heads one after the other, but as each fell another grew in its place. Finally, Rama drew a magic weapon given him by Agastya, the renowned sage.[16] This weapon, known as the Brahma weapon, was infused with the energy of many gods, with the wind in its wings, the sun and fire in its heads, and the weight of Mount Meru and Mount Mandara in its mass. Rama consecrated the weapon and sent it flying, whereupon it went straight to the breast of Ravana and killed him. This was the moment of great rejoicing among the gods, who showered Rama with heavenly garlands.

The remainder of the myth deals with Sita's ordeal to prove her innocence. The people of Rama's kingdom find it hard to believe that she had been able to preserve her virtue while a captive of Ravana. She submits to a test of fire and Rama is reassured that his wife has been faithful. Rama states that he knew of her loyalty all along (after all, he is a god) but that he put Sita through the test of fire in order to eliminate any doubts or rumours from his subjects that might stain her reputation or his, and because of his heroic commitment to truth above all else. Finally Rama and Sita are united and Rama calls a great assembly in order for her to declare her innocence publicly. Sita calls upon Earth, her mother, to attest to the truth of her words. Earth makes a sign, but it takes the form of opening up beneath Sita and swallowing her up.

Rama is now heartbroken, for Sita was his only wife and he wishes to follow her. The gods have mercy upon him in his despair and send Time, in the guise of an ascetic, with the message that he must either stay on earth or ascend to heaven and rule over the gods. Rama proceeds to the banks of the sacred river, walks into it thus forsaking his body, and ascends to his heavenly home.

In this myth Vishnu has transformed himself into Rama in order to save the world from the oppression of the demon Ravana. Rama represents and upholds morality and law (*dharma*) while Ravana symbolizes evil and wickedness (*adharma*). Rama combines the virtues of faithful husband, brave leader, and beneficent king, exhibiting heroism and nobility. The bliss of the royal couple and Sita's loyalty have become models of true love and devotion among Hindus. Rama is regarded as one of the greatest Avatars, a being of noble character, both human and divine, and his name has become a favourite one for the deity.

Throughout Indian history the popularity of Rama has been the subject of devotional stories and hymns. The poet Kalidasa (5th–6th century A.D.), devoted one of his poems, the 'Raghuvamsa', to this story. Tulsi Das (A.D. 1543–1623) composed his own version in literary Hindi called the 'Holy Lake of the Acts of Rama'. Every year in the autumn, Hindus celebrate a ten-day festival commemorating Rama's victory over Ravana. It is generally thought that Hindus who read and study the *Ramayana* with devotion will become free, those who recite it gain merit, and all Hindus are encouraged to hear it, for it is very pleasing to the Avatar Rama.

4. KRISHNA AND THE *BHAGAVAD GITA*

My Krishna has nothing to do with any historical person . . . I believe in Krishna of my imagination as a perfect incarnation, spotless in every sense of the word, the inspirer of the *Gita* and the inspirer of the lives of millions of human beings.

(Mahatma Gandhi)

The eighth Avatar is Krishna, the most popular of Vishnu's Avatars and often regarded as a perfect incarnation. With Krishna we have the most elaborate mythology of all the Avatars. Among Hindus Krishna is commonly regarded as a full or complete Avatar (Purnavatar), and the mythology surrounding him gives rise to numerous avataric motifs. In Hindu literature sometimes Krishna is the eighth Avatar and Balarama is his accomplice, at other times Krishna is the Avatarin (the source of Avatars), and Balarama is the eighth Avatar. According to the tradition, Krishna lived for 125 years, and his life can be divided into three stages, (1) birth and childhood, (2) youth and adolescence, and (3) middle age and death.

(1) Krishna's Birth and Childhood

At the end of Dwapara yuga, there lived a peace-loving, agricultural people, the Yadavas, ruled by a king and a queen. One day the queen was raped by a demon who had assumed the appearance of her husband. The demon announced that the son to be born, Kamsa, would rule the earth and struggle against one whose name would be Krishna. As Kamsa grew up his evil nature revealed itself: he murdered children, deposed his father the king,

ascended the throne, and banned the worship of Vishnu. He
extended his kingdom by conquest and committed many crimes.
The gods decided that it was time to intervene and called upon
Vishnu. Vishnu plucked a white hair from Sesha, the serpent on
whose coiled body he lay, and a black hair from his own head,
declaring that these would become Balarama and Krishna, the
seventh and eighth sons of Devaki.

When Kamsa learned that Devaki would give birth to a child
whose destiny was to kill him, he ordered that every child of hers
be put to death as soon as it was born. His orders were carried out,
and Devaki's first six children were killed. But when Devaki was
expecting her seventh child, Vishnu had the child in her womb
transferred to that of Rohini. In due course Balarama was born to
Rohini, and Kamsa was led to believe that Devaki had miscarried.

When the time came for Devaki to conceive again, Kamsa took
the precaution of imprisoning both Devaki the mother, and Vasudeva, the father. He had them manacled together and set men,
elephants, and lions to guard the prison. But the eighth child was
Krishna, and when he was born he assumed the form of Vishnu,
made the manacles fall off, and put the guards to sleep. Then he
ordered his father to take him to the house of Nanda, where
Nanda's wife had just given birth and to exchange the babies.

Krishna's dual nature was revealed even in childhood. At times
he seemed to be just an exceptionally lovable boy, and at other
times he began to show his strength and was recognized as a god.
During his first year Krishna was attacked by three demons: a
child-killing ogress, a monstrous flying demon, and a whirlwind
demon. As Krishna grew up he amused himself with various
pranks, such as stealing butter and sweets, and upsetting the dairy
maids' milk pails. But Krishna's idyllic childhood in the forest of
Vrindavana was interrupted by the efforts of Kamsa, who sent
demons to attack all children of Krishna's age. Again and again
Krishna was attacked by Kamsa's demons, but on each occasion,
assisted by his constant companion, Balarama, he extricated himself, fighting the jackass demon, the snake demon Kaliya, and
swallowing up a fire sent to consume him. In addition to these
demons, he also conquered evil-willed horses, bulls, and flying
creatures.

In what may be his most famous battle in Vrindavana, Krishna
encountered the many-headed serpent Kaliya. Kaliya lived in a
nearby stream and had poisoned its waters, causing the death of

many cattle. Krishna arrived on the scene, surveyed the situation, climbed into a tree, and leaped into the poisonous waters, where he began to bait the monster by swimming and playing there. The enraged Kaliya emerged from his lair beneath the waters and the battle began. Kaliya seemed to get the upper hand at first, gripping Krishna in his coils, but Krishna was only humouring him. Freeing himself from Kaliya's coils, he began circling the demon until his heads began to droop with exhaustion. Seeing his chance, Krishna jumped onto the heads of the serpent and began to dance. By rhythmically stamping his feet on the serpent's heads he trampled his enemy into submission. Battered and bloody, Kaliya finally admitted defeat and sought refuge. Krishna, at the pleading of Kaliya's wives, granted him his life but banished him to the periphery of the cosmos, sending him back to the sea where he belonged.[17]

Originally Vishnu rested on the serpent Sesha; now Krishna dances on the serpent Kaliya, indeed both gods have their pet serpents. Krishna's elder brother, Balarama, also has a close association with the world of serpents, and Indian sculpture portrays the cobra arching over him. In the Hindu text called the *Harivamsa*, Krishna treats Kaliya as if he were Sesha, and it becomes necessary for Balarama to remind him that this is not the golden age, and the time to relax on the serpent's back has not yet arrived.

(2) **Krishna's Youth and Adolescence**

One day when Krishna and his companions were hungry they smelled food and found that it was being cooked by Brahmins in preparation for a sacrifice. They asked to eat but were refused. The Brahmins' wives, however, eager to oblige disobeyed their husbands and brought Krishna food, feasting their eyes on him and recognizing him as God. Krishna's amorous adventures with the Brahmins' wives began when he was quite young and developed naturally from his teasing of the married dairymaids, known as *gopis*. One day when a group of them went bathing in the Jumna River, Krishna came across them as they were calling his name. He stole their clothes and climbed a tree. The gopis were horrified and tried to hide their nakedness beneath the water; but Krishna told them that a god-like aspect of himself inhabited the water so they were no better off in it. He insisted that each of the dairymaids

come to the tree to receive her clothes. Sending them away after all
this teasing, Krishna mollified them by promising that he would
dance with them in the autumn.

When autumn came Krishna went into the forest of Vrindavana
and played his flute to call the dairymaids, who slipped away from
their husbands and joined him. After some teasing on his part the
dance began, sending the girls into ecstasies of delight, each one
dancing with Krishna as if he were her lover. But Krishna slipped
away with one of them and when the other girls realized that they
were abandoned they set out to find him by following his footprints. Soon the girl with Krishna asked him to carry her, and
annoyed, he abandoned her. The others found her, and after their
endless search and entreaties that he return, Krishna relented.

The dance began again and the girls became desirous. Krishna
made each girl believe that he was dancing with her, embracing
and loving her. The dance and its erotic delights continued for six
months and ended with the whole company bathing in the Jumna
River. The girls returned to their homes and discovered that no
one knew that they had ever been away.

The idea of Krishna having an appropriate consort gradually
developed from the 7th to the 12th centuries when Jayadeva in his
Gita Govinda depicted the playfulness of Krishna with a gopi
named Radha.[18] For the Bengali Vaishnavas, Krishna and Radha
are the most passionate of lovers, and their passion is intensified
by periods of separation. Theirs is an ideal love, the epitome of
love, and Radha is praised as the true consort and real beloved of
Krishna. The mythic imagination carried the love of Krishna and
Radha to the fullest extent by imagining that their love was eternal
and had existed in each of their previous lives, even that they were
really one individual rather than two, and that Krishna differentiated the Radha aspect of himself solely for the purposes of joy
and playfulness.

In Vrindavana Krishna is eternally young.[19] His skin is dark
blue and he wears golden-yellow robes just like Vishnu. His
dancing expresses the charm and grace of the divine, for his
movements are fluid and harmonious and his figure is lithe.
Krishna's flute is an extension of his beauty, for it makes heavenly
music and imparts the essence of his blissful nature. The sounds
that it produces are no earthly sounds; they fill the heavens and
distract even the gods.[20] Krishna's flute echoes throughout Vrindavana, beckoning all to join him there. Its sound is like a

summons calling the souls of men back to their Lord. Its pure, clear notes sound as if they came from another world. Even the gopis, who are married women, cannot resist its sensuous charm and succumb to its bewitching call. The whole of creation can concentrate on nothing but the sound of Krishna's flute. Nature itself is intoxicated by his flute and the lion lies down with the lamb. When the clouds hear his flute they provide shade for him, rivers slow down to listen to its sounds and grow lotuses, and the reeds from which the flute grew shed tears of delight.[21] With his flute Krishna fills the universe with bliss and ecstasy. His flute incites the world to dance as natural laws are suspended and the stars dance in the heavens. The sound of Krishna's flute elicits devotion to its divine melody.

(3) Krishna's Middle Age and Death

Kamsa continued to attack Krishna by sending his demons in the form of a bull, a horse, and a wolf, but Krishna was able to overcome them all. Kamsa now abandoned such tactics and cast Krishna's parents into prison in an effort to lure Krishna to Mathura and ultimately kill him there. Kamsa sent his prime minister to invite Krishna to a great sacrifice in honour of Shiva at Mathura. But the prime minister was a secret devotee of Krishna and warned him of Kamsa's plan to kill him. Krishna, Balarama, and a few gopis set off for Mathura. At the gate of the city Krishna picked up the great bow of Shiva and broke it into pieces (just as Rama had done before), and killed all the guards. As he entered Mathura he was attacked by Kamsa's wild elephant but killed him, and he and Balarama paraded around with the elephant tusks. Kamsa was now desperate, so he ordered the demons to bring Krishna's parents and have them put to death along with Krishna and Balarama as soon as they were overcome. When news of this reached Krishna he slew the remaining demons and killed Kamsa and his brothers. Krishna had now achieved the main purpose of his life, to kill Kamsa, but Kamsa's allies were still at large and upsetting the balance of power between good and evil.

Upon the death of Kamsa, two other powerful demons took his place. At least seventeen times did Krishna and Balarama fight against these demons and defeat them. Krishna decided to build a new capital which would be easier to defend and he commissioned Visvakarma, the divine architect, to build it in one night.

Krishna was now ready to settle down and sought wives for himself and his brother Balarama. Balarama married a princess while Krishna fell in love with the princess Rukmini upon hearing a description of her beauty. This was to set the stage for a great romantic passion, but not before certain obstacles were overcome. Demons frequently interfered with Krishna's wedding plans, but they were taken captive. Krishna married Rukmini and celebrated the defeat of still more demons at his nuptials. In the same way he married seven additional wives, each marriage being opposed in some way by demons and resulting in the destruction of yet more evil. Thus, Krishna married the daughter of the king of the bears, and the daughter of the sun, in each case after struggles with demons.

At that time a powerful king conquered all the rulers of the earth. He stole the earrings of the mother of the gods, and took into captivity 16100 virgins. Finally, taking the form of an elephant, he raped the daughter of Visvakarma, the divine architect. Krishna attacked and defeated this king and took all the virgins back to his capital and married them, for they had fallen in love with him. Krishna settled down with his 16108 wives, was able to cater to their whims and desires, and each of them bore him ten sons and one daughter. The climax of Krishna's long battle with the forces of evil occurred in the struggle between the Pandavas and the Kauravas which is related in the *Mahabharata* epic. Krishna took no active part in the battle, only giving advice and letting the warriors fight it out. Krishna's most important advice is found in a section of the *Mahabharata* comprising book 6, section 25 to 42, called the *Bhagavad Gita*, the *Song of the Lord*. The setting of the *Gita* is the battlefield of that war and its content is a discourse that takes place between Arjuna, general of the army of the Pandavas, and Krishna, who is both an Avatar of Vishnu and Arjuna's charioteer. As the battle is about to begin, Arjuna loses his nerve and refuses to fight because he sees his kinsmen in both armies and thinks that the war will lead to the destruction of the families, and hence to the destruction of the laws (dharma) of the families. Destruction of dharma will lead, according to Arjuna, to the destruction of society, the mixture of caste, and to the corruption of women. Lord Krishna assumes the task of convincing Arjuna to fight, using an array of arguments including (1) disgrace if he does not fight since he is a warrior; (2) appealing to his sense of duty (*dharma* or *svadharma*); (3) assuring him that a man of wisdom knows that in war he is not really killing the soul of anyone, since the soul is separate from the material body (jnana yoga); (4) that it is legitimate to perform required action so long as one is not attached to the fruit of reward of the action (karma yoga); and (5) that it is also legitimate to perform required action so long as one acts in a spirit of complete devotion to God (bhakti yoga). Thus, the *Bhagavad Gita* presents Krishna as recommending three major yogas: jnana yoga, karma yoga, and bhakti yoga.

Krishna decides that he should return to heaven. However, portents of impending destruction appear in Krishna's capital, and the Yadavas, frightened by storms and lightning, deformed babies, and other horrors, appeal to Krishna for aid. On his advice the men set out on a pilgrimage and perform various rituals. When the Yadavas quench their thirst at the river they drink the waters of fury and a battle ensues in which they kill each other. Now Krishna and Balarama are free to leave the earth. Balarama performs austerities at the seashore and the serpent Sesha, from whose white hair he was born, comes out of his mouth. The ocean with various serpents in its midst comes to meet him and carry him back to his watery home.

Krishna assumes a yogic posture beneath a fig tree. A passing hunter mistakes Krishna's foot for a deer and shoots an arrow at it, piercing Krishna's only vulnerable spot and mortally wounding him. The hunter, recognizing Krishna, asks his pardon, is forgiven, and is granted liberation. A great funeral is held for Krishna and Balarama and for their parents who died of grief upon learning of their deaths. Krishna's eight principal wives and Balarama's wives immolate themselves on the funeral pyre.

The Krishna myth portrays him as a full and complete Avatar. He has a miraculous birth, a playful relationship with the gopis, establishes his androgyny by uniting with Radha, is a teacher of the law, and is a saviour who repeatedly defeats evil forces. When he plays his magic flute he sends celestial currents reverberating down the centuries for later Avatars to hear, revere, and imitate.

5. BUDDHA, THE DECEPTIVE AND COMPASSIONATE AVATAR

. . . Buddha, though forgotten on the surface, is still the secret breath of life in modern Hinduism. He is suffered at least to be an avatar of Vishnu.[22]

(C. G. Jung)

Hindus came to regard the Buddha as an Avatar of Vishnu between A.D. 400 and A.D. 500.[23] Lists of Vishnu's ten Avatars traditionally have the Buddha Avatar as the ninth. In the *Mahabharata*
the Buddha is not mentioned because he is not yet considered an
Avatar. However, later Hindu thinkers had to admit that a person
who could influence men as Buddha did could not have been other
than an Avatar, and he is alluded to in some of the Puranas.

It was the Hindu text called the *Vishnu Purana* (A.D. 400–500)
which first identified the Buddha as an Avatar of Vishnu. The
Vishnu Purana states that:

> the demons, led by Prahlada, had stolen the sacrificial portions
> of the gods, but they were so full of svadharma (attending to
> their own duties), Vedic worship, and asceticism that they could
> not be conquered. Vishnu created a man of delusion to lead the
> demons from the path of the Vedas; the man was naked, bald,
> carrying a peacock-feather fan; he went where the demons were
> practising asceticism on the banks of the Narmada and made
> them all into Arhats, discouraging them from their asceticism
> and teaching them contradictory tenets about dharma (good).
> Then the man put on red garments and taught the rest of the
> demons that the sacrifice of animals was an evil act. He said, 'If
> the animal slaughtered in the sacrifice is assured of arrival in
> heaven, why does the sacrificer not kill his own father?' Then
> the demons became Buddhists, and they caused others to
> become heretics, abandoning the Vedas and reviling the gods
> and Brahmins, discarding their armor of svardharma. The gods
> attacked them and killed them.[24]

In this account Vishnu has sent an illusory form of himself to the
gods telling them that this deceptive form will beguile the
demons[25] and turn them away from the Vedas, and that due to
their willingness to believe in errors and lies they will be easy to
subdue. He induces some demons to deviate from their religious
duties and become Buddhists. Having strayed from the path of the
Vedas, the demons are inwardly weak and the gods take courage
and defeat them. Vishnu in his deceptive form as Buddha has
exposed the inner weakness of the heretics and put them at the
mercy of the gods. Buddha is portrayed as a deceptive Avatar of
Vishnu who will separate Veda-following devotees from Veda-
rejecting heretics.

The Hindu text called the *Bhagavata Purana* states that:

> when the Kali Age has begun, in order to delude the enemies of
> the gods, Vishnu will be born as the Buddha, son of Ajana. . . .
> When the enemies of the gods come to know the Vedic rites and
> begin to oppress people, then he will assume an attractive and
> deluding form and teach adharma (evil) to the demons . . .
> making them heretics. . . . With words he will delude those who
> are not deserving of the sacrifice. . . . Homage to Buddha, the
> pure, the deluder of the demons.[26]

Furthermore, the *Agni Purana* relates that 'during the battle between gods and demons, the gods were defeated and sought
refuge with the Lord; he became the son of Suddhodana, the very
form of Mayamoha, and deluded the demons, who became Buddhists and abandoned the Vedas'.[27]

These Puranic myths make the purpose of the Buddha Avatar
evident. While the demons come to know the Vedic rites, they are
not deserving of the Vedic sacrifice and it is necessary for them to
be corrupted as well as destroyed. The inclusion of the Buddha as
a deceptive Avatar seems to have been intended to keep Hindus
away from Buddhism. The portrayal of the Buddha Avatar in the
various Puranas reflects the tension between Hindus and Buddhists and the gradual elimination of Buddhism from India. The
Buddha Avatar may represent an attempt by priestly (Brahmin)
Hindus to slander the Buddhists by identifying them with the
demons. This suggestion is supported by the fact that the Buddha
Avatar, who deludes the demons, is followed by the Kalki Avatar,
who exterminates the heretics and barbarians in the Kali yuga.
These myths indicate a political situation in the pre-Gupta age
(precisely when the myth of the Buddha Avatar first appears),
when orthodox Hindus had their prestige threatened by foreign
invaders and a thriving Buddhist community at home. The
Buddha Avatar, which appears in Puranic texts composed after the
initial idea of human Avatars has been accepted, is portrayed in
order to discredit the Buddhist doctrines. In the myth of the
conversion of the demons to Buddhism, the teaching is always
intended to be destructive, to be preached by God in bad faith.

The Hindus who appropriated the Buddha in the Puranas did so
to suit their own purposes. For them, the Buddha Avatar stood for
the God-man who would bring about the apocalypse, the final

cosmic catalysm, by leading men toward evil ways and heretical teachings. As his influence supported a teaching opposed to their own, the Hindu writers cleverly said that Buddha promulgated his doctrine to mislead the enemies of God, and that those who were weak and wicked would easily fall prey to his doctrine. His avatarhood portrays a deceptive spiritual path that can lead weak and evil men away from the true path of Hindu spirituality. It heralds the time when the final Avatar, Kalki, will have to end the age of darkness and inaugurate a resplendent golden age. Because Kalki came to destroy heretics and barbarians, these same heretics may have been personified as Buddhists during the Gupta period, when Buddhism posed a threat to the Hindu revival, and precisely when Buddha first appeared as the Hindu Avatar. It has been suggested that the Buddha Avatar may have been inspired by the Kalki Avatar.[28]

Thus far the Buddha Avatar has been presented negatively, as a deceptive figure. However, the Buddha Avatar has a positive side as well.

This Avatar has been an enigma to scholars for nearly two hundred years. In 1790, Sir William Jones noted the contradiction between Jayadeva's praise of the Buddha Avatar in his *Gita Govinda* and the *Bhagavata Purana*'s reference to a deluding Buddha Avatar. European scholars emphasized the positive element of the Buddha Avatar, correctly when applied to later texts (for example, those of Kshemendra and Jayadeva), but incorrectly with reference to the early works dealing with Puranic mythology. The confusion is due in part to a change in attitude. In the main corpus of Puranic myths, Buddha and Buddhists are associated with demons and barbarians. However, in the post-Puranic period some Indian writers came to accept the Buddha Avatar as a positive aspect of Vishnu. This attitude is reflected in later Puranas such as the *Varaha Purana*, where it is said that the worshipper should sacrifice to Krishna when he wants sons, to Kalki when he wants to destroy enemies, and to Buddha when he wants beauty.[29] Similarly, the *Matsya Purana* notes that the Buddha Avatar is lotus-eyed and beautiful as a god, and offers homage to the peaceful Buddha.[30] Kshemendra in the 11th century described the Buddha Avatar in a positive sense, and this is thought to be the earliest known favourable reference to the Buddha Avatar by an orthodox Hindu.[31] Jayadeva, a 12th century Hindu, said that Vishnu became the Buddha Avatar out of compassion for animals, to end bloody sacrifices.[32] The *Devibhagavata Purana* supported Jayadeva's statement, saying that Vishnu 'became incarnate as the Buddha in order to stop the slaughter of animals and to destroy the sacrifices of the wicked' (or possibly 'to destroy wicked sacrifices').[33]

From the 5th to the 12th century in India, the Buddha Avatar went from a negative to a positive transformation. However, in neither case was he presented as a historical person in a historical setting. The Buddha Avatar of Hinduism bears little resemblance to the Buddha of the Buddhist religion who is revered as the Enlightened One.

6. KALKI, THE APOCALYPTIC AVATAR

> To slay barbarian hosts you draw
> Bright comet – scimitar of fire
> How vastly blazing! Full of fire
> In Kalkin's body you appear,
> The primal virtues you restore
> Hail, Hari, Ruler of the World!
>
> (Jayadeva, *Gita Govinda*)

The tenth Avatar of Vishnu is Kalki, who, it is believed, will appear on earth in the future when it is time for the evil age to end and a righteous age to begin. For many centuries in India there have been numerous prophecies and myths predicting whom the Kalki Avatar will be. This has led to hope and expectation, and whenever a new God-man makes his appearance, the suspicion arises that he is the Kalki Avatar.

The basis for the Kalki prophecies derives from a Puranic text called the *Kalki Upapurana*. From this work many Hindus have come to believe that Kalki is due to appear on earth at the juncture of the two ages, the present dark age known as the Kali yuga, and the Krita yuga, the golden age to be resuscitated.

According to traditional Hindu mythology, toward the end of the Kali yuga, wealth and power will be the standards for ruling, hypocrisy will dominate business dealings, and carnal pleasures will rule the relationships between men and women. Virtue and religion will have disappeared, as rulers, outwardly arrayed in the apparel of justice, but inwardly evil, will harass the people. The people will begin to leave the wicked cities and greedy rulers and take refuge in the valleys where they will overpopulate the earth, endure harsh weather, and many will die young.

At the conclusion of the Kali yuga, Vishnu will appear as Kalki. He will be born into the family of the Vishnuyashas, the chief Brahmin of the village of Shambala. He will be revealed in the sky seated on a winged white horse with a drawn sword blazing like a comet. He will be endowed with eight supernatural faculties. He will destroy the wicked and barbarian and save the righteous. A remnant of humanity will be transformed and will repopulate the earth. The new offspring will follow the correct ways of Hindu spirituality under the leadership of Kalki, and the golden age will begin. The purpose of Kalki Avatar is to create a new generation of people, God-fearing and righteous.

Prophecies of Kalki's return haunt the minds of many modern Hindus. For example, Pandit Rajnarayan Sastri, an astrologer from the Punjab, forecast that Kalki would be born in 1924 and would conquer East Asia in 1941. When this prophecy failed to happen, Swami Jagadiswarananda had a vision of Kalki who told him about his imminent advent. Swami Jagadiswarananda wrote a book explaining that Kalki will come in 1985 when one-eighth of the Kali yuga remains. Kalki will establish the kingdom of heaven on earth and shower peace and prosperity on all deserving people irrespective of caste, colour, or creed. He will rule for 125 years and die in the year 2110.[34] There is also a contemporary claimant to the Kalki Avatar in Java, a guru by the name of W. Hardjanto Prad-japangarsa who has begun a new religious movement.[35]

Just as the Kalki mythology flourishes in the East, so has it penetrated the West and been picked up in popular literature, a current example being the mythopoesis of Gore Vidal in his novel *Kalki*.[36] Vidal portrays the Kalki Avatar as a 35-year old American Catholic, who astride his white horse, announces the end of the Kali yuga in Madison Square Garden. He brings about the apocalypse with the demise of all human beings except the 'five perfect masters' from whom a new breed of beings is to emerge and inaugurate the golden age. However, Kalki's plan goes hay-wire and the Kalki Avatar is subjected to an ironic twist of fate. Kalki resigns himself to his final role as Shiva, the destroyer, instead of Brahma, the creator, and a new age begins with the origin of a non-human species.

The Kalki Avatar is part of a vibrant mythic image that con-tinues to develop and spread. Vidal has reanimated the Hindu myth of Kalki and presented it in a contemporary American setting in accord with the popular Hindu belief that Western degeneracy will bring to fruition the apocalypse at the end of the Kali yuga. The prophecy of the return of Vishnu's tenth Avatar continues as an apocalyptic image of a world saviour who will end the evil era and inaugurate the golden paradisal age.

The Kalki myth bears striking resemblance to various apocalyptic visions. In the apocalypse of the New Testament, the Book of Revelation, the author sees

> heaven opened, and behold, a white horse! He who sat upon it is called Faithful and True, and in righteousness he judges and makes war. His eyes are like a flame of fire, and on his head are many diadems; and he has a name inscribed which no one knows but himself. . . . From his mouth issues a sharp sword with which to smite the nations, and he will rule them with a rod of iron. . . . On his robe and on his thigh he has a name inscribed, King of kings and Lord of lords
> (Rev. 19: 11, 12, 15, 16)

The German *Book of a Hundred Chapters* written in the early 16th century gives another example of a Christian apocalypse. The messiah in this instance is a king who

> will come on a white horse and will have a bow in his hand, and a crown shall be given him by God so that he shall have power to compel the whole world; he will have a great sword in his hand and will strike many down. . . . At the same time this saviour will establish a messianic kingdom for the benefit of his followers, in which their every need, spiritual and material, will be amply supplied.[37]

Apocalyptic saviours and Avatars arrive on white horses, brandish flaming swords, bring an end to the decadent era, and herald a golden age.

CONCLUSION – CLASSICAL AVATARS AND CHRIST

When we entered the great temple of Vishnu-Narayana in Vrindavana, a merchant in his modest shop offered us his wares. The consecrated signs and marks of Vishnu were there, the *Gita* and other holy Scriptures. There was also a little pamphlet there with a strange title, in the midst of the Indian books. It was the Gospel of Luke. 'Of whom does this book treat?' 'Of Jesus. He is the last Avatar of Vishnu.' So think many in India.[38]

(Rudolf Otto)

Is there a connection between the classical Avatars of India and Jesus Christ? Many people have noticed similarities between the lives of Jesus and Krishna and have suspected and searched for cross-cultural influences. For centuries there has been confusion concerning the names Christ (Christos) and Krishna (Christna), with the added suggestion that the *New Testament* may have influenced the *Gita*. This confusion can be corrected by observing how Hinduism gradually came to be known in the West.

The comprehension of Hinduism by Westerners before the 18th century was negligible. The prevailing belief among Europeans throughout the 18th century was that the Hindus and other 'pagans' had originally been part of a single and undivided human race that accepted the truth of the unity of God. However, it was believed that after the building of the Tower of Babel the peoples of the earth became scattered, and while the Jews and the Christians remained faithful, any trace of monotheism on the part of other religions could be attributed to a distant recollection of the remote past. Various elaborate 'historical' arguments were proposed to explain the existence of elements in Hinduism that could be praised from a Christian point of view. Some Christians maintained that after the dispersal of the nations at Babel, Hinduism had come under the influence of either Jewish or Christian beliefs. Scholars noticed the similarity between Hindu myths, such as the Matsya Avatar myth, and the accounts of the flood and the ark in *Genesis*. Travellers and missionaries to India also took note that Hindus revered a god in three aspects, and concluded that Hinduism had been influenced by the Christian trinity. Any evidence that Hinduism contained some trace of Jewish or Christian influence was of particular interest to missionaries. For example, when the German Lutheran missionary Bartholomaeus Ziegenbalg learned about Vishnu's incarnations he inferred that the Hindus had heard of Christ and that they had modelled their Avatars upon Christianity's Incarnation.[39]

In the mid-18th century British scholarship began to uncover the richness of Sanskrit literature and scriptures. The enthusiasm for India was so intense that certain radical theories arose, one of which was that all the world's religions were versions of an original Indian religion that God had delivered to man via Brahma.[40] Some British scholars also speculated that Christ and Brahma were perhaps separate appearances on earth of the same person with the same message, or that Christ's teaching was merely a restatement of Brahma's message.[41] In 1790, Sir William Jones, writing 'On the Gods of Greece, Italy, and India', stated that the name of Crishna and the general outline of his story is 'long anterior to the birth of our Saviour, and probably to the time of Homer . . .'.[42] Jones suggested that some 'spurious' Christian gospels were brought to India and repeated to the Hindus who 'ingrafted them on the old fable of Cesava, the Apollo of Greece'[43] and thus there developed the stories of Crishna. (In the 18th and 19th centuries the name Krishna was often spelled with a 'C'.)

In France around the time of the revolution, Hinduism was regarded as the basis of all the world's religions including Christianity. It was even thought that the five books of Moses were an abridgement of Egyptian books which originated in India.[44] In 1796 the French traveller, writer, politician and philosopher, Constantine De Volney, argued that Christ was a solar myth derived from the Hindu god Chris-en or Christna.[45] And a century later Louis Jaccoliot who was French Consul at Calcutta wrote 'Si la légende du Christna indoo est authentique, la légende du Christ juif ne peu qu'être apocryphe',[46] (If the story of the Hindu Krishna is authentic, then the story of the Jewish Christ can only be apocryphal).

In the late 18th and early 19th centuries, industrialization and scientific knowledge brought about a widening of the gap between Indian and European standards, and there grew a greater confidence in the superiority of everything Western, including the books of Moses and the Gospels of Jesus. The positive attitude toward Hinduism began to diminish and the Hindu religion was now seen as a debased and superstitious faith practised by immoral people. While Western scholars began to see Krishna as a corruption of Christ, to Hindu writers of the 19th century Christ could be none other than a later Krishna or Rama.

The debate raged on. In 1823 there occurred a theological debate between the Indian nationalist and reformer, Ram Mohan Roy, and the British missionary to India, Rev. R. Tytler. In this debate

Roy asserted that the common basis for Hinduism and Christianity is the incarnation of the deity, and argued that if an incarnation occurred in Judea it could just as reasonably occur in India and assume any colour and name. Roy's statement to Reverend Tytler is noteworthy:

> I am more particularly astonished that a man of your reputed learning and acquirements, should be offended at the mention of the resemblance of your belief in the Divinity of Jesus Christ with a Hindoo's belief in his Thakoor, because you ought to know that our religious faith and yours are founded on the same sacred basis, *viz.*, the MANIFESTATION OF GOD IN THE FLESH, without any restriction to a dark or fair complexion, large or small stature, long or short hair. You cannot surely be ignorant that the Divine RAM was the reputed son of Dushuruth, of the offspring of Bhuggeeruth, of the tribe of Rughoo, as Jesus was the reputed son of Joseph, of the House of David, of the Tribe of Judah. RAM was the King of the Rughoos and of Foreigners, while in like manner Jesus was King of the Jews and Gentiles. Both are stated in respective sacred books handed down to us, to have performed very wonderful miracles and both ascended up to Heaven. Both were tempted by the Devil while on the earth, and both have been worshipped by millions up to the present day. Since God can be born of the Tribe of Judah, how, I ask, is it impossible that he should be born of the Tribe of Rughoo, or of any other nation or race of men?[47]

To this attack Rev. Tytler responded that the Avatar legends, including those of 'Chrishna', were 'perverted and corrupted copies of the Holy Scriptures in the possession of Christians', which had no relation whatsoever to the ancient religion of India.[48]

At the end of the 19th, and into the 20th century eminent Sanskrit scholars such as Albrecht Weber and Sir Monier-Williams were still suggesting the possible influence of Christianity on the Hindu legends of Krishna, and even a parallel in the names of Christ and Chrishna. Since dates for the composition of the *Gita* ranged from 300 B.C. to as late as A.D. 400, it was possible to imagine that copies of the New Testament had found their way into India and influenced the *Gita* and the name of Chrishna.

Certain motifs which Christ and Krishna shared in common seemed to support this contention. Did not Christ and Krishna have a miraculous birth? Were they not both mediators and saviour figures who battled against evil? Did they not both inspire love and devotion? Indeed, in 1875, Kersey Graves published a list of 'three hundred and forty-six striking analogies between Christ and Chrishna'.[49] It was not difficult to imagine some cross-cultural influence.

Today we are in a somewhat better position to realize that there was probably little or no influence of Hinduism upon Christianity nor of Christianity upon Hinduism in the early centuries, and that the two religions developed primarily independently. While the names Christ and Krishna may sound alike, the word Christ is derived from the Greek *Christos*, and is a title meaning the anointed, while Krishna is a name meaning the dark one. Furthermore, today we realize that the spirit of Hinduism has been unconcerned with history and historicism until perhaps the 20th century, while Christianity has been an historical religion from its inception and values things in terms of historicism. For Christianity, Jesus Christ is an historical God-man who was born, lived, and died in a given time and place as a singular and unique historical event. Christ as interpreted by Hinduism, on the other hand, is an aspect of the divine appearing repeatedly throughout the ages.

For the Hindus the historic existence of the Avatars is not as important as their spiritual efficacy. They tend to view Christ in the same spiritual way, as the Logos, the Word of God, and thus, they have no difficulty relating Krishna and Christ, for they accept them as the divine Logos or Spirit. While Christians tend to be exclusive and emphasize the uniqueness of their faith, Hindus prefer to be inclusive and see all religions as part of a larger whole. Mahatma Gandhi is a good example of this inclusiveness. He expresses the characteristic Hindu attitude in his statement, 'I cannot ascribe exclusive divinity to Jesus. He is as divine as Krishna or Rama or Mohammad or Zoroaster.'[50] When Gandhi was asked about the historical person of Jesus he responded, 'I should not care if it was proved by someone that the man called Jesus never lived, and that what was narrated in the Gospels was a figment of the writer's imagination. For the Sermon on the Mount would still be true to me.'[51]

Some Westerners tend to exalt the historical Jesus and degrade the mythic Avatars, and consequently consider Hinduism inferior to Christianity. An example is found in the book *Avatar and Incarnation* where the author, Geoffrey Parrinder, concludes that:

> The Avatars of Hinduism lead up to Christ and they are valuable preparations for him. More easily than Jews or Greeks, Indians can understand the coming of God in human form. Yet this very ease has great dangers, and the casual way in which many modern Hindus consider Christ as just another Avatar thereby deprives him of significance and challenge. The Avatars, after all, were a flashing kaleidoscope of theophanies, coming and going in the endless cycle of ages. They were never really men.[52]

Here it can be observed that historical men are judged to be significant, while avataric theophanies recurring in mythic cycles as portrayed in ancient Indian religion are regarded as ephemeral. Occasionally when contemporary Hindus convert to Christianity they base their decision upon the historicity of the Christian God-man. For example, when Rabindranath Maharaj is reminded that 'You don't have to become a Christian because you believe that Jesus is a god', Rabindranath responds by saying,

> Well, I can't agree with that . . . Jesus said that he is *the* way, not a way; so that eliminates Krishna and everyone else. He did not come to destroy sinners – like Krishna said of himself – but to *save* them. And no one else could. Jesus is not just one of many gods. He is the only true God, and he came to this earth as a man, not just to show us how to live but to die for our sins. Krishna never did that. And Jesus was resurrected, which never happened to Krishna or Rama or Shiva – in fact, they never existed.[53]

Having dealt with the comparison between classical Avatars and Christ, let us now turn to what is perhaps a more appropriate comparison, Jesus Christ and modern Avatars.

2
Modern Avatars of India

INTRODUCTION ON VAISHNAVISM

The time has long since passed when scholars of Indian religion should have begun to consider seriously the nature of Indian sainthood and more particularly the so-called 'living saints.' As it is, the knowledgeable reader has very little choice of published material upon which to base his judgments. For many of the living saints there is a fairly extensive body of apologetic writing. In the nature of primary sources such works are invaluable but remain unanalyzed. There are also publications available in the occult market; but there the motives of the writers differ from those of scholarly inquiry in many cases, however interesting their contributions may be in their own right. Analytical works on modern Hinduism and its saint leadership are negligible in number. . . . Regarding the living saints, what is presently most necessary is that there should be thorough reporting of their behavior, preferably from first hand observation, and an objective clarification of their biographies according to certain motifs and structures. The specifically religious nature of their activities must also be investigated. . . . In the case of the study of modern Indian saints one cannot overemphasize the need to evolve criteria that will make it possible to describe our understanding of these individuals in language other than that of the adoring devotee or the hostile sceptic.[1]

(Charles S. J. White, 'Approaches to the
Study of Indian Saints')

This chapter will describe six modern historical Avatars of India. It will show how they came to an awareness of their divinity, the nature of their avatarhood, other Avatars whom they acknowledge as divine, and their relationship with the Vaishnava tradition of Hinduism. Although there have been many books written about each of the following God-men individually, thus far these six

51

have not been studied collectively. This study views the Indian Avatars serially and collectively. Themes, motifs, and the mythic substructure of avatarhood are examined. Before proceeding to the study of the Avatars, let us pause to explore the tradition which provided the context within which avatarhood developed, Vaishnavism.

Vaishnavism is the major tradition within the Hindu religion. It centres its faith upon the god Vishnu and his numerous incarnations. In Bengal, Vaishnavism has existed for many centuries. Although it appears to be homogenous, in reality it is a complex product, embodying worship of the gods Vishnu, Narayana, and Vasudeva-Krishna.

Two fundamental elements that form the texture of Bengal Vaishnavism are *bhakti*, the emotional service of love and devotion used for divine realization, and the Krishna cult, that forms the ground of this devotional attitude. The practice of *bhakti* is basically dualistic in nature, reflecting the yearning of the devotee to attain communion with a deity. Devotion is paid to one or more of the Hindu gods who are conceived of as personal. *Bhakti* means adoration of *Bhagavan* the 'Blessed One'.

Throughout the history of religion in India there has been a tension between dualistic and monistic interpretations of God and Reality. The monistic interpretation posits only one reality to the world, spirit (*Brahman-atman*), and declares matter to be an illusion (*maya*). The dualistic interpretation, on the other hand, sees matter as real and evolving toward the spiritual. The imposing theology of Shankara in the 8th century advocated monism (*Advaita*). This gave rise in subsequent centuries to a revival and refinement of dualistic theologies such as Vaishnavism. The Vaishnavite dualism underwent some reconciliation with the monistic interpretation, and a variety of schools developed, each diverging in part from Shankara's monism and expounding various degrees of qualified dualistic views, thus permitting the practice of piety and *bhakti*. The subsequent history of Vaishnavism as a religious tradition follows the lines of worshipping God in the form of a person, along with his symbols and manifestations. Vaishnavites believe in a personal creator (Vishnu), in his energy (Shakti), in his incarnations (Avatars), and in eschatology. They believe in the complete surrender to divine grace, and in emotional and mystical forms of adoration that they feel are superior to intellectual convictions adduced by mere knowledge.

As the Vaishnava faith was essentially personal, one or another of Vishnu's incarnations was in actual practice chosen as the principal object of devotion. The Ramanuja sect mostly preferred Vishnu and Lakshmi, or the Rama Avatar, while in Northern India other Vaishnava sects chose to exalt Krishna. They saw Krishna as the youthful hero of wonderful feats and amorous exploits at Vrindavana, different from the Krishna of the *Bhagavad Gita*, yet still identifiable with him. The Krishna mythology was exalted with a wealth of devotional legends in the writings called the Puranas, and all its mystical and emotional possibilities were elaborated. Yet in the background of all the Vaishnava literature stood Krishna the God-man as portrayed in the *Bhagavad Gita*.

In the medieval period the Puranas embellished the Krishna mythology and reached their fullest expression in the *Bhagavata Purana* (also called the *Srimad Bhagavatam*). This text came to be regarded as one of the major scriptures of Vaishnavism. Its chief purpose was the glorification of *bhakti* and the divine playfulness (*lila*) of Krishna. It came to exercise enormous influence on the development of *bhakti*, and marks a turning point in the Vaishnava faith. The *Bhagavata Purana* does not deal with the entire life of Krishna, focusing mainly upon his childhood and youth. It weaves its theory and practice on intensely personal and passionate *bhakti*, which is somewhat different from the speculative *bhakti* of the *Bhagavad Gita*. Although Radha is not mentioned, the *gopis* figure prominently in the romantic legend, and their dalliance with Krishna is described in highly emotional and sensuous lyrics. The utter self-abandonment of the *gopis*, the romantic love of the mistress for her lover, becomes the accepted symbol of the soul's longing for God, and the vivid portrayal of Krishna in Vrindavana is supposed to create the model for a passionate love and devotion to the deity. By transfiguring the sex impulse into a passionate religious emotion, the *Bhagavata Purana* introduces as the leading spiritual ideal a type of mysticism where eroticism and poetry bring warmth and colour to the religious life.

Another aspect of the Vaishnava tradition and the transfiguring of the sex impulse is a form of *bhakti* known as *tantra*. Tantra is a synthesis of yoga and *bhakti*. The tantric vision is based upon the belief that each god has a spouse, a Shakti, who is his energy. The Shakti is an emanation of the god that brings divine power to humanity and makes god approachable. In Tantrism, Shakti is a vital, personal entity that is called Pure Consciousness

(Chaitanya), or Supreme Being of Power (Para Shakti). Shiva and Shakti form a pair, with Shiva embodying wisdom and Shakti embodying energy, productivity and growth. The union of Shiva and Shakti represents wisdom and energy, whereas Shiva alone is wisdom lacking strength, and Shakti alone is energy lacking direction. Shiva can also be understood as an androgyne, half man and half woman in one body.[2] Shiva, the deity especially associated with Tantrism, has 1008 names, and for each name he has a Shakti. The Shaktis of Shiva most frequently prayed to are Kali, Durga, and Bhairavi. Shakti as a cosmic Being is the Divine Mother, the productive dynamism of all creation. But Shakti is also understood in a broader sense to be every woman, and some tantrics hold that woman is essential for the liberation of man.

Evidence clearly demonstrates an indigenous growth of Tantrism within Hinduism and its enthusiastic revival in the 9th and 19th centuries. One of the greatest supports for Tantrism came from Vaishnavism, according to which Shakti is an essential attribute of the deity. In some Vaishnava sects, Radha, who personifies Shakti, was seen as having no existence separate from Krishna, while others saw her as the object of worship and exalted her over Krishna. However, in the *Bhagavata Purana* Krishna delights in his own Shaktis, the powers inseparable from himself. In any case, Tantrism and Vaishnavism supported each other.

Tantric yoga is the union of Shiva and Shakti, the divine wisdom and divine energy, resulting in the recovery of a lost identity. In Tantrism the human body is understood to be the microcosm of the universe and the agency of a spiritual discipline based upon an esoteric physiology known as the *kundalini*. The kundalini is modelled upon a subtle spiritual body within the human body. To Hindus, kundalini is the cosmic energy latent in man, the Shakti. The word 'kundalini' means serpent power, and many Hindus believe that the energy is in the form of a serpent which lies coiled at the base of the spine. The kundalini can be 'awakened' by *prana* (the vital breath) being directed upon it through appropriate yogic techniques, causing it to ascend through the *sushumna* column situated within the cerebro-spinal axis, illuminating the *chakras* which are subtle energy centres. These chakras are located approximately at the pelvis, stomach, solar plexus, heart, throat, and brow. To each chakra is assigned a fundamental sound, colour, shape, element, animal symbol, specific number of lotus petals, and a deity, but the important feature of each chakra is the physical and mental function it governs. The ultimate aim of the kundalini is liberation (*moksha*), and this is attained when the energy ascends through all the chakras and reaches the apogee, the *sahasrara*, the centre with a thousand lotus petals situated at the crown of the head. The sahasrara is the microcosmic correlative of the macrocosmic Shiva–Shakti union. When Shiva finally unites with Shakti the union is completed, and the missing identity is uncovered as man regains his true divine reality.

Within the context of the Vaishnava tradition the spiritual practices of *bhakti*, *tantra*, and *kundalini*, play a significant role in the lives of the six Avatars that are now described.

1. CHAITANYA (1486–1533) – THE GOLDEN AVATAR

The one ever ancient who has taken form as Krishna Chaitanya for the purpose of teaching the knowledge and practice of non-attachment, *Vairagya Vidya*, and his own method of devotion, *Bhaktiyoga*, his shelter I seek, the ocean of mercury; may my mind like a bee cling closer to his lotus-feet, who is born to restore *Bhaktiyoga*, destroyed by time!

(Vasudeva Sarvabhauma)

Let the son of Sachi shine in the hollow of my heart, the Hari, who is lighted up by an assemblage of lustre lovelier than that of gold, and who in his compassion has descended at last in the Kali Age in order to bestow that wealth of his own bhakti, which was never bestowed before and which consists of the exalted sentiment of love.

(Rupa Gosvamin)

The first historical Indian Avatar and the one who sets the tone for later God-men in India is Chaitanya. Chaitanya was born Visvambhara Misra at Navadvipa, in Bengal, India, February, 1486. This was a time when the Islamic religion had control in Bengal, causing Hindus to view this period as the dark age (Kali yuga). Visvambhara's father, Jagannatha Misra, and his mother, Saci, were pious Brahmins of the Vaishnava faith. Visvambhara was their ninth child, and his name means 'he who sustains the world', a reference to Vishnu the sustainer. All but one of his older brothers and sisters died in childhood. That one surviving brother, Visvarupa, became a monk, left home, and was never heard from again. Thus, all the affection and love of the parents fell upon Visvambhara. It was said that he had a lovely golden complexion, and so he was later called the golden Avatar.

Visvambhara was a precocious child with above average intelligence, and by his mid-teens had proven his intellectual acumen and graduated from a Sanskrit school. However, his greatness did not lie in scholarship but in other directions. While Visvambhara was still quite young his father died, and the responsibilities of the household fell on the boy's shoulders. He married a girl named Lakshmi, became a householder, and set up a Sanskrit school like most learned Brahmins of his day. While Visvambhara belonged to a Vaishnava family, he rejected the efforts of relatives to interest him in serious worship of Vishnu in any form, and was quite contemptuous of the *bhakti* path that many people of the region practiced. He made an extensive tour of East Bengal and while he was away his wife Lakshmi died of a snake-bite. On his return he took the news quite calmly and soon remarried. At the age of 22, Visvambhara undertook a pilgrimage to Gaya to perform a ritual on behalf of his father's spirit. What happened at Gaya was certainly one of the greatest moments of his religious life and shaped the remainder of his years. In pursuit of his duty it was necessary for him to enter a shrine displaying the footprints of Vishnu made when that god descended upon earth to insure the preservation of man. The footprints of Vishnu are symbolic of the benevolence of this deity. At the shrine, Visvambhara happened to meet the ascetic Bengali monk, Isvara Puri, who reminded him of the claims of his Vaishnava faith. He voluntarily accepted Isvara Puri as his guru and was given a mantra that initiated him into the worship of Krishna. In 1510, at the age of 24, having renounced his wife, he was initiated as a *sannyasin* (a pilgrim totally detached from worldly matters), and upon him was bestowed the name Krishna Chaitanya, meaning 'he who has consciousness of Krishna'. He returned to his birthplace a transformed man, paying no attention to his appearance and talking of nothing but Krishna. He soon had to close his school, for when he taught his pupils, the subject was always Krishna. He ignored his scholarly friends, slept on the ground, hardly ate, and spent his time laughing, weeping, and shouting Krishna's name. From this time on, mystical encounters became a striking feature of his religious experience. He saw visions of Krishna in the clouds and ran after them with his eyes full of tears. Even his mother thought that he had lost his sanity.

In the town of Navadvipa where Chaitanya was born there was a group of Krishna devotees who were able to appreciate, accept, and support Chaitanya's behaviour. Its members were accustomed to assemble nightly to sing songs in praise of Krishna. Chaitanya now became the leader of this devout Vaishnava group and came to be regarded as the very embodiment of their spirit of devotion. His extraordinary capacity for emotion had the power of evoking similar feelings in others, and his sincerity and charm made him the natural leader of the group. While many outsiders were questioning his sanity, the devotees of this circle were saying that he might be Krishna in a new body, or Krishna himself.

One of Chaitanya's most important creations was the stimulation of an emotional and unritualistic mode of musical singing known as *Kirtana*. A *Kirtan* is a congregational song that magnifies a deity by mentioning his honorific names or praise-worthy deeds. Chaitanya took the leadership in such singing, and he is believed to have been the creator of several types of Kirtan. His personal contributions included a clear expressive voice of great charm and a passionate acceptance of the message of the songs. The method of enthusiastic chorus singing to the accompaniment of drums and cymbals, along with rhythmical body movements ending in an ecstatic abandon of dancing, proved very fruitful in utilizing group emotion, and soon became a distinctive feature of the faith. Its physical and sensuous appeal was not only congenial to the essentially emotional faith, but it was also utilized effectively for spreading the contagion of love and devotion to Krishna. When the emotion in the crowd and in himself reached a certain tension, Chaitanya would spring up from his seat, raise his arms high and wide and move among the crowd, dancing, singing, and shouting words in ecstasy until perspiration ran down his face and the veins stood out on his brow. Fits often came on him in which he would stiffen and fall. He would sometimes jump up and bound out of the crowd and climb a nearby tree, or he would lie for a long time on the ground in a frothing fit, or in exhausted stupefaction. He came out of these trances as if torn away from happy visions.

The biographies of Chaitanya do not detail Chaitanya's later life, except to say that up to about the age of 30 he made numerous pilgrimages throughout India and converted some highly respected people to his views, thus adding to his prestige and charisma. From the age of 30 until his death at 48 he settled at the Vaishnava pilgrimage centre at Puri, on the seacoast of Orissa, and continued singing and dancing in ecstatic emotional fervour. This eventually led to his death at Puri in 1533, where he either drowned by plunging into the sea in one of his ecstatic visions or died of an infection in his foot which he injured while dancing in frenzied emotion. Before his death he sent some disciples to Vrindavana, the legendary dwelling place of Krishna, to identify the sacred sites, restore the area, write and compile scriptural works, and build a new city there to the glory of Krishna.

Three characteristics led to his being recognized as an Avatar: first, the efficacy of the chanting of the name of Krishna; second, his devotion to Krishna as if he were Radha, Krishna's ecstatic lover, following the example of Jayadeva's poem the *Gita Govinda*; and third, his belief that he was possessed by Krishna. His contemporaries affirmed his belief in the very name that they gave him: he who has consciousness of Krishna. The scriptural support that buttressed the belief in his possession by Krishna was the incarnational passage in the *Bhagavad Gita*, chapter 4, verses 6–8.

Did Chaitanya ever proclaim himself to be an Avatar or God-man? There is no record of his having done so, and his glorification as an Avatar is largely the result of the writings of the poet-devotees who became the 'theologians' of the movement, known as the six Gosvamins of Vrindavana. These theologians were greatly inspired by Chaitanya's life, which furnished them with a vivid portrait, and they embellished it. One of these theologians, Rupa Gosvamin, developed an incarnational theology based upon the name of God, in which chanting the names of God is not merely a human activity, but is an occasion for the descent of God into the presence of His devotees.[3] The chanting of the names of God brings actual realization of God's presence because a name of God is not just a name, but is an approach to the essence of the thing named. For the Chaitanyites, the true name of God is a genuine modality of God's being or is God Himself. That is why, in the reciting of sacred names, the mysterious presence is often felt, i.e. God is there.

Various are Thy Names, O Lord,
In each and every Name Thy power resides.
No times are set, no rites are needful, for chanting of Thy Name,
So vast is Thy mercy.[4]

Another Chaitanyite theologian adapted incarnational theory
into a new form by connecting the name with a possessed
individual who thus became an Avatar 'by adoption'. This
classification of Avatar was called *avesa*, and the God-man was an
Avesavatar, creating a divine incarnation by the fact that the god
entered into him and possessed him. Thus the view developed
that Chaitanya became an Avesavatar, possessed by Krishna
through the singing of Kirtan. There also evolved the belief that
Chaitanya was possessed by both Krishna and his lover Radha,
forming an androgyne. This is another explanation of the golden
hue of Chaitanya's body (*Gaurahari*), which would have been dark
blue like Krishna's had it not been for the incorporation of Radha.

However, a difficulty arose in the minds of the Chaitanyite
theologians. Since an Avesavatar is not quite the full being of God,
but is divine by analogy only, limited to the degree of immanence
of the divine power, the Bengal Chaitanyites gradually moved
away from the Avesavatar interpretation, and identified
Chaitanya with Krishna himself. They came to the conclusion that
no doctrine would suffice that claimed that less than the Name is
the very essence of the Lord. Eventually an essential identity
between Chaitanya and Krishna became the definitive formula,
and his followers were led to declare that Chaitanya manifested
himself as God in the womb of his mother, that is, even before his
human birth.

In conclusion, although Chaitanya did not explicitly proclaim
himself to be an Avatar, worship of him as a special being began
during his lifetime,[5] and his mode of religious expression stimu-
lated his disciples into regarding him as a God-man. In a number
of ways his religious practices helped establish the belief among
his compatriots that he was the incarnation of Krishna. The belief
that Chaitanya was an Avatar became generally accepted, and
three hundred years later when the next Avatar appeared (Ramakrishna), some thought that Chaitanya had made a reappearance.
Chaitanya's avatarhood has found favour right up to the present
among Chaitanyites, and renewed enthusiasm recently among the

Krishna-Consciousness movement better known in America as the Hare Krishna people. The Hare Krishna Avatar and his relationship to Chaitanya will be discussed in Chapter 3.

2. RAMAKRISHNA (1836–86) – THE COSMIC CONSCIOUS AVATAR

The story of Ramakrishna Paramahamsa's life is a story of religion in practice. His life enables us to see God face to face. No one can read the story of his life without being convinced that God alone is real and that all else is an illusion. Ramakrishna was a living embodiment of godliness. His sayings are not those of a mere learned man, but they are pages from the Book of Life. They are revelations of his own experience. They therefore leave on the reader an impression which he cannot resist. In this age of scepticism Ramakrishna presents an example of a bright and living faith which gives solace to thousands of men and women who would otherwise have remained without spiritual light.[6]

(Gandhi)

Ramakrishna is a phenomenon both extraordinary and mysterious. He has been called 'Vedanta Incarnate', and also 'the consummation of 2,000 years of the spiritual life of 300 million Hindus'.[7] He was one of the key figures in India's renaissance movement in the 19th century, and is one of her greatest religious mystics. Although he has been dead for a century, his spirit continues to animate Indian spirituality, and he has left an indelible legacy.

Ramakrishna was born on 18 February 1836, in the village of Kamarpukar in Bengal, India. His parents were poor, pious Brahmins by the name of Kshudiram and Chandra Chatterji. According to a legend his father had a vision of Vishnu who told him that he would be reborn as his son. At the same time, Chandra, his mother, dreamt that she was being possessed by a god. They named their child Gadadhar, meaning bearer of the mace, in honour of Vishnu, the mace bearer.

Gadadhar attended school somewhat irregularly from the ages of 5 to 17, and as he was creative and intelligent he mastered what interested him, and the rest he ignored. At the age of six the sight of snow-white cranes against dark rain clouds inspired his first ecstatic mystical experience. He began worshipping the god Rama when he was nine, and frequently remained for a long time totally in rapture and oblivious of all outward surroundings. He sought solitude, frequently went into the woods, and meditated for hours. From his tenth year on, such ecstasies became common, in fact so frequent that his family feared that he was an epileptic; but as his health did not suffer, they came to accept his experiences as possession by the Divine.

When Gadadhar was seven years old his father died and his eldest brother, Ramkumar, went to Calcutta and opened a Sanskrit school to earn a living and support the family. Ten years later he sent for Gadadhar in order to teach him, but Gadadhar refused what he called 'bread-winning education'. The only learning that interested him was knowledge of God.

In 1855, a wealthy woman named Rani Rasmani built a temple on the banks of the Ganges at Dakshineswar, just north of Calcutta. It was dedicated to the goddess Kali, a shakti of Shiva. Ramkumar was invited to be the priest of the temple, and he took Gadadhar with him. Gadadhar liked the serene atmosphere by the sacred Ganges River, and spent the remainder of his life there. Ramkumar died after serving as the temple priest for only one year, and Gadadhar, appointed in his brother's place, performed the priestly duties. Gradually there developed in him a yearning for direct realization of Kali and life became unbearable without her. He would rub his face on the ground like one gripped by pain, and cry for a vision of Mother Kali. Finally he had his first vision of Kali, was overcome with waves of light, lost awareness, and upon regaining consciousness uttered the words, 'Mother, Mother'.

After his first vision of Mother Kali, Gadadhar longed to see her continuously. A 'divine madness' seized him, and he soon began to see Kali peeping from every nook and cranny. After this he could no longer perform his priestly duties, and people thought that he had lost his sanity. They watched as he gave the food offering for Kali to a stray cat that had entered the temple, for he had recognized the presence of the Divine Mother in the cat.

Gadadhar's behaviour became increasingly bizarre and word reached his mother who wished to see him. At the age of 23 he returned to Kamarpukar and to his mother, but continued to live in a God-intoxicated state, indifferent to worldly matters. His mother and brother decided that marriage would cure him, and set out to find him a wife. They searched unsuccessfully until it was Gadadhar himself who revealed to them where they could find his bride-to-be. Sarada Devi was found and they were married, but because she was only five years old she was sent back to her parents, and Gadadhar returned to his temple at Dakshineswar where he plunged deeper and deeper into spiritual practices. Gadadhar remained married to Sarada Devi for the remainder of his life. He worshipped her as the Divine Mother, and they both agreed to live celibate lives.

In 1861, at the age of 25, Gadadhar noticed a female ascetic enter the temple courtyard and he sent for her. She greeted him with tears of joy, saying, 'My son, you are here! I have been searching for you so long, and now I have found you at last.'[8] The ascetic's name was Bhairavi Brahmani and she came from Bengal. She was a woman of great spirituality, well versed in the Vaishnava and Tantric traditions. Gadadhar told her of his spiritual struggles, visions, and attainments, and that many people considered him mad. She assured him that it was divine madness and not to be concerned, that it had happened to Krishna's lover, Radha, and to Chaitanya. Gadadhar accepted the Brahmani as his first spiritual teacher (guru), and she instructed him in the 64 disciplines of the Tantra. He progressed rapidly with his visions and experienced superconscious states, known as *samadhi*. For three years Gadadhar practised Tantric and Kundalini disciplines and demonstrated that even the severest of these practices could be accomplished in complete chastity, without a sex-partner, or *shakti*.

After attaining the goal aimed at in the Tantric practices, Gadadhar began in 1863 practising in the Vaishnava tradition, under the guidance of his second guru Jatadhari. As a Vaishnavite he was to follow the path of devotion to a personal God, one who was an incarnation of Vishnu. Gadadhar first chose to worship Rama, and later he chose Krishna. He worshipped Krishna as if he were Radha, assuming the dress and life style of a woman for several months, both to relate to the beloved Krishna, and to overcome the idea of sexual difference.[9] Through each of these Avatars he achieved union. His first guru, the Brahmani, came to the staggering realization that Gadadhar was more than human, that he was actually an incarnation of God upon earth, an Avatar. She came to this conclusion based upon her familiarity with Bengali Vaishnava books on Chaitanya, in which it was said that

Chaitanya would assume a body again and come down to earth for the deliverance of men. The Brahmani compared the conduct of Gadadhar to Chaitanya and found a great similarity between them.[10] She became convinced that Chaitanya dwelt in Gadadhar's body,[11] and she proceeded to inform everyone who came to Dakshineswar that Gadadhar was an incarnate deity.

The Brahmani first expressed her view of Gadadhar's avatarhood to Gadadhar himself. It seems as if he did not know what to make of it, and tested it out on Mathur Mohan, the son-in-law of Rani Rasmani, who rejected it saying, 'Father, let her say whatever she likes; the incarnations of God cannot be more than ten. Therefore, how can her words be true?'[12] The Brahmani replied, 'Does not the *Bhagavata* speak at first of twenty-four principal incarnations and, afterwards, of innumerable ones? Besides the coming again of the great lord (Sri Chaitanya) is distinctly mentioned in the Vaishnava books, and a great similarity of the principal characteristics is found to exist between him and Sri Chaitanya.'[13] Mathur was dumbfounded. To prove her conviction the Brahmani held a formal debate inviting two holy men, Charan and Gauri. Thinking that the Brahmani's claim would be successfully refuted, Mathur consented to attend. Meanwhile, Gadadhar took a child-like pleasure in the whole proceeding and when the debate began he sat there happily eating seeds. Evidently Charan recognized Gadadhar's divinity at once and proceeded to cite scriptural evidence for his avatarhood. At this, Gadadhar turned to Mathur playfully and said: 'So he really thinks that! Well, anyway I'm glad it's not a disease.'[14] Shortly thereafter Gadadhar said, 'The One who became Rama and Krishna is now within this case (showing his body). But His advent this time is secret.'[15]

In 1864 a naked ascetic by the name of Tota Puri came to Dakshineswar. He was a Vedantic monk belonging to the order of Shankara. He recognized Gadadhar's advanced spiritual state and invited him to learn Vedanta from him. Gadadhar received Kali's permission and became a disciple of Tota Puri, learning the teachings of the Upanishads on the unity of the soul with the Godhead. Tota Puri initiated Gadadhar into the monastic life and bestowed upon him the theophoric name of Ramakrishna,[16] uniting the names of the two Avatars whom Gadadhar had worshipped. Ramakrishna proceeded in his spiritual quest and severing a visual representation of Kali in half, he soared beyond duality and entered into the highest mental state, known as the seedless supramental state (*nirvikalpa samadhi*) which is the goal of Vedantic practice, and considered comparable to cosmic consciousness (the mind of the universe). In essence Ramakrishna had attained in one day what it had taken Tota Puri forty years to achieve. After Tota Puri left Dakshineswar, Ramakrishna spent six months in the state of *nirvikalpa samadhi*, oblivious to all external surroundings, even having to be force-fed. Thereafter he lived in a realm between normal consciousness and samadhi, known as *bhavamukha*, and he would enter into *samadhi* about once a day.

Thus far we have seen how Ramakrishna fulfilled various strands of Hindu discipline: Saivism, Tantrism, Vaishnavism, and Vedanta, and if his life had ended here it would have been magnificent enough. However, in 1866, Govinda Roy (or Ray), a Hindu convert to Islam, who was practising Sufi mysticism, came to Dakshineswar and began instructing Ramakrishna in the Islamic faith. Ramakrishna began to repeat the name of Allah, pray five times a day, dress in Moslem garb, and even eat Moslem food. Finally he had a powerful vision of 'a radiant person with a long beard and a solemn countenance'[17] who was recognized as the prophet Muhammad. Using this vision as a way station, he proceeded to enter into communion with Brahman, showing how the river of Islam could carry him back to the ocean of the Absolute. Within three days he had realized the goal of his Islamic devotions.

Some years later, in 1874, Ramakrishna wished to experience Christianity. He was exposed to Christ and Christianity through a Hindu devotee by the name of Shambhu Charan Mallik, who was a student of the scriptures of various religions. Mallik read the Bible to Ramakrishna and spoke to him of Jesus, Sri Isha, as the Hindus call him. One day Ramakrishna chanced upon a picture of the Virgin Mary with the child Jesus sitting on her lap, and became especially attracted to this image. He felt that the figures of the Mother and Child began to shine, and that the rays of light flowed forth from them and entered his heart. He was filled with love for Jesus and for Christianity and began to see visions of Christian priests burning incense and lighting candles before images of Jesus. On the evening of the fourth day he saw a tall, stately man with fair complexion coming toward him. A voice from within told him,

'This is Jesus the Christ, the great yogi, the loving Son of God and one with his Father, who shed his heart's blood and suffered tortures for the salvation of mankind!' Jesus then embraced Ramakrishna and passed into his body. Ramakrishna remained convinced, from that day onward, that Jesus was truly a divine incarnation.[18]

Ramakrishna's mystical experience with Jesus in 1874 is highly significant, as it marks the beginning of the assimilation of Jesus Christ into the Hindu religion on a par with the Hindu Avatars. From this time forward, the Hindu God-men have a spiritual brother in Sri Isha, another Avatar to contend with, and a Western one at that.

Ramakrishna's only direct contact with Christianity was his brief encounter with the Reverend Joseph Cook during his Oriental tour. In February of 1882, in the presence of Reverend Cook and others, Ramakrishna went through all the phases of spiritual discipline which characterized him, including a long period of supraconsciousness, praying, singing, and discoursing on spiritual subjects. A newspaper reported that:

Mr. Cook, the American evangelist, who came to his country a few years ago, once witnessed Ramakrishna's divine exercises. He expressed his great surprise and remarked that he was not aware before that a man could become so immersed in divine spirit as to lose all perception of the external world.[19]

This contact took place eight years after his mystical experience with Jesus, and we may note that Ramakrishna had little or no contact with historical Islam or Christianity. His universalism did not arise out of his knowledge of these other religions so much as out of his widely inclusive mystical experiences.

Toward the end of Ramakrishna's life he taught his close disciples about the characteristics of Avatars. He instructed them that Avatars have six special traits: (1) they are born free of karma, (2) they have perfect memory from the moment of birth (even of previous lives), (3) they are able to transmit knowledge to others at will, (4) they are able to perceive immediately the karma of human beings, (5) they are conscious of their mission throughout their lives, and (6) they are discoverers of new paths in religion and can transform a whole group of persons to a higher plane of existence.[20] Ramakrishna taught that on the tree of Sachchidananda grow innumerable fruits such as Rama, Krishna, Christ and others: one or two of them come down now and then to this world, and they work wonderful changes in society . . . the Avatara is always one and the same. Plunging into the ocean of life, He rises up in one place and is known as Krishna; diving again and rising elsewhere, He is known as Christ.[21]

Ramakrishna's disciples continued to expound this message, and took added delight in demonstrating that it applied to Jesus Christ as well.[22]

The rest of the story of Ramakrishna's life is rather accessible. One can read about it in numerous books – his spiritual relationship with his wife, Sarada Devi; the gathering of the disciples; his favourite disciple Naren, who was to become the famous Swami Vivekananda; and his association with Keshab Chandra Sen, founder of the Brahmo Samaj of India.

In January of 1886 Ramakrishna distributed twelve ochre robes and rosaries of rudraksha beads to his twelve disciples.[23] Before he died he explicitly proclaimed himself an Avatar before two disciples, Naren and Rakhal.[24] He was suffering from cancer of the throat, and on 16 August 1886, he died. While Ramakrishna never wrote anything, accounts of his life were written by disciples such as Vivekananda, Saradananda, and Brahmananda, who accepted his avatarhood, and therefore accepted miraculous tales connected with his divinity. Vivekananda recognized his master as an Avatar, travelled to the Parliament of Religions in Chicago in 1893, spread the message of Ramakrishna to the West, and helped transform Hinduism from a national religion to a universal one. Perhaps Ramakrishna's greatest contribution of all was indirect: his disciples were inspired to spread and popularize his avatarhood to the West as well as in the East, and as a result a plethora of Avatars arose.

Concerning Ramakrishna, two aspects of incarnation are especially noteworthy: (1) he is the first historical Hindu holy man to accept his own avatarhood; and (2) as a Hindu Avatar he acknowledges Jesus Christ on a par with other Avatars. In so doing, Ramakrishna helped bring together two religions that emphasize incarnation, and since his time each Indian God-man has been quite cognizant of his Christian counterpart.

3. AUROBINDO (1872–1950) – THE SUPRAMENTAL AVATAR

Sri Aurobindo incarnated in a human body the supramental consciousness and has not only revealed to us the nature of the path to follow and the method of following it so as to arrive at the goal, but has also by his own personal realisation given us the example; he has provided us with the proof that the thing can be done and the time is now to do it.

(The Mother, Mira Richard)

Sri Aurobindo has been ranked by many a scholar as one of the outstanding figures of the modern world, and has been compared with such philosophers as Bergson, Hegel, and Bradley. Yet his thought is clearly situated in the context of the Indian philosophical and spiritual traditions. He deals with the classical problems of the phenomenal world and the transcendent Absolute, the relative merits of the different states of consciousness, and the ultimate goal of human life. He accepts traditional Indian orientation on many points: the non-dual nature of ultimate Reality, its identification as Sat-Chit-Ananda (Being-Awareness-Bliss) in abstract terms and as the divine incarnation of Lord Krishna in personal terms. He develops the Tantric Shakti tradition and reconciles the various yogas. He offers interpretations of the Hindu scriptures and demonstrates the orthodoxy of his doctrine in conformity with them. Among his countrymen he is classed with Tagore and Gandhi as a leader of modern India, with Ramakrishna and Ramana Maharshi as a yogi and holy man, and with Radhakrishnan as a philosopher. His reputation is international and his works, written in English, have been translated into French, Spanish, German, and Chinese, as well as into the Indian languages of Bengali, Gujarati, and Hindi. Aurobindo study centres have been established in India, the United States, and in Africa. Let us focus in on Aurobindo in order to comprehend his avatarhood and his metaphysical beliefs.

Sri Aurobindo was born Aravinda Ackroyd Ghose on 15 August 1872, in Calcutta. His father was Dr Krishnandhan Ghose and his mother was Swarnalata Devi Ghose. His father had studied medicine in England and felt that the West was far superior to his native India. He did not wish that any of his sons be 'contaminated' by what he called the smokey and retrograde mysticism in which his country was running to waste. Therefore Aurobindo was originally given an English name, Ackroyd, and at the age of five he was sent to a Catholic school, and at twelve to London to study at St. Paul's school. He went to Cambridge University on a scholarship, but became deeply involved in politics and did not complete a degree. He returned to India at the age of twenty, and for the next fifty years attempted to work out a synthesis between East and West, as well as between the spiritual and the material worlds.

In April of 1901, Sri Aurobindo married Mrinalini Bose, in Calcutta. Two years later he had a powerful spiritual experience at the Hill of Sankaracharya in Kashmir in which he experienced 'the infinite', and began the practice of yoga. In 1908 he met Vishnu Bhaskar Lele, a yogi who instructed him in yoga, and following Lele's instructions, Aurobindo silenced his mind and experienced the Absolute, suprapersonal Brahman. Sometime after this experience he was incarcerated for a full year of solitary confinement for his alleged sedition. He was locked up in a cell with only the *Gita* and the *Upanishads*, and these he studied assiduously. It was in jail that an overwhelming event occurred in his life: a vision of Krishna appeared to him and transformed him. His vision is best expressed in his own words:

I looked at the jail that secluded me from men and it was no longer by its high walls that I was imprisoned; no, it was Vasudeva who surrounded me. I walked under the branches of the tree in front of my cell, but it was not the tree, I knew it was Vasudeva, it was Sri Krishna whom I saw standing there and holding over me His shade. I looked at the bars of my cell, the very grating that did duty for a door, and again I saw Vasudeva. It was Narayana who was guarding and standing sentry over me. As I lay on the coarse blankets that were given me for a couch, I felt the arms of Sri Krishna around me, the arms of my Friend and Lover. This was the first use of the deeper vision He gave me. I looked at the prisoners in jail, the thieves, the murderers, the swindlers, and as I looked at them, I saw Vasudeva, it was Narayana whom I found in those darkened souls and misused bodies.[25]

While in jail Aurobindo had intimations of various levels above the conscious mind, above even the highest level attained by the standard yoga. He took it upon himself to realize those supramental levels, and for this purpose he withdrew from the active political life of Bengal and took up residence in the French territory of Pondicherry south of Madras on the east coast of India, where he lived and worked for the rest of his life. There, in 1914, he met a French woman, Mira Richard, who joined him six years later to become the partner in his life-work and in the life of his ashram. It was she who became his co-Avatar, and was known to the disciples as 'The Mother'.

On 24 November 1926, Aurobindo experienced the culmination of his spiritual discipline, which is referred to as 'The Day of Siddhi'. As a result of this experience, Aurobindo retired into solitude and devoted his life to spiritual pursuits, and to Mira Richard was given charge of the ashram and guidance of the disciples. Twenty-three productive years followed in which Aurobindo produced his philosophical works as well as many essays and poetry. He made one public appearance per year and it was attended in total silence.

Aurobindo's teachings are chiefly contained in his major works *The Life Divine* and *Essays on the Gita*. His works are an attempt to form a synthesis between Hindu and evolutionary concepts. His emphasis upon evolution is an attempt to come to terms with modern scientific theory, and bears a striking resemblance to that of the Catholic mystic and paleontologist, Teilhard de Chardin. Like Teilhard, Aurobindo's philosophy is grounded in personal spiritual experience. Aurobindo rejects the Hindu concept of the material universe as an illusion (*maya*). Rather, he perceives a definite purpose in matter, life, and mind, which is revealed in the ongoing process of evolution. For Aurobindo, man is evolving both physically and consciously toward higher and higher forms. Man's quest for freedom, truth, immortality, and bliss is an aspiration for the next stage in human evolution. Aurobindo expresses it clearly this way:

In my view the body as well as the mind and life has to be spiritualized or, one may say, divinized, so as to be a fit instrument and receptacle for the realization of the Divine. It has its part in the Divine *lila*, even, according to the Vaishnava *sadhana*, in the joy and beauty of Divine Love.[26]

The highest form of consciousness for Aurobindo is union with what he calls the 'Supermind', and the manifestation of that in the physical world. This is not the union with Brahman accompanied by loss of consciousness which is traditional in Hinduism and was noticeable in the case of Avatar Ramakrishna. It is, rather, the creation of individuals of a higher order, who, through a type of training called Integral Yoga, become vessels for the descent of the supermind.

The goal of Aurobindo's yoga is to help one become a conscious collaborator in the process of the continuing evolution of matter and consciousness. As Aurobindo's own spiritual development occurred with very little outside stimulus or guidance, his integral yoga is geared towards helping each individual find his own spiritual path, rather than imposing a series of moral or psychological disciplines. Integral yoga is composed of the traditional Hindu yogas, *bhakti* yoga (devotion), *karma* yoga (deeds), *jnana* yoga (knowledge), and *raja* yoga (spiritual discipline), plus the opening of the *chakras* of the *kundalini* yoga. It attempts to attain a calm, ultimately silent mind, and an extremely well-developed physical body, in order to effect the manifestation of spirituality in matter.

Aurobindo's metaphysics is a spiritual evolution in which both matter and spirit are real and evolving to higher and higher forms. He does not accept man in his present condition as the highest form. Rather, he sees stages of human life, each representing an ascending movement of the consciousness to reach the divine. The higher that one ascends on his spiritual journey the more the divine is impelled to descend, there being a corresponding pull from above and below. The goal of human existence is to transcend the mental and achieve the supramental level, thus bringing about a corresponding descent of the supramental consciousness into the refined human vessel. Thus the Supermind is the bridge between the lower and the higher hemispheres of existence, and Aurobindo proposes a seven-fold chord of Being, illustrated as follows:

Involution	Existence (Sat)
	Consciousness-Force (Chit-Shakti)
	Bliss (Ananda)
	Supermind (perfect unity in diversity)
	Mind (intellect and intuition)
Evolution	Life (vital, organic)
	Matter (physical, inconscient)

It is the impulse toward perfection and human transformation that Aurobindo calls evolution or ascent. This brings about a corresponding descent or involution of the pure Spirit (Sat-Chit-Ananda), and this transformation is the goal of human existence. Sat-chit-ananda is the indispensable term for what human consciousness is seeking. The involution and the evolution work together, and as one moves forward so does the other. Each successive level in the descent of the Divine is to man a stage in his ascension. The involution and the evolution of the supermind are the *lila*, or sport of the gods, and can be graphically illustrated in the *yantra* (see Figure), the Hindu geometrical diagram used for meditation. The yantra works simultaneously in two directions, forward as a source of evolution, and backward as a process of involution. As Heinrich Zimmer says, 'It restates in miniature the stages or aspects of the manifestation of the Absolute in the evolution and involution of the world.'[27] It also symbolizes the sexual union of Shiva and Shakti.

According to Aurobindo the evolution of unconsciousness to consciousness has already occurred. Further human evolution involves the progressive development through ordinary consciousness, to religious consciousness, to spiritual consciousness, to the ultimate stage of supra-mental consciousness. Before one can attain the supramental level one must ascend from the higher mind to the illumined mind, to the intuitive mind, and to the overmind. These are the graded approaches to the real source of the Supermind. As one ascends from level to level there develops an integrating transformation within oneself and a harmony with others, a sense of being in touch with reality, and of being in communion with the divine. The ascent to the overmind requires the introduction of a new dimension, the replacement of the ego-sense by the cosmic-sense. As his selfhood expands, the spiritual man realizes the harmony of his individual will with the cosmic will. Aurobindo believed that the next stage in human

The *yantra* is a dynamic symbol of Hinduism. It is a geometric device that is used as a support to meditation. In this example, there are nine interpenetrating triangles. The five downward-pointing triangles symbolize the female creative energy and the four upward-pointing triangles symbolize the male creative energy, forming the male/female pair known as Shiva-Shakti. This Shri-Yantra, as it is called, symbolizes Life, both universal life and individual life, as an incessant interaction of co-operating opposites. The five female triangles expand from above and the four male triangles emerge from below, signifying the continuous process of creation. It is also important to note that while the female and male are represented, the Absolute is not, for It cannot be represented since It is beyond form and space. The Absolute is to be visualized as a vanishing point or dot, 'the drop' (*bindu*), amidst the interplay of the triangles.

SOURCE   Heinrich Zimmer in Joseph Cambell (ed.), 'Shiva-Shakti', *Myths and Symbols in Indian Art and Civilization* (Princeton University Press, 1974) pp. 137–48.

FIGURE   *Shri-Yantra*

evolution, heralded by man's urge for spirituality, would take him ultimately to the supramental level and the life divine. He expresses this poetically in *Savitri*:

> A mightier race shall inhabit the mortal's world.
> On Nature's luminous tops, on the Spirit's ground,
> The Superman shall reign as king of life,
> Make heaven almost a mate and peer of heaven
> And lead towards God and truth man's ignorant heart
> And lift towards godhead his mortality.[28]

The key to the final transformation lies in the descent or involution of Sat-Chit-Ananda, which by its nature is unity. Even the Overmind does not have this power of transformation, for it has built its unity out of the play of multiplicity. A truly integral transformation must come from the original unity itself, the unity that is the ground of all possible diversity. Such a level of reality is what Aurobindo calls the Supermind. His knowledge of this is based upon the experience that he had in 1926, which he described thus:

> The 24th of November, 1926, was the descent of Krishna into the physical. Krishna is not the supramental Light. The descent of Krishna would mean the descent of the Overmental Godhead preparing, though not itself actually, the descent of the Supermind and Ananda. Krishna . . . supports the evolution through the Overmind leading it towards his Ananda.[29]

The final victory, the descent of the Supermind, was not attained on 24 November 1926, but the Overmind was experienced, and this was felt to be a prediction of the descent of the Supermind at a later date. There were annual celebrations on 24 November at Aurobindo's ashram in commemoration of this great event.

Sri Aurobindo regarded himself as having achieved overmental consciousness. He was convinced that his yogic discipline, by virtue of his near ascent to the supermind, did indeed remove the play of a separative ego and enabled him to be one with the will of Brahma–Vishnu–Shiva. His thoughts and actions were not fully supramental, but he did approach this state in its essential points. He lived in and for the Divine in himself, in society, and in humanity; in short, he exemplified the early stages of the perfections generated by the supermind. But by his own admission it was to be the Mother, Mira Richard, who was to be the instrument of the supramental descent.

Aurobindo's belief in the descent of the supramental can be termed 'incarnationist', and in *Essays on the Gita* he proposed ideas about Incarnations and Avatars. He stated that the full implication of the divine Incarnation was not appreciated in the West because it had not entered the general consciousness of the people but had been restricted to a single instance, namely Jesus. He felt that the West had never understood incarnation properly because it had been presented through exoteric Christianity as a theological and historical dogma without roots in the general consciousness and attitude toward life. If there had been more teaching on the immanence of God and his 'living within our spiritual being', then belief in incarnation would have taken deeper root in the West, he believed.[30]

Aurobindo taught that the Avatar is a divine descent and a taking on of the human form. The Avatar comes to reveal the divine nature in man above his lower nature, and shows the divine acts to be full of light, power, and love. It is to assist the ascent and evolution of man that the descent of the Avatar is made, so that man may observe what it is and take courage to grow toward divinity. The Avatar demonstrates that human birth with all its limitations can be an instrument of the divine, and through a heightening of such human powers as love, strength, and purity, can be drawn into closer proximity with the divine consciousness.

Evolution is central to Aurobindo's model and he envisions history as an evolutionary progression toward the divine. He interprets the incarnational message of the *Gita* to mean that when there is a crisis and consequent setback to evolution, the Avatar incarnates to set the world on the proper evolutionary path. For Aurobindo avatarhood would have little meaning if it were not connected with evolution, and he interprets the ten Avatars of Vishnu as a parable of evolution in the following way. Matsya, Kurma, and Varaha represent progression from aquatic to amphibious to terrestrial forms. Narashimha, the man-lion, is the transition from animal to human form. The dwarf Avatar, Vamana, is seen as a partially developed human. The first full stage of man is Parasurama Avatar, but he is violent and uncivilized. Next comes Rama, who stands for the mental consciousness. The eighth

Avatar is Krishna, the spiritual Avatar and the one who leads the evolutionary process toward bliss (*Ananda*), as he represents the over-mind. Krishna is 'the Avatar of the Overmental Superman'.[31] Concerning the ninth Avatar, Buddha, Aurobindo says that he is full of compassion for life, and works for the redemption of mankind, but 'Buddha tries to shoot beyond to the supreme liberation but that liberation is still negative, not returning upon earth to complete positively the evolution.'[32] Kalki, the tenth Avatar, is to complete the Buddha's evolutionary mission by bringing the divine kingdom upon earth and destroying the opposing evil forces. According to Aurobindo, the evolutionary progression among Avatars is 'striking and unmistakable'.[33]

Aurobindo's evolutionary conception of the Avatars has been quite popular in contemporary India. In the early 1970s the Spiritual Academy Exhibition at Delhi employed multi-media techniques including films, photographs, charts, and pictures to demonstrate the science of evolution, and the ten Avatars of Vishnu were 'strikingly depicted in their relation to Darwin's theory of evolution, giving evidence of the continual progressive change in man's nature'.[34] In this exhibit the ten Avatars of Vishnu were portrayed as supplying the missing link between Darwin's material evolution and Aurobindo's spiritual evolution.

Interestingly enough, the aforementioned historical Avatars did not fit into Aurobindo's evolutionary model. He stated that Chaitanya and Ramakrishna were highly evolved spiritual personalities, but that they appeared to be unconscious of their avatarhood, and frequently seemed to be striving to become divine. He called into question their avatarhood, referring to them as 'reputed' Avatars.[35] However, his attitude toward Mira Richard was strikingly different. He saw her as the power of divine omniscient will and omnipotent knowledge, spontaneously perfect in every process, and standing above the gods.[36] He identified her with the Divine Mother, the supramental divine conscious force, and she in turn regarded him as the eternal supramental Avatar. Aurobindo explained that 'The Mother's consciousness and mine are the same, the one Divine Consciousness in two, because that is necessary for the play. Nothing can be done without her knowledge and force, without her consciousness – if anyone really feels her consciousness, he should know that I am there behind it and if he feels me it is the same with hers.'[37] And the Mother reciprocated in her pronouncement that every descent of the Supramental upon earth was the embodiment of the eternal spirit of Aurobindo. She stated that: 'Since the beginning of earth history, Sri Aurobindo has always presided over the great earthly transformation, under one form or another, one name or another.'[38] She let it be known that Aurobindo was to be the 'last Avatar in a human body'.[39] They regarded each other as co-divinities, a glorious pair of supramental Shiva-Shakti Avatars.

Sri Aurobindo died of a kidney disease on 5 December 1950, at the age of 78. Normally the funeral and burial would have taken place on the same day, but The Mother announced that 'his body is charged with such a concentration of Supramental light that there is no sign of decomposition and the body will be kept lying on his bed so long as it remains intact'.[40] It was not until 9 December that his body was laid to rest in a marble tomb. A few months later the Mother told of a conversation that had taken place between Aurobindo and herself on 8 December: 'When I asked him to resuscitate he clearly answered: "I have left this body purposely. I will not take it back. I shall manifest again in the first supramental body built in a supramental way."'[41]

With Aurobindo begins a 20th-century phenomenon in which Avatars analyse and discriminate between those who they think are and those who they think are not really Avatars. The fluidity of the mythic phase of Avatars gives way to an exclusivity in which historical Avatars consciously choose who they think are true Avatars. Aurobindo acknowledges all ten Avatars of Vishnu as authentic, and he sees them as progressive stages of evolution ending with the supramental Shiva–Shakti Avatars, himself and The Mother.

THE MOTHER OF PONDICHERRY (1878–1973) – THE LEAP YEAR AVATAR

The mother comes in order to bring down the Supramental and it is the descent which makes full manifestation here possible.

(Aurobindo)

The Mother Goddess has held a special place in Indian devotion for centuries. Although the early Vedas contain a few references to female deities, the doctrine of the Mother Goddess is most fully developed in the Tantras. The Tantras present the Supreme Deity as one universal spiritual power known as Shakti, called the Divine Mother. The Divine Mother pervades the entire world giving birth to all things. For the purpose of creation she divides herself into the dual aspects of male and female. Of these, Shiva is the male principle and the cosmic consciousness, while Shakti is the female principle and the primordial energy. Shiva and Shakti are inseparably connected.

The Divine Mother is venerated in parts of India today as incarnations of Shakti. One such manifestation, and the only female Avatar, is Mira Richard, known as The Mother of Pondicherry. The Mother of Pondicherry was born in Paris on 21 February 1878. Her name was Mira Alfassa, and her wealthy parents were of Egyptian descent. In her youth she studied occultism and received spiritual training from gurus in her dreams. As a teenager she had a dream that repeated itself for a year in which she saw herself clad in a magnificent golden robe in which she rose out of her body, above her house, and covered the entire town. Men, women, and children gathered under the golden robe, and as they touched it were healed.[42] She reports empathetic experiences with both plants and animals,[43] ability to calm violent storms at sea, and at the age of thirteen used the power of her mind to overpower a cobra that was about to strike her.[44] Indian myths and legends attracted her from early childhood, and she read books on yoga and the *Gita*.

She first met Aurobindo in 1914 when she sailed to India with her second husband, Paul Richard, a French diplomat. Immediately she recognized that Aurobindo was Krishna and that she was Radha, and she proceeded to learn Sanskrit and Bengali. During World War I she and her husband lived in France and Japan where they made the acquaintance of the renowned Hindu poet Rabindranath Tagore. The Richards returned to Pondicherry in 1920 at which time their marriage was dissolved, and Mira remained for the rest of her life at Aurobindo's ashram. For the next 53 years she was the dominant force behind the Sri Aurobindo Ashram, which Aurobindo placed in her charge in 1926, the year of his seclusion. At the time of her death the ashram supported 1500 resident members, including 100 Westerners, all practising Integral yoga.

Mira Richard had a special attraction for the 29 February. On this day in 1956, six years after Aurobindo's passing, she announced the fulfilment of her avatarhood, the descent of the supramental into herself. She recounts it in this manner:

This evening the Divine Presence, concrete and material was
there present amongst you. I had a form of living gold, bigger
than the universe, and I was facing a huge and massive golden
door which separated the world from the Divine. As I looked at
the door, I knew and willed, in a single movement of consciousness, that 'the time has come', and lifting with both hands a
mighty golden hammer I struck one blow, one single blow on
the door and the door was shattered to pieces. Then the supramental Light and Force and Consciousness rushed down upon
earth in an uninterrupted flow.[45]

Henceforth she was regarded as the Divine Mother by her followers. On 29 February 1960, in commemoration of her avatarhood
she gave a performance of spiritual music on the organ, and then,
dressed in a golden sari she distributed 2500 golden medallions
with Aurobindo's lotus on it. And on 29 February 1968, when she
was 90 years old, she established the international township called
Auroville, a spiritual community that she diligently worked to
develop during her lifetime, and that she hoped would become an
ideal society in a propitious spot for the flowering of the race of the
Sons of God. She 'withdrew from her body' on 17 November 1973,
at the age of 95.

What is the authority for Mira Richard's avatarhood? She is an
Avatar according to Aurobindo, and an Avatar according to her
devotees as well as a self-proclaimed Avatar. Aurobindo, the
supramental Avatar, acknowledged her as the Mahashakti (great
female energy) Avatar.[46] According to him, she is the consciousness-force (chit-shakti) of the Divine, who has descended from
above and has been divine since childhood. She was born with the
Divine Mother's consciousness, and all spiritual disciplines that
she had to perform were for the perfection of that consciousness.
Reports of her practicing yoga from the age of four and gathering a
group of spiritual seekers about her as a teenager are offered as
evidence of her early divinity.

What is the nature of Mira Richard's avatarhood? Her divine
aspect incorporates the embodiment of two Hindu goddesses,
Durga and Savitri. As Durga she embodies the divine mother's
power of protection. The Shakti (force) of Durga empowers her
with yoga-force, occult-force, curing-force, knowledge-giving
force, and light-giving force.[47] She was known to cure illnesses
miraculously and to save people from untimely death. As the

goddess Savitri she is the source of light, and radiates the divine. However, her light cannot be imagined by the mind and can be seen only with inner vision. She is the light-giver for the inner world and her aura is white, whereas Aurobindo's is blue.[48]

According to Aurobindo, he and the Mother are really one, but manifest as the divine Shiva and the energy Shakti. The dynamic Shakti is necessary in order to reach the immutable Shiva. The Shakti has no single form of its own, but adopts multiple forms, and the Mother has four. They are (1) Maheswari, the wisdom which opens to the supramental, (2) Maha-lakshmi, beauty and harmony radiating a golden hue,[49] (3) Maha-kali, energy and strength, and (4) Maha-saraswati, order and perfection. These four aspects testify to the uniqueness of a female divinity for the Hindu and indicate a diversity of patterns for her worship.[50] In the supramental domain all four are reunited into one, the Maha-shakti, or Divine Mother. As such she is transcendent and universal, the divine in its consciousness-force.

Aurobindo said that the way to the Divine is through the Mother, and the Mother is the force of the Shakti. Total surrender to the Mother is the way toward freedom and liberation. She manifests a trinity of emanations (or *Vibhutis*): (a) an individuality, in which she mediates between human personality and divine nature, (b) a transcendence, as original supreme Shakti, and (c) a universality, as cosmic Mahashakti. According to Aurobindo she is Truth, Light, Life, and Bliss.[51]

Aurobindo associates kundalini symbolism with the shakti of the Divine Mother. He indicates that the Mother's power is felt in the chakras (energy centres). In his poem *Savitri* he describes the kundalini waking up from its slumber, raising its hood and standing ready for the tremendous ascent, while the lotus centres are awakened and fragranced by the touch and power of the shakti, in this ascent and evolution of consciousness.

A flaming serpent rose released from sleep.
It rose billowing its coils and stood erect
And climbing mightily stormily on its way
It touched her centres with its flaming mouth:
As if a fiery kiss had broken their sleep,
They bloomed and laughed and surcharged with light and
  bliss . . .

And the mystic serpent
Then at the crown it joined the Eternal's space.[52]

As the kundalini ascends, the supermind descends, and the two
meet at each of the energy centres (*chakras*), opening them for the
eventual transcendent victory.

The disciples of the Mother speak of her powers, such as her
aura, her extra-sensory perception, and her ability to transform
herself in and out of her four major forms. Her presence was
thought to emanate through a fragrance that was a mixture of
flowers and incense. She was said to have a heavenly smile like the
enigmatic Mona Lisa, and a special vision that could see into one's
innermost depths. She was the 'Mediatrix', the female link between heaven and earth, and the bestower of grace. She was
known to intervene from afar to help people in danger and
sickness by sending her divine power, sometimes in the form of
her fragrance.[53] The flowers that she gave to her followers were her
blessings, and each flower had its own spiritual significance.[54]

The Divine Mother's human existence was regarded by her
disciples as extraordinary. They report that she would sleep about
two hours per night, spend part of each night in *samadhi*,[55] eat
very little, and never eat meat. She would engage in physical
exercise for one hour a day and enjoyed tennis most of all. She did
a tremendous amount of work each day, which was her karma
yoga. This included interviews with her disciples, answering her
mail, meditation, teaching classes in French, as well as supervision of the ashram and Auroville. At the ashram the disciples and
visitors would gather daily just before noon and form a long row
extending to a central room containing a throne beside which were
young girls holding trays of flowers. The Mother would enter
wearing a white silk cap from which was suspended a gold ring
dangling on her forehead. A visitor writes, 'She is the image of the
Eternal Return, of all the beings and things within the Great Wheel
of Life. Her face seems to contain all mineral, vegetable, animal,
and human life mixed together.'[56] After seating herself on the
throne she distributed flowers to the pilgrims who came to see
her. The ceremony was conducted in total silence.

Aurobindo and the Mother recognized and authenticated each
other as supramental Avatars. According to Vasant V. Merchant,
'No one other than Sri Aurobindo and The Mother, who dedicated
their entire lives to their stupendous work on the Supermind, its

discovery and manifestation, and the transformation of Earth through the power of Supramental Truth, have ever been known to have received the living splendour of puissance of the Super-mind.'[57] The Mother died 23 years after Aurobindo, and they are buried side by side in the courtyard of the ashram at Pondicherry.

MEHER BABA (1894–1969) – THE SILENT AVATAR

I am the Ancient One whose past is worshipped and remem-bered, whose present is ignored and forgotten and whose future (Advent) is anticipated with great fervor and longing. . . . God has come again and again in various Forms, has spoken again and again, in different words and different languages, the same One Truth – the outer life and habits of an Avatar reflect in some degree the habits and customs of the people of that time, and in his teachings he stresses the aspects that call for improvement. In essence every Avatar embodies the same ideals of life. . . . I have come to sow the seed of *love* in your hearts so that, in spite of all superficial diversity which your life in illusion must experience and endure, the feeling of oneness, through Love, is brought about amongst all the nations, creeds, sects, and castes of the World.[58]

(Meher Baba)

Meher Baba is the only modern male Avatar who was not born a Hindu. His parents were Persians of the Zoroastrian religion, and they named him Merwin Sheriar Irani when he was born on 25 February 1894, in Poona, India, the second of seven children. His mother's name was Shirinbanoo, and his father was Sheriar Mun-degar Irani, the son of the keeper of the Zoroastrian tower of silence, where corpses are hung to be devoured by vultures. The name Irani is a common designation meaning from Iran. In Mer-win's youth his favourite haunts were burial grounds and the towers of silence. He attended a Roman Catholic school in Poona for five years and graduated in 1911. Then he went to the Deccan College where he concentrated upon the study of poetry. Mean-while his spiritual training was under the supervision of what he calls Perfect Masters, and there were five of them.

The first Perfect Master whom Merwin met in May of 1913 was Hazrat Babajan. She was a Moslem holy woman, reputed to be 122 years old. He visited her every night and their meetings were held in silence. In January of 1914, she kissed him on the forehead and he was transformed into a superconscious state, the effects of which lasted nine months. It was thought that he had gone insane, and medical treatment was of no avail. Hazrat Babajan declared that 'this child of mine will shake the world to a great upheaval'.[59]

The second Perfect Master whom Meher Baba met was the Hindu holy man Narayan Maharaj, and their brief meeting occurred in 1915. His third teacher was Tajuddin Baba, a Moslem Perfect Master who spent 17 years in an asylum for the insane, could perform miracles and resurrections, and was regarded as very holy. Meher Baba's fourth spiritual teacher was Sai Baba of Shirdi, who bears the distinction of having played an important role in the lives of two Avatars, Meher Baba and Satya Sai Baba. In 1915, Shirdi Sai Baba recognized Meher Baba as the 'Parvardigar', meaning God-Almighty-Sustainer.

The fifth Perfect Master was Upasni Maharaj (1870–1941). He was a disciple of Sai Baba of Shirdi who assisted him in becoming God-realized. For six months Meher Baba lived with Upasni, and in December of 1921 Upasni Maharaj announced that Meher Baba was the Avatar. Thus at the age of 27, Meher Baba had acquired the status of an Avatar and began his life-long mission. He said that the first Perfect Master gave him divine bliss, the fourth Perfect Master gave him divine power, and the fifth Perfect Master gave him divine knowledge. He then took on his new Avataric name, Meher Baba, meaning compassionate father.

Meher Baba is the inheritor of four religious traditions. Born a Zoroastrian, he was educated in Christian schools, trained in Islam by Hazrat Babajan and Tajuddin Baba, and in Hinduism by Upasni Maharaj. Many of his disciples, called *mandali*, were Zoroastrians, Moslems, and Hindus, as well as American Christians, but Baba said that he belonged to no religion, rather every religion belonged to him.

Perhaps the most distinctive aspect of Meher Baba's life was his silence. In 1925 he began the golden silence which would last for the remaining 44 years of his life. At first he communicated by pointing to letters on an alphabet board, but in 1954 he even gave up this device. From 1954 until the end of his earthly life he conversed through his own unique shorthand system of representative gestures. Using his own system of gestures, he directly recorded his spiritual message in booklets called 'discourses', 'beams', and 'darshan hours', and he even dictated a book entitled *God Speaks*, published in 1955. Although he made frequent claims that he would break his silence and utter the only real and divine word, he never did. He remained a tower of silence to the very end.

Meher Baba did not indulge in altered states of consciousness (*samadhi*), yoga, or meditation, and was vehement in his denunciation of the use of drugs. In addition, he did not believe in the Avatar's role in performing miracles, and disavowed ever having performed one. His message was for the heart, not the head, and he insisted that he came not to teach but to awaken. His favourite colour was not golden but pink. In 1931 he had three meetings with Gandhi, and beginning in that year he commenced his six journeys to America where a Meher Baba spiritual community was established in Myrtle Beach, South Carolina.

Baba had many male and female disciples but he is the first historical Avatar not to marry. The fact that Meher Baba did not have a close relationship with a woman may afford a clue to his prolonged silence. In Hinduism it is generally acknowledged that Vishnu represents wisdom while his wife Lakshmi is speech. Meher Baba, having no female partner or wife, thus typically refrained from speech. Or perhaps his silence was modelled upon Zoroaster, of whom it is said that he maintained silence for seven years.

Meher Baba was in two severe automobile accidents in which he suffered a broken nose, arm, and hip. The first was in 1952 in America and the second in 1956 in India. The suffering and pain were accepted as part of the divine plan whereby the Avatar suffers on behalf of humanity. The injuries received in these two accidents became the cross which he had to bear, and he did so resignedly. Even though he repeatedly said that he would break his silence and utter the word of words before he left the earth, Meher Baba 'dropped his body' on 31 January 1969, without speaking. It is proper to say 'dropped his body', for Baba said that the Avatar is immortal and returns when needed. Those who came into contact with Meher Baba during his advent reported that his wishes were beyond man's mind to fathom, for the requests that he made upon his disciples forced them to hurdle obstacles and hold fast to their devotion in spite of everything. It was the Avatar's *lila*, and a test of the disciples' *bhakti*. Meher Baba was indeed inscrutable, imponderable, and totally unpredictable.

Of all the modern Avatars, Meher Baba has proposed the most elaborate model of spiritual evolution, consisting of a spiritual hierarchy comprised of seven levels of consciousness, ten states of God, and time cycles divided into eleven ages. Diagrams, charts, and tables appear in his books to explain it. In the evolution from the material world to the spiritual world, one progresses from Islam to Hinduism, to Christianity and to Zoroastrianism. The spiritual hierarchy consists of 7001 souls. At the pinnacle stands the Avatar surrounded by 120 disciples. There are 56 god-realized beings in the world, and five are Perfect Masters and three are Majzoobs. According to Meher Baba, the 48 remaining god-realized ones 'are on the waiting list ready to help in any spiritual contingency cropping up through one or more of the functioning members dropping their body'.[60] The main distinction between an Avatar and a Perfect Master is that the Avatar is a descent, or God-man, while the Perfect Master is an ascent, or man-God. Otherwise their consciousness is on the same level, known as God-consciousness or infinite-consciousness. The Perfect Masters render spiritual service to humanity as a whole, while the Majzoobs render it to the few who come into contact with them. The following enumerates upon the spiritual hierarchy:[61]

In the first plane, and also between 1st and 2nd, between 2nd and 3rd, between 3rd and 4th, between 4th and 5th, between 5th and 6th and between 6th and 7th	5600
In the second plane	666
In the third plane	558
In the fourth plane	56
In the fifth plane	56
In the sixth plane	56
In the seventh plane (i.e., Majzoobs in the body)	3
Perfect Masters (Sadgurus)	5
	7000
The Avatar, in the eleventh age of each cycle, brings the number to	7001

According to Meher Baba the Avatar comes when the thread of spiritual truth begins to fray and there are crises in world affairs. The Avatar comes during Avataric periods which are every 700 or 1400 years, and the Avatars have been (1) Zoroaster, (2) Rama, (3) Krishna, (4) Buddha, (5) Jesus, (6) Muhammad, and (7) Meher

Baba. According to Meher Baba the eighth Avatar will incarnate in Japan in 700 years.[62]

The God-man is a representative of the eternal Logos and thus all God-men possess the same consciousness, yet each Avatar is an individual with a unique personality. Meher Baba claimed to possess this avataric consciousness, and he spoke of having been all the previous Avatars. He said, 'I am one with God. I live in Him, like Buddha, like Christ, like Krishna. They know Him as I know Him.'[63] Baba said that the Avatar functions on all seven levels simultaneously, but stations himself on one level in order to accomplish his work. Thus Buddha chose the sixth level, while Jesus chose the fourth level in order to perform miracles.

The titles that Meher Baba used for the Avatar were Christ, Buddha, Rasool, the Ancient One, the Perfect One, the Messiah, and the Highest of the High. He referred to himself most frequently as the Avatar and the Highest of the High. Meher Baba claimed to be in the state of Christ-consciousness and to have been Christ. He said, 'At the time of Jesus, I uttered many warnings, yet none could grasp in advance the necessity of my crucifixion.'[64] Baba's focus on Jesus revolves around his crucifixion. According to Meher Baba, Jesus wanted to be crucified, and 'he performed the miracles to make certain of being crucified'.[65] The explanation that Baba offered was that the Avatar allows himself to be persecuted, tortured, humiliated, and condemned by humanity in order to allow mankind to assert the existence of God in his infinite state.[66] Thus, all acts and events in Baba's life that led to his humiliation and suffering were regarded as further proof that he was the Avatar of the present age. His followers relate that on the day of his passing Baba wrote, 'Today is my crucifixion.'[67] Indeed, numerous sayings of Baba, as well as many rituals that he performed, such as the washing of the feet, remind one of Jesus.

Concerning Meher Baba's view of the other modern Hindu holy men, he claimed that Ramakrishna was not an Avatar but rather a Perfect Master, and offered as proof that Ramakrishna had to slap himself and pull his hair in order to remain conscious, which was behaviour unbecoming to a true Avatar.[68] Baba also said that 'a Perfect Master is one who has gone through a process of cosmic evolution and involution and become a Man-God. An Avatar, or God-man, is one who does not pass through those processes but is born as a man who knows himself to be God'.[69] According to this theory, Aurobindo is a Perfect Master and not an Avatar. And

Baba indicated that the Avatar always incarnates in the body of a male,[70] which would deny Mira Richard her avatarhood.

In conclusion, Meher Baba is the least 'Hinduized' of the Avatars in this chapter for the following reasons: (1) he is not born a Hindu; (2) he is the first Avatar not to marry and to have no observable Shakti; (3) his extended silence is antithetical to the Hindu belief in the efficacy of sound (mantras); (4) he does not connect the Avatars with the yugas, but has them appear at avataric periods of 700 or 1400 years; (5) his spiritual path requires no alteration of consciousness; and (6) he ignores the ten Avatars of Vishnu. On the other hand, he is the most universal of the Avatars for transforming the traditional concept of Hindu Avatars by identifying them with founders of world religions, namely Zoroaster, Muhammad, Jesus Christ, and Buddha.

The noted scholar, theologian and priest, Raymond Panikkar, had this to say about Meher Baba:

> The astounding affirmations of a Meher Baba: 'I am the Christ', 'I am infinite consciousness', 'I am the Highest of the High', 'Before me was Zoroaster, Krishna, Rama, Buddha, Jesus and Mahommed' and the all-pervading love he has infused to his disciples, for instance, constitute a serious problem which an unbiased theologian cannot dismiss as simple hallucinations or aberrations.[71]

SATYA SAI BABA (1926–2022) – THE MIRACLE-WORKING SAI-CO-THERAPEUTIC AVATAR

> Since I move about with you, eat like you, and talk with you, you are deluded into the belief that this is but an instance of common humanity. Be warned against this mistake. I am also deluding you by my singing with you, talking with you, and engaging myself in activities with you. But, any moment, my divinity may be revealed to you; you have to be ready, prepared for that moment. Since divinity is enveloped by humaness [sic.] you must endeavor to overcome the maya (delusion) that hides it from your eyes. This is a human form, in which every divine entity, every divine principle – that is to say, all the names and forms ascribed by man to God – are manifest.[72]

(Satya Sai Baba)

There are few homes and shops in South India that do not have a picture of Satya Sai Baba, India's living Avatar, a self-proclaimed God-man about whom many biographies have been written and a number of films produced.[73] In many places on Thursday evenings prayers are said to him, and a shrine has been erected in Bombay where he is worshipped. A world conference was held in his honour in Bombay in 1968, with devotees coming from all over the world to gather at his lotus feet.

Satya Sai Baba proclaims that he is the embodiment of all forms and aspects of God that have manifested on earth, a full and integral Avatar. He is regarded by his devotees as the advent of the Christ here on earth, and he claims to be a rebirth of Jesus Christ. Author Robert Ellwood comments that seeing Satya Sai Baba walking through rows of his devotees, healing, distributing *vibhuti* (sacred ash), teaching, 'the scene suddenly makes the New Testament seem contemporary'.[74] Satya claims to know all of the past, present, and future, including the time of his death in the year 2022 at the age of 96.[75] In addition he bears two birthmarks that are regarded by his followers as physiological proof of his divinity, a circular mark the *Samku Chakram*,[76] on the soles of his feet, and a birthmark in the shape of a garuda bird on his chest.[77] He playfully says 'God is no where; God is now here', and his Afro hairdo looks very much like a halo.

Satya Sai Baba was born on Monday, 23 November 1926. Devotees of Avatars might be inclined to see more than mere coincidence in the fact that the very next day Aurobindo experienced the Overmental, the event known as 'The Day of Siddhi'. Satya was born in the village of Puttaparthi, Andra Pradesh, South India, into the Brahmin caste. He was the last of four children, born when his father, Pedda Venkappa Raju, and his mother, Eswaramma, were old, and his brothers and sisters were already married. Special signs attended his birth, such as a cobra found lying under his bed, and musical instruments playing by themselves.

Satya's birth name was Satyanarayana Raju. The name Narayana refers to Vishnu and Satya means truth. Sai refers to the divine mother. Baba means father in Hindi, and is a term used for respect. Thus this Avatar's name signifies the true union of the male and female aspects of the universe.

In his youth Satya was bored by school and at the age of 10 formed a group for the presentation of songs of love and devotion to God. At the age of 14 he announced his avatarhood.[78] On 8 March 1940, he seemed to have been stung by a scorpion although neither a scorpion nor a snake was uncovered. He was unconscious for a while and when he revived he began behaving in an extraordinary manner. He stopped eating and speaking and began shrieking. This was explained as the possession of his body by Sai Baba of Shirdi. Two months later, on 23 May, Satyanarayana announced, 'I am Sai Baba', and on 20 October he said to his brother, 'I am no longer your Satya. I am Sai. I don't belong to you, my devotees are calling me. I have my work, I cannot stay any longer'.[79] It was during his fourteenth year that he supposedly materialized his first object. He offered to give his sister who was hospitalized something to make her well. Holding both hands above his head, a lime appeared suspended in air, then dropped into his hands. All kinds of miraculous powers have been attributed to him since that time. For example, since the age of 14, Satya has continued to materialize objects *ex nihilo*. The most famous of these materializations is his *vibhuti*, sacred ash, which flows daily from the palms of his hands, and which is used as a sacramental substance for the working of his miracles. *Vibhuti* is taken as a sign of Satya's avatarhood and it is used to effect cures by being rubbed on the skin or by being swallowed. Devotees throughout the world have told of having found *vibhuti* on their pictures of Satya.

Since 1940 Satya Sai Baba has been amazing people with his manifestations and powers, which Hindus call *siddhis*. He said that the first 32 years of his incarnation would be marked by *siddhis*, which he refers to as his calling cards. The nature of his *siddhis* seem to transcend the laws of time and space. For example, it is alleged that he can read the minds of people who are far away, see into the future and the past, cure diseases by miraculous means, perform spiritual surgery and resurrect people from the dead. It is said that he possesses the powers of omniscience, omnipotence, omnipresence, and omnifelicity, and that he understands and speaks all the languages of the world. He left India only once, in 1968, when he visited Uganda in Africa and told the Indian population there to leave before Idi Amin came to power. His American devotees have been pleading with him to come to this country but to no avail. His devotees believe, however, that he travels throughout the world on the astral plane to be near those who think of him and love him.[80]

Satya Sai Baba's ashram in southern India is called *Prasanthi Nilayam*, the Abode of Eternal Peace, and his summer residence is in northern India at Vrindavana, where Krishna is thought to have resided. The five pillars that undergird his message are truth, righteousness, peace, love, and non-violence, but the greatest of these is love: 'Begin the day with love, spend the day with love and end the day with love: that is the way to God.'[81] His mission is to restore India to its former spiritual glory and usher in a golden age.[82] Satya says that the nations of the world are like a railway train, that India is the engine that draws it on its spiritual path, and he himself is the engine-driver.[83] His confidant, Dr. V. K. Gokak, has explained that

> there is going to be a world crisis around the 1980s, after which there will be a definite turn toward what we call the Golden Age. At this time, it will be clear to man that any more entering into world power games will end in disaster for the whole world; and this will not be done. Simultaneous with this realization, there will be a descent of Grace. This descent of Grace is what will really bring forward the 'Hour of God.'[84]

Satya Sai Saba manifests what is known as 'Sai Power'. This power is physical, psychic and spiritual, and there are outward manifestations of each. On the physical level he presents miracles which fall within two divisions, apports and non-apports. In the psychic realm Sai power produces psi phenomena such as tele-pathy, clairvoyance, and psychokinesis. In the spiritual domain Satya effects the spirit, and thereby performs 'spiritual' surgery and resurrects people from the dead.

Volumes have been written about Satya Sai Baba's manifes-tations and miracles. One of his many biographies, called *Sai Baba, Man of Miracles*,[85] designates Satya's 'miracles' into the categories of 'apports' and 'non-apports'.[86] An apport is the materializing of an object by psychic force, and this is well-known in spiritualist and occult circles. The non-apport is rarer and occurs when objects are produced by mysterious means. Examples of Satya Sai Baba's apports include the materialization of (1) rudraksha, a talisman made from the berries of a tree that grows in the Himalayas, (2) statues and lockets of Hindu gods and goddesses (Vishnu, Krishna, Shiva, Parvati, etc.) made of wood and metal,[87] (3) photographs, drawings, and paintings of Avatars, (4) food and candy to feed the multitudes,[88] (5) amrita, an ambrosia-like elixir, the 'drink of the gods' that comes from the churning of the ocean of milk,[89] (6) an American gold coin minted in the year of the birth of the devotee,[90] (7) rings made of 22 carat gold,[91] (8) oblong stone linga, the symbol of Shiva and his generative power, that Satya Sai Baba produces from his mouth once or twice a year,[92] (9) the *Bhagavad Gita* manifested out of sand.[93] Examples of Satya's non-apports are (1) changing granite rock into edible rock candy,[94] (2) changing a flower bud into a glittering diamond,[95] (3) leaving his body to be with a disciple elsewhere (astral travel),[96] (4) manifesting on a single branch of a wild tree a mango, apple, orange and pear,[97] (5) changing a stone figure set in jewelry to another figure of an entirely different character while fully within view,[98] (6) producing about one pound of sacramental ash (vibhuti), per day.

Since Satya Sai Baba is living in a scientific age he has been scrutinized by skeptical Western scientists. To understand how carefully Satya has been scrutinized, one may refer to the study of Erlendur Haraldsson and Karlis Osis entitled 'The Appearance and Disappearance of Objects in the Presence of Sri Satya Sai Baba',[99] Based upon eleven examinations of Satya from 1972 to 1976, their findings are as follows:

1. Lengthy history without clear detection of fraud. According to those who have had a long association with Sai Baba, the seemingly paranormal flow of objects has lasted for some 40 years, or since his childhood. Most of the persons we met who had had even just one meeting with him reported having observed some ostensible materialization phenomena. We did not meet anyone who claimed personal observations indicative of Sai Baba having produced the objects by normal means.

2. Reports of the occurrence of other psi phenomena, such as ESP over distance, giving messages in dreams, healing, out-of-body projections collectively perceived, and PK (psychokinesis) of heavy objects.

3. Variety of circumstances in which objects appear: during private interviews, while traveling in a car, outdoors in the presence of crowds, in private homes, etc. Almost every time we saw Sai Baba, in public or in private, objects were produced.

4. Production of objects apparently in response to a specific situation or on the direct demand of the visitor. We encountered

many witnesses who testified as to such occurrences: the appearance of statuettes of a deity on request, a ring with a picture of a visitor's favorite deity, etc.

5. Reported production of large objects. e.g., a bowl the size of a dinner plate, and a basket of sweets 20 inches in diameter.

6. Production of objects at a distance from Sai Baba, such as prayer beads appearing on the windshield of a car being driven along an open country road, holy ash appearing on Sai Baba's pictures (observed by two senior research scientists), fruit appearing directly in the visitor's hand, etc.

7. Several prominent scientists in India have had the opportunity of observing Sai Baba extensively and have become convinced about the genuineness of the phenomena. . . . We have met all these men, and they told us of a number of phenomena that they had observed in a variety of circumstances.[100]

Haraldsson and Osis conclude that they were unable to detect any evidence of fraud, and were led to regard Satya Sai Baba's materializations as 'possibly paranormal'.

The famous professional magician Doug Henning viewed a movie about Satya Sai Baba. He felt certain that he could duplicate all the cases he saw on the film with his magician's art. However, he considered Satya's feat of making a picture in a ring disappear and then reappear (non-apport number 5), to be beyond the skills of magicians. Henning also said that if Satya does produce objects upon demand, that this would be an accomplishment that no magician could duplicate.[101]

The type of object that Satya Sai Baba materializes is significant since many of them, such as the *Gita*, *amrita*, and statues of Vishnu and Krishna, are aspects of the Vaishnava tradition. Satya materialized a copy of the *Gita* out of sand, and the incarnational passage of chapter four is as follows:

For the protection of the virtuous, for the destruction of evildoers and for establishing righteousness on a firm footing, I incarnate from age to age. Whenever asanthi, or disharmony, overwhelms the world, the Lord will incarnate in human form to establish the modes of earning prasanthi, or peace, and to reeducate the human community in the paths of peace.[102]

Satya Sai Baba has an accepting and all-embracing attitude toward Hinduism's many Avatars. He acknowledges all the mythic Avatars including Buddha and Balarama, the 22 Avatars named in the *Bhagavata Purana*, and Shankara, Ramakrishna, Aurobindo, and Jesus Christ, as *amshavatars*, or partial Avatars. However, he designates himself as a *purnavatar*, like Krishna, a full and integral Avatar.[103] To the *purnavatar* are attributed seven divine qualities: (1) the power to bestow grace on the deserving, (2) the power to bestow grace on the undeserving, (3) the power to awaken new states of consciousness and a new order of society, (4) the power to support what is good but defenceless, (5) the power to destroy what is evil, (6) a form which when recalled mentally invokes the spiritual or physical presence of the Avatar, and (7) a name which has divine potency.[104]

Satya claims that all forms of God are the same and that he is a reincarnation of Christ. On Christmas day, 1972, he pointed to a lamb and said,

> the lamb is merely a symbol, a sign. It stands for the voice: 'Ba-Ba'; the announcement was of the advent of Baba. . . . The lamb is the sign and symbol of love. Christ did not declare that He would come again; he said, 'He who sent me will come again.' That 'Ba-Ba' is this Baba.[105]

In addition, Satya materialized a wooden cross with a silver statue of Jesus on it which he claims to be wood from the original cross upon which Christ was crucified.[106] He said that the hole at the top of the cross was where the cross was hung on a standard.[107] And regarding the image of Christ on the cross, Satya said that it is 'not as artists have imagined Him and as historians have told about Him, but as he actually really and truly was, with stomach pulled way in and ribs all showing because He had had no food for eight days'.[108]

Satya Sai Baba claims to know intimate details about Jesus and to exhibit the same mysterious powers. Some of Satya's Christ-like powers are feeding the multitudes, not with loaves and fishes, but with *amrita*, the nectar of immortality,[109] and the ego-less love which flows from 'the divine fount of his nature'.[110] Satya's maxim, 'Whatever you feel should not be done to you by others, you should avoid doing to others',[111] is reminiscent of Jesus' golden rule.

Satya's various forms of healing can remind one of Jesus. For example, the touch of his robe produces healing effects,[112] and he exorcises demons out of people.[113] Most amazing of all, are reports that Satya has brought people back from death. There are accounts of his having resurrected an Indian man in 1953,[114] and an American by the name of Walter Cowen in 1971.[115] In addition, reports tell of Satya curing cancer and gall stones with *vibhuti* taken internally,[116] and curing cerebro-spinal meningitis and blindness by the external application of *vibhuti*.[117] He has vicariously accepted in his own being such ailments from his devotees as heart attacks, strokes, fever, paralysis, and blindness, in order to atone for them and spare them the suffering.[118] Furthermore, there are accounts of Satya materializing surgical instruments and bandages, removing tumours and cancer through spiritual surgery,[119] and performing mediumistic surgery by operating through the body of a reputable surgeon.[120]

Another striking similarity between Satya Sai Baba and Jesus is that both are part of a trinity. As Jesus is the second person of the Christian trinity, and Vishnu is the second member of the Hindu trinity, so Satya is the second person of an avataric trinity consisting of Shirdi Sai Baba, Satya Sai Baba, and Prema Sai Baba. The claim is made that eight years after Shirdi Sai Baba died in 1918, he reappeared as Satya in 1926. And the *Vibhuti* that pours out of Satya is believed to come from Shirdi, who kept a fire burning perpetually in the Zoroastrian style, and also used the ashes as a sacramental substance. Furthermore, Satya believes that he will die in 2022 and reappear as Prema Sai Baba in the Mandya district of the Karnataka state of India.[121] His devotees believe that this last manifestation of the Sai Baba phenomenon will occur in the golden age (Krita yuga).

The following myth has been offered to explain the trinitarian Sai Baba claim. Thousands of years ago the sage Bharadwaja was advised by Indra, ruler of the gods, to perform a Vedic ritual. Eager to have Shakti, the consort of Shiva, preside over the ritual and receive her blessing, Bharadwaja travelled to their Himalayan abode to convey the invitation. Finding them coupled in the cosmic dance, Bharadwaja waited eight days without getting their attention, although failing to notice the smile cast at him by Shakti. Disappointed, he returned home and on the way had a stroke. Shiva cured him by sprinkling him with water, and consoled him by promising that he and Shakti would assume human form in the Bharadwaja lineage: Shiva as Shirdi Sai Baba, Shiva and Shakti as Satya Sai Baba, and Shakti as Prema Sai Baba.[122]

Many Hindus believe today that Satya Sai Baba has come at the present time as the second manifestation of the Sai Baba trinity, and as 'the Hindu Christ'. Accounts abound of people who have apparently seen Satya turn into Jesus Christ, and interpret this as his divine capriciousness (*lila*).[123] In some American spiritualist churches ministers have been known to proclaim that the coming of Satya heralds the second advent of the Christ.[124] It is not too surprising that a rumour has circulated saying that Satya received a telegram from the Vatican asking him to grant an interview to the Pope.[125]

CONCLUSION: MODERN AVATARS AND CHRIST

Prayer to Jesus

O! RAY OF LIGHT
that ever came
To save men by thy Holy Name,
Through Yugas, Thou Anointed One
Who lit decaying Dharma's sun,
O! Brooding Love, that raised the dead,
On sinning sick, kind healing shed,
Christ, quelling demons by Thy Might
And filling multitudes with Light.
We long to see Thee come again,
To gather and transfigure men!
Hail! Avatar of Holy Birth,
Come, reign in Peace and Love on earth.
Om! Om! Om![126]

(Sister Sushila Devi)

Before discussing the relationship of the modern Avatars to Jesus Christ, let us first notice that this chapter has illustrated the evolution of an awareness of divinity, starting with Chaitanya who is unconscious of being an Avatar, then Ramakrishna who is semiconscious of his divinity, followed by Aurobindo and The Mother who are conscious of each other as Avatars, then Meher Baba who is self-conscious of his Avatarhood, and ending with

Satya Sai Baba who is unself-conscious about his divine status. A gradual evolving of the cognizance of divinity has transpired among these historical God-men and God-woman.

Now let us reflect on the relationship between India's modern Avatars and the Christian God-man Jesus Christ. The year 1874 marks a watershed in Hindu spirituality, for in that year Ramakrishna had a mystical vision of Jesus Christ and 'validated' Jesus as a genuine spiritual master upon whom the aspirant could meditate and be transported to the ultimate Hindu spiritual goal. From that time forth, Ramakrishna believed in the divinity of Jesus Christ as an incarnate God and kept a picture of Jesus in his room, burning incense before it each morning and evening. The significance to Hindus of Ramakrishna's experience was to place Jesus on a par with Krishna, Rama, and the other Avatars including Chaitanya and Ramakrishna himself. Later, some Indian Christians would view Ramakrishna as a direct manifestation of the Christ and go into ecstasy before him.[127] But for Ramakrishna, the Avatars were essentially one and the same, appearing under different names and forms, now as Krishna, now as Christ, and even as Ramakrishna. Toward the end of Ramakrishna's life he gathered twelve disciples around him, and insisted that two of them, Ramakrishnananda and Saradananda, had been disciples of Christ in a former life.[128] The points of similarity between Ramakrishna and Jesus Christ became striking. The title of Mahendranath Gupta's biographical diary of Ramakrishna, *The Gospel of Sri Ramakrishna*, further suggests the equivalence between this God-man and the God-man of the Christian Gospels. The disciples of Ramakrishna viewed him as a divine incarnation or Avatar, and recognized in him the same spirit which had animated Jesus. Ramakrishna's most renowned disciple, Swami Vivekananda, felt that God had made himself manifest in the person of Ramakrishna more vividly and more humanly than he had in Jesus. Vivekananda expressed many doubts about the historicity of Jesus. For example, Vivekananda had a strange dream in which a bearded old sage told him that he was one of the Theraputae, sons of the Buddhist monks, who had once lived on Crete where Christianity had its origin. The ideals of the Theraputae had been proclaimed as the teachings of Christianity, and the old sage said 'there was no such personality of the name of Jesus ever born'.[129] Swami Vivekananda pondered over this dream, wondering whether it was merely a dream or whether it was reality. However, there could be no question in Vivekananda's mind about the historicity and divinity of his master, Ramakrishna.

Ramakrishna as a Hindu God-man was the first to acknowledge Jesus Christ on a par with other Hindu Avatars, thus beginning the Hinduization of Jesus Christ. Both Ramakrishna and Vivekananda tended to emphasize the divinity of Christ to the exclusion of his humanity. Ramakrishna's familiarity with Jesus Christ came from Indian Christian converts, paintings of Jesus, and through visions that he experienced. He knew very little about Jesus the man of Nazareth, and was not especially concerned with his historical existence. This attitude helped to set the tone for the Hinduization of Jesus Christ in which Jesus is understood as the divine Christ-Spirit with whom the Hindu may merge and enter into a superconscious state.

About fifty years after Ramakrishna's Hinduization of Jesus Christ, a shift occurs with Meher Baba. According to Meher Baba, the Avatar possesses an avataric consciousness that animated the founders of most of the world religions. Meher Baba connected Christ-consciousness with Buddha-consciousness, Muhammad-consciousness, Zoroaster-consciousness, and Meher Baba-consciousness, thus making it one repeating divine consciousness. Meher Baba's statement that he was Jesus Christ can be interpreted in this light to mean that he possessed the same divine consciousness that Jesus possessed, which repeats during 'avataric' cycles.

Satya Sai Baba's relation to Jesus Christ takes a different turn. This Avatar claims to possess the miraculous powers (siddhi) and healing ability that is attributed to Jesus Christ. Satya is the first Hindu Avatar to approach Jesus not through a mystical experience, nor through Christ-consciousness, but as an historical divine incarnation, one who produced miracles and healed people. Whereas Ramakrishna was largely unaware of the historical Jesus, Satya claims to be a reincarnation of the historical Jesus, reporting things about Jesus that are recalled from his past life. In fact, some of Satya's deeds and sayings are so reminiscent of Jesus that many people are left with a 'willing suspension of disbelief'. Satya appears to be repeating many of the feats that Jesus Christ accomplished two thousand years ago, and skeptics and scientists are left without an adequate explanation of his Christ-like abilities. Many Hindus regard him as a modern-day Christ and in many ways his charisma and miracles rival those of Jesus. Is this really a comparable miraculous phenomenon?

Epilogue: Criteria for Avatarhood Based on Mythemes

Throughout Part One we have seen a recurrent pattern of certain themes and motifs central to the classical and modern Avatars. Certain motifs are used by the Indian Avatars repeatedly and they are found as common characteristics of the God-man, although all of the characteristics may not be used by each God-man. These 'mythemes' are central to the Avatar and are isolated and described below.

THE DIVINE AURA

The aura associated with the Avatars is golden. Vishnu creates the world in the golden age by sprouting a golden lotus from his navel, and Vishnu's incarnations have golden imagery. Matsya the fish Avatar has golden scales, and the man-lion Avatar kills golden-garment. Among modern Avatars Chaitanya is known as the golden Avatar, the Mother of Pondicherry encircles herself with golden imagery, and Satya Sai Baba wearing golden robes materializes golden rings. A major centre of the Vaishnavite faith in India is Bengal, referred to by its inhabitants as *Sonar Bengla*, 'golden Bengal', and those who belong to the *Sonar* caste traditionally work as goldsmiths.[1]

The golden aura relates the Avatar to his progenitor, Vishnu, the solar, golden deity, and the Avatars are his emanations, or golden sun-beams. This golden imagery may be a reflection of what is stated in the Isa Upanishad, 'The door of the True is covered with a golden disk' (verse 15), and the Avatar's golden aura is a reflection of his transcendence. Furthermore, since gold is not part of the colour spectrum it appears to emanate from a transcendent source, as in Russian icons where 'gold of the midday sun remains the color of colors and the miracle of miracles', and 'only God' "brighter than the sun", emits this royal light'.[2] The Avatars encircle themselves with golden imagery, for a golden hue is the symbol of God and denotes divine splendour. It seems that the

Avatars would like to appear as spiritual alchemists, able to
transubstantiate the material elements of the earth into gold, and
to possess the Midas-touch.

THE DIVINE SERPENT

A major determinant of the Avatar is the royal serpent, the cobra.
The cobra is intimately related to Vishnu and the Avatars. In India
the snake (*naga*) is regarded as part of God's essence and composed of divine substance.[3] It is the symbol of the life-energy that
motivates birth and rebirth, and the shedding of its skin suggests
immortality. In India the cobra is regarded as a very special
creature, not only for its speed and deadly venom, but for its hood
which looks like a crown, and gives it the appearance of royalty.
The hood of the cobra is portrayed as polycephalous (i.e. comprised of many heads), and it is generally thought in India that
within each hood lies a precious jewel.

In the Hindu imagination the cobra and the Avatar are both
manifestations of the one divine substance. They function harmoniously, demonstrating a mutuality between the God-man and
the forces of nature. The cobra acts to protect and sustain the
Avatar, and the Avatar seems to possess a supernatural relationship with the cobra that makes him invulnerable to its potential
danger.

The gods Vishnu, Krishna, and Shiva are closely connected with
cobras. Vishnu reclines on the serpent Sesha and the hood of this
cobra protects him. Krishna also has a special relationship to
cobras. When he danced on the cobra Kaliya he left his footprint
on Kaliya's head, and this is thought to account for the marks on
the cobra's hood. In Indian lore the cobras are considered born
dancers, and it is thought that Krishna's flute taught them to
'dance', and they have been dancing ever since to the Indian
snake-charmer's flute. Shiva wears a necklace of cobras, which are
associated with the sacred lingam, the emblem of Lord Shiva. The
lingam, symbolizing the creative principle of the universe, is
sometimes depicted on stone sculptures as guarded by many-
headed cobras, further establishing the relationship between man
and nature and the snake who is the ruler of fertility.

Worship of the snake is part of the Vaishnava tradition. Scholars
have shown how a Vaishnava cult has been grafted on to a snake

cult, the Vaishnava deity being identified with the resident serpent.[4] The serpent deity is the residing deity of field and home,
and psyche of man, an elemental, natural, indwelling lord. Amorous and marriage alliances between men and snakes occur in
Indian literature. One such marriage is that between Arjuna and
Ulupi in the *Mahabharata*. It has also been explained that one of
the roles of the cobra in ancient Hindu literature was to guard
gold.[5] The earth was considered to be the depository of jewels and
precious metals, and snakes, which are the sons of earth, are the
rightful owners of the treasures concealed in the womb of their
mother.

Modern Avatars seem to exhibit a spiritual empathy with cobras, and any Avatar who does not possess some relationship with
a cobra is a rare exception. When Chaitanya was a toddler he
caught hold of a snake. Everyone was terribly frightened but he
released it and it crawled away.[6] Mira Richard was able to overpower a cobra with the strength of her mind. Meher Baba
instructed his disciples that the name Baba is effective in subdu-
ing the cobra.[7] And devotees considered it significant that a cobra
was discovered under Satya Sai Baba's bed when he was born.

Ancient Sanskrit literature designates snakes with more than 25
names. One of these names is Kundalin, and from this is derived
Kundalini, meaning the serpent power, the major image behind
the Kundalini yoga. Some modern Avatars have transformed the
cobra by internalizing it in the form of the serpent power, Kundalini. The yoga of Kundalini begins by arousing the coiled cobra at
the base of the spine, and allowing it to ascend through the
chakras until it reaches the top of the skull where it bursts forth
and unites with God. Ramakrishna, Aurobindo, and Satya Sai
Baba were familiar with the internalized cobra in the form of the
Kundalini. In one way or another the royal cobra is intimately
related to the Avatar.

PREORDAINED BIRTH AND SUFFERING DEATH

The paradigm for the Avatar's birth is supplied by Krishna. While
accounts of Krishna's birth vary, in the *Bhagavata Purana* it is said
that Vishnu enters the mind of Krishna's father. Likewise, thirteen
months before Chaitanya's birth his father felt a divine light enter
his heart and then pass on to his wife, who saw many gods

worshipping her. Ramakrishna's father had a vision in which Vishnu informed him that he was going to be reborn, and Ramakrishna's mother dreamt that she was being possessed by a god.

Concerning the Avatar's death, Krishna died from a wound to his heel, reminiscent of Achilles, but this manner of dying has not been imitated by modern Avatars. Chaitanya's death is similar to Rama's as both of them walked into a river and drowned. However, two Avatars in particular have experienced great suffering in their dying. Ramakrishna suffered with throat cancer, and Meher Baba suffered through two automobile accidents that maimed him, and he accepted this as his cross to bear. Both Ramakrishna and Meher Baba are likely to have had Christ's agony in mind when they departed this earth.

DIVINE NAME AND PARENT FIGURE

Each of the Avatars takes or receives a spiritual name which is his or her divine epithet. The following is a list of each modern Avatar's birth name, divine name, and explanation of the divine name:

Birth name	Divine name	Meaning of divine name
Visvambhara Misra	Krishna Chaitanya	He who has consciousness of Krishna
Gadadhar Chatterji	Ramakrishna	Combination of Avatars Rama and Krishna
Aravinda Ackroyd Ghose	Aurobindo	Lotus
Mira Alfassa	The Mother	Divine Mother
Merwin Sheriar Irani	Meher Baba	Compassionate Father
Satyanarayana Raju	Satya Sai Baba	Truth Mother Father

The Avatar functions in the mind of His followers as divine parents.[8] The Avatar is 'Baba', the father, and Shakti, the mother. Chaitanya was thought to embody Krishna and his consort Radha, Ramakrishna was both Krishna, the god, and Kali, the goddess. Aurobindo and The Mother are a father–mother, Shiva–Shakti pair, and Sai Baba means mother–father. The Avatar embodies in himself the qualities of the divine mother along with those of the heavenly father. In effect, the Avatar is an androgyne, a vision of wholeness encompassing both male and female aspects.

DISCIPLES

The Avatar asks that humanity respond to him with the love that a child gives its parents. It is customary for a small band of disciples to gather around the Avatar and offer themselves selflessly. This small group is composed of individuals who recognize the Avatar's divinity and receive his esoteric message. The paradigm for the inner circle of disciples may be the milkmaids (gopis) that surrounded Krishna, or the twelve apostles who encircled Jesus. Chaitanya and Ramakrishna each had a small circle of close disciples; Aurobindo and The Mother had the 'ashramites'; Meher Baba gathered his 'mandali'; and Satya Sai Baba had devotees called *bangaru* (golden ones). The disciples offer all their love and devotion to the Avatar and serve as models for others.

SUPERNATURAL POWERS

Among the supernatural powers (*siddhis*) that Avatars claim are extra-sensory perception, telepathy, and the ability to perform astral travel. Avatars claim to enter into altered states of consciousness such as *samadhi* or overmental consciousness. Some Avatars perform 'miracles' such as healings, spiritual surgery, and the resurrecting of people from the dead, as signs of their divinity. Further examples of these divine signs are the apports and non-apports of Satya Sai Baba, and the lengthy silence of Meher Baba. These powers of the Avatar seem to extend beyond human ability and offer evidence for superhuman status.

Another example of the Avatar's supernatural power is *Vibhuti*. In the Hindu Vaishnava tradition the Avatars manifest *vibhuti* as a sign of divine omnipotence. *Vibhuti* is related to Vishnu's universal power, for in the *Mahabharata* Vishnu is often called Vibhu, a reference to his imperishable source of existence. The substantive form of *Vibhu* is *Vibhuti*.[9] The Avatars tend to interpret *vibhuti* in their own distinctive ways. For example, the Mother of Pondicherry refers to an emanation of her inner self as Vibhuti, while for Aurobindo vibhuti is one who rises to the uppermost spiritual heights.[10] Satya Sai Baba manifests vibhuti from the palms of his hands in the form of ash, which is declared to have healing powers. Vibhuti is given various interpretations by the Avatars, but it is a link with the gods and a form of divine omnipotence.

APOCALYPTIC EXPECTATION

Most of the Avatars in Chapter 2 have been viewed by their devotees as Kalki, the Avatar who will end the dark age and inaugurate the new age. The *Gita* foreshadows this apocalyptic tone, for in it the Lord says that he will come again whenever evil increases and goodness grows weak. In the Hindu view the present cycle of time is moving inexorably toward the final cataclysm and Kalki will come to end it. Because the tenth and final Avatar, Kalki, is supposed to arrive in times of decadence and decline, it is frequently thought that the Avatar who makes an appearance is Kalki in disguise. Kalki will function first as Shiva, the destroyer, causing the majority of mankind to perish, and then as Brahma, the creator, saving a righteous remnant.

The Kalki Avatar fulfils the apocalyptic expectations of Hindus who contemplate the end of a cycle in the Kali yuga. The hope that God will end the age of quarrel and save a righteous remnant is a recurrent theme among various religious movements who await the advent of a God-man in times of materialism, immorality, and decadence, which many Hindus feel we are currently witnessing. The Kalki Avatar in Hinduism, Maitreya Buddha in Buddhism, the Mahdi in Islam, the messiah in Judaism, and the Saviour in Christianity, all fit the pattern of a divine agent who will arrive at the apocalypse. From Chaitanya to Satya Sai Baba, each modern Avatar has been regarded as Kalki, the final Avatar.

To summarize, the mythemes of the Avatars are related to the paradigmatic model for all Vaishnavites, Lord Vishnu and his anthropomorphic incarnation Krishna. The predominant characteristics of avatarhood are a golden-hue, the royal cobra, divine androgyny, disciples, supernatural powers, and his expected presence at the apocalypse.

Part Two
The God-Man in the West

3

The Avatar Incarnates in the West

INTRODUCTION: THE ADVENT OF THE AVATAR AND THE *GITA* UPON THE WEST

The pure Walden water is mingled with the sacred water of the Ganges.[1]

(Thoreau)

Passage to more than India!
Are thy wings plumed indeed for such far flights?
O Soul, voyagest thou indeed on voyages like those?
Disportest thou on waters such as those?
Soundest below the Sanscrit and the Vedas?
Then have thy bent unleash'd.
Passage to you, your shores, ye aged fierce enigmas!
. . . Passage to more than India!
O secret of the earth and sky![2]

(Whitman)

Whereas Part One demonstrated how the Avatar stems from an Indian tradition and has a mythic imagery that gives it reality and popularity in the East, Part Two focuses upon the influence that the avatar concept has had on the Western world (particularly Ireland, England, and America), and the differences in the way avatarhood has manifested itself. In this chapter we shall see certain transformations which the avatar concept underwent as it was transplanted to the West.

Western missionaries to India began taking notice of Vishnu's numerous Avatars in the mid-17th century. The first chaplain of the Dutch East India Company, Abraham Rogerius, described the Hindu gods and Vishnu's Avatars in his book *The Open Door to* the Hidden Heathen Religion in 1651.³ Twenty-one years later another Dutchman, Philip Baldaeus (1632–71), portrayed Vishnu's ten Avatars in detail. It is now known that practically everything in Baldaeus' account was plagiarized from an anonymous manuscript written in the mid-17th century.⁴ But while Baldaeus cannot be regarded as an independent investigator, he did function as a popularizer, his Dutch work being highly regarded and translated into both German and English. The German missionary Barthalomaeus Ziegenbalg reported in 1706 that the incarnations of Vishnu indicated that these 'deluded people have heard some imperfect Rumour of Christ, but taking it all in a huddle, have interlaced it with a World of Fables and Fictions'.⁵ This statement was based upon the similarity between the sound of the name Krishna and the sound of the name Christ, a likeness that some Hindu religious thinkers still assert.

In the last quarter of the 18th century, great advances in general knowledge of Hindu culture were made in Bengal by a small group of enthusiastic Englishmen who had taken up the study of Sanskrit language and literature. In 1784 Sir William Jones, Charles Wilkins, Nathaniel Halhed, Henry Thomas Colebrooke, and others, organized an association of vast importance for the future of Asian studies, the Asiatic Society of Bengal. This society was devoted to the antiquities, arts, sciences, history, and literature of Asia. The contagious interest in the study of the classical Indian languages generated by this group spread eventually to the Western universities, where it continues to this day.

The founders of the Asiatic Society of Bengal studied the Hindu heritage primarily as historians and men of letters. Sir William Jones was a jurist, a poet, a classicist, and a scholar whose works were praised by such men as Ben Franklin, Samuel Johnson, Edmund Burke and William Pitt. Jones, already a master of Arabic, Hebrew, and Persian, left for India in 1783, and there he began the study of Sanskrit. His use of the word 'Avatar' in 1784, in reference to the descent of Vishnu,⁶ was the first in the English language. Sir Charles Wilkins was an associate of Jones who mastered Sanskrit and in 1785 became the first translator of the Bhagavad Gita, which he called the 'Bhagvat Gheeta'. This was the first published translation into any European language of any major Sanskrit work, and the artist/poet William Blake did a drawing of 'Mr. Wilkins translating the Geeta'. Three years later in 1788 a Russian translation of the Gita was completed, followed by a German translation fourteen years later. The *Gita* has been translated more than 25 times since 1785.

It was the Wilkins translation of the *Gita* that delighted the New England transcendentalists in the 19th century. Arthur Christy has said that 'No one Oriental volume that ever came to Concord was more influential than the Bhagavadgita.'[7] For years Ralph Waldo Emerson was one of the very few Americans who owned a copy of the *Gita*, and his copy was even more widely used than the one in the Harvard College library.[8] Emerson wrote in his *Journal* in 1848 that:

> I owed – my friend and I owed – a magnificent day to the *Bhagavat Geeta*. It was the first of books; it was as if an empire spake to us, nothing small or unworthy, but large, serene, consistent, its voice of an old intelligence which in another age and climate had pondered and thus disposed of the same questions which exercise us.[9]

To Emma Lazarus, Emerson wrote, 'And of books there is another which, when you have read, you shall sit for a while and then write a poem – the 'Bhagavat Geeta' but read it in Charles Wilkins's translation.'[10]

Emerson's friend Henry David Thoreau also had high admiration for the *Gita*, saying, 'The reader is nowhere raised into and sustained in a higher, purer, or *rarer* region of thought than in the *Bhagvat-Geeta*', and 'Beside the vast and cosmogonical philosophy of the *Bhagvat-Geeta*, even our Shakespeare seems sometimes youthfully green and practical merely.'[11] In *Walden* he wrote:

> In the morning I bathe my intellect in the stupendous and cosmogonal philosophy of the *Bhagvat Geeta*, since whose composition years of the gods have elapsed, and in comparison with which our modern world and its literature seem puny and trivial; and I doubt if that philosophy is not to be referred to a previous state of existence, so remote is its sublimity from our conceptions.[12]

Another Transcendentalist, Walt Whitman, incorporated the Avatar concept in his *Leaves of Grass*, writing:

I see the site of the old empire of Assyria, and that of Persia,
    and that of India,
I see the falling of the Ganges over the high rim of Saukara. [13]
I see the place of the idea of the Deity incarnated by avatars in
    human forms . . .[14]

and again,

I receive now again of my many translations, from my avatars
    ascending, while others doubtless await me,
An unknown sphere more real that I dream'd, more direct,
    darts awakening rays about me, *So long!*[15]

Thus, in the early and mid-19th century there was considerable
experimentation in American literary works with the avataric
concept. Indeed, an example of its misuse was in Edgar Allen
Poe's *The Masque of the Red Death*, written in 1842. Poe wrote 'The
"Red Death" had long devastated the country. . . . Blood was its
Avatar and its seal – the redness and the horror of blood.'[16]

J. P. Parroud translated the *Gita* into French in 1787, and the
word 'avatar' entered the French language in the year 1800, the
same time that Paris became a centre for Sanskrit studies. At least
four French literary works have focused upon the avatar theme.
The first of these is a story entitled 'Avatar' published in 1856 by
the author and artist Théophile Gautier (1811–74).[17] In Gautier's
tale Hindu holy men divulge certain magical monosyllables for
transferring souls from person to person. Gautier lists all ten
mythological Avatars of Vishnu, and refers to Krishna as Kitona,
'in which some recognise a Hindoo Christ'.[18] In 1906 the French
dramatist Charles Marion wrote a one-act comedy called *Les
Avataries* (the Avatarized Ones).[19] In this comedy of errors, the
inspiration for the idea of soul transference is found in an
unspecified Hindu book, and souls get into the wrong bodies as
people get 'avatarized'. A third French work, *L'Avatar d'Yvan Orel*,
was written by Omer Chevalier in 1919.[20] In this novel the avatar
possesses esoteric knowledge that he receives from a fakir of
Benares, empowering him to transcend time and space through
endless incarnations, inhabit superterrestrial planets, and observe
men at different levels of evolution. This novel is reminiscent of
the science fiction of Jules Verne, and is also a polemic against
socialistic government. A fourth French literary work is the play

Les Avatars de Juste Palinod[21] written in 1973 by Gaston Cherpillod. In these French literary works the Hindu concept of avatar is understood as transference of a soul or possession of supernatural powers, but not descent of a deity.

However interesting these literary works may be, our concern is to follow the trail of the Avatar, the God-man, and the imagery of a divine descent as announced in the *Gita*. In the West the first example of an Avatar is to be found in the spiritual movement known as Theosophy.

THE AVATARS OF THE THEOSOPHICAL SOCIETY

America, England, and India

Yogibogeybox in Dawson chambers. *Isis Unveiled.* . . . Cross-legged under an umbrel umbershoot he thrones an Aztec logos, functioning on astral levels, their overshoul, mahamahatma. The faithful hermetists await the light, ripe for chelaship, ring-roundabout him. . . . Hesouls, shesouls, shoals of souls.

(James Joyce, *Ulysses*)

The concept of the Avatar, having crossed the ocean from India to the West in the late 18th century, found its first personification in a God-man among a spiritual group known as the Theosophical Society. Theosophy means the wisdom of God, and this movement sought to unlock the secrets of divine wisdom.

Through occult science the Theosophical Society attempted to uncover hidden laws in nature and latent powers in man. These laws and powers were thought to lie hidden in the lore of ancient cultures and religions, and the early Theosophists tried to find evidence for these laws by studying esoteric religions. Various leaders within the Theosophical Society developed a 'science of occultism' and 'laws of the higher life' by which to recognize higher beings and understand the ladder stretching from man to God. Theosophists sought 'great teachers', and evolved the notion of a spiritual hierarchy composed of sages, teachers, initiates, adepts, masters, mahatmas, and world teachers. They believed that high on the ladder stood the World Teacher who is a founder of a great religion, an Avatar, and a transmitter of divine wisdom.

The founder of the Theosophical Society was the exotic, eccentric, and enigmatic Russian, Helena Petrovna Blavatsky (1831–91). From her youth she was curious about everything mysterious and uncanny and came to believe strongly in a world of supernatural beings. Often exaggerating and embroidering her environment, she embarked upon psychic escapades, saying that she had a double existence – in her physical body during the day and in her astral body at night. She claimed knowledge of an ancient 'Lemuro-Atlantean wisdom', that she said was the fount of wisdom. Her two massive literary works, *Isis Unveiled* (1877) and *The Secret Doctrine* (1888), show the influence of numerous occult teachings related to Kabbalism, Pythagoreanism, astrology, alchemy, numerology, mesmerism, and esoteric Christianity, Hinduism, Buddhism, and Gnosticism. Blavatsky's theosophy was an attempt to synthesize Orientalism and occultism into a new universal religion.

Helena Petrovna Blavatsky (known as HPB) was intrigued by the mystique of the East, its antiquity, abstruse terminology, and strange tongues. She travelled to India and Nepal (and claimed to have entered Tibet); claimed to have contacted 'shells of departed beings' called 'elementals'; and practised spiritualism in the form of mediumistic communications, psychokinesis, spirit-rapping, out-of-body experiences, poltergeists, and materializations called 'ectoplasm'. Like many late-19th century spiritualists, she believed in a spiritual world-centre concealed in the heart of Asia, that she connected with the home of the Masters and the place of the world's creation. She regarded herself as an adept of Eastern spiritualism, or 'Brahma Vidya', and spoke of controlling 'elementals' by 'mayavic' power. She believed that she was guided by Masters who bore the names Koot Hoomi and Morya. These Masters, also known as Adepts, although their attention was world-wide, focused on spiritual India, mysterious Tibet, and beyond it to an even more esoteric Shambala. (Shambala is the village from which the Kalki Avatar is expected to arrive.) Blavatsky spoke of contacting these Masters by leaving her physical body and entering the 'astral', 'subtle', or 'etheric' plane. She said she had spoken to Masters who had once inhabited the bodies of Christ, Pythagoras, and Plotinus. She wore a symbolic brooch containing the Aryan Swastika and the Star of David surrounded by an encircling serpent, and this became the seal of the Theosophical Society.

In 1873 when almost 42 years old, HPB arrived in America on the advice of her 'mysterious Hindu'. The following year she met Col. Henry Steel Olcott (1832–1907), and these two spiritualists, known as 'the theosophical twins', organized the Theosophical Society in 1875 in New York City with Olcott as president and Blavatsky as secretary. Thus began a movement which was to attract such notables as Thomas Edison, G. B. Shaw, W. B. Yeats, Scriabine, Rudolf Steiner, Gandhi, Christmas Humphreys, Edward Conze, Abner Doubleday, and many others. HPB introduced Col. Olcott to her 'phenomena' and taught him about an Egyptian branch of a mystic brotherhood, the 'Brotherhood of Luxor' composed of Eastern Adepts living on both earthly and astral planes. Olcott, under Blavatsky's guidance, began as a student of the Luxor branch of the occult brotherhood but was rapidly transferred to the Indian section.[22] In 1875 his book *People from the Other World* was published.

In 1877 Blavatsky published her first major work, *Isis Unveiled*, saying that she received much of it directly from Masters of the Great White Brotherhood in Tibet, and it helped establish her as an occult priestess of Isis. Two central themes that emerged in *Isis Unveiled* were disdain for Christianity and the belief that the source of all ancient wisdom was India.

In 1876 and 1877 the Theosophical Society was moribund in New York and its future looked bleak. India, thought to be the major storehouse of wisdom, became more and more prominent in the conversations between Blavatsky and Olcott, and the Masters whom Blavatsky introduced to Olcott increasingly wore turbans. Drawn by the spiritual magnetism of India, HPB and Olcott felt that the Masters were ordering them to leave America for India and so they went. Olcott recorded in his diary that in India he was 'on sacred soil . . . the cradle country of religions, the dwelling place of the Masters'.[23] In 1878 the society affiliated itself with the Indian Arya Samaj, founded by Swami Dayananda Sarasvati, and called itself 'The Theosophical Society of the Arya Samaj'. HPB affirmed that Swami Sarasvati was none other than a Himalayan Master inhabiting the Swami's body. Blavatsky and Olcott met the Swami and tried to strengthen the ties between the two societies. But by 1880 Swami Sarasvati disaffiliated himself with the Theosophists, referring to them as atheists believing in spirits and witches.

In India, Olcott and Blavatsky were the guests of maharajahs, pandits, and the British elite. While Blavatsky mysteriously kept in touch with the Masters, Olcott lectured to Hindus on the virtues of their own religion and performed 'magnetic' healings. They instilled in many Hindus a pride of their indigenous culture and promoted education and the learning of Sanskrit, hoping to counter the influence of Christian missionaries. In 1882 they moved the headquarters of the Theosophical Society from America to Adyar, just outside of Madras. It was here in the shrine room, sometimes referred to as 'the astral post office', that messages from the Masters were regularly 'precipitated' to the Theosophical leaders, and these epistles became known as the Mahatma letters. The theosophical twins had entered the mysterious East and brought with them mythical mahatmas and a fanciful fant-asia.

In 1880 Blavatsky and Olcott travelled to Ceylon (Sri Lanka) where they were both formally accepted into the Buddhist religion. This was the first of 37 visits by Col. Olcott, and there he busied himself in revitalizing Buddhism, establishing schools where Buddhism was taught, and organizing branches of the Theosophical Society. He was regarded by many of the Buddhists of Ceylon as a Buddha-to-be (*Bodhisattva*), and a unique honour was bestowed upon him as he became the very first layman granted authority to administer vows to persons wishing to convert to Buddhism. He was responsible for designing the Buddhist flag and for writing the Buddhist catechism. He was admired as a restorer of Buddhism and became a national hero in Ceylon with his picture on its postage stamp, and he has evolved into something of a saviour figure as well.

In 1888, three years before her death, HPB published her second major work and magnum opus, *The Secret Doctrine*. Her stated intention in this work was to translate and reveal an archaic Tibetan manuscript called the *Stanzas of Dzyan*, which was supposedly written in a language unknown to philology, called Senzar. However, according to William Emmette Coleman, her chief sources were H. H. Wilson's *Vishnu Purana* and other works including Donnelly's *Atlantis*, Dowson's *Hindu Classical Dictionary*, Myer's *Qabbala*, and some twenty other works.[24] *The Secret Doctrine* is Blavatsky's account of how the universe was created, the forces fashioning it, and what it all means. In it Hindu and Buddhist concepts were 'theosophized', i.e. correlated with astrological and esoteric wisdom. In this multivolume work Blavatsky revealed a doctrine of Avatars that she said were uncovered from the *Stanzas of Dzyan*. She wrote of a mysterious principle in nature containing the seed of 'Avatarism,'[25] in which all the Avatars are trees that grow from the seed (*Bija*) and its principle (*Maha Vishnu*). According to Blavatsky, all the Avatars are sons of the Father who is the 'Causal Soul', and she identifies them as Buddha, Shankara, Jesus, and a few others.[26]

In the last few years of Madame Blavatsky's life she established a Lodge of the Theosophical Society in London and created within it an Esoteric Section where initiates had to pledge allegiance to both her and the Mahatmas, and practice celibacy, asceticism, vegetarianism, and occultism. She stratified the Esoteric Section by establishing an Inner Group composed of six men and six women, these select few comprising her twelve apostles. When Mohandas Gandhi was introduced to her in 1889 she had before her a genuine mahatma, but ironically she failed to recognize the real thing. In London HPB became enormously popular and influenced the Irish revival and such luminaries as AE (George Russell) and Yeats. Towards the end of her life she engaged in an exhausting power struggle with Col. Olcott who had been leading the Theosophical Society from the East. At the very end of her tempestuous life she is said to have asked for last rites in the Russian Orthodox Church.[27] As for her contribution, in some sense she revolutionized Western occultism, which had been derived largely from Gnostic and alchemical sources, by reformulating it in terms of Eastern texts that had recently become available in Europe and America. Thus she prepared the way for a Western interest in Hindu gurus, swamis, and Avatars.

Before Madame Blavatsky died in London in 1891, she had won the loyalty of a very energetic and enthusiastic individual, Annie Besant, the friend of G. B. Shaw and Susan B. Anthony. Besant had been a leader in social and educational reform, a union organizer, a prolific author, and a feminist who fought for birth control. Besant became intrigued with Theosophy while reviewing *The Secret Doctrine* for the *Pall Mall Gazette*. On 10 May 1889, she applied for membership in the Theosophical Society and kneeling before Madame Blavatsky received the blessing of Master Koot Hoomi. Besant would become his disciple and would study under HPB as a member of the Esoteric Section. From that day to the day she died 44 years later, she never wavered in her faith in Theosophy nor was her faith in HPB ever shaken. Upon the death of HPB a second generation of Theosophists arose, composed of Annie Besant and Charles W. Leadbeater, both born in 1847.

Besant became the custodian of HPB's notes and papers, including the fragmentary third volume of *The Secret Doctrine*. Besant was a born leader and the possessor of phenomenal energy and endurance. At first she suffered from unusual shyness in her contacts with people, but when she mounted the platform to speak she was gripped by an enthusiasm that gave her invincible and reckless courage. She has been acclaimed as the greatest woman orator of the nineteenth century.

In 1893 Besant represented the Theosophical Society at the World's Parliament of Religions in Chicago where she was an enormous success. The Hindus whom she met at the Parliament helped convince her that she should return to India, 'her motherland'. She travelled to India, took up the study of Sanskrit, and declared herself a Hindu of the ancient Aryan type, though not of the corrupted modern variety. In India Besant wore native clothing, ate according to strict Hindu rules, meticulously followed Hindu regulations for cleanliness, and performed the religious ceremony (*puja*) as an orthodox Brahmin would. Her enthusiasm even led her to preach the desirability of the caste system. She declared that Hinduism was 'the first-born daughter of the ancient Brahma-Vidya, and its least imperfect representative'.[28] In 1895 she translated the *Bhagavad Gita* into English, and this popular translation, awarded as a prize to Hindu students of merit, impressed Gandhi when he read it for the first time in London at the insistence of some Theosophists. Besant's 1896 Adyar lectures were entitled 'Four Great Religions', and included Hinduism, Buddhism, Zoroastrianism, and Christianity, each looked at from an occult point of view. In 1898 she founded the Central Hindu College in Benares and continued to arouse the Indian's sense of self-respect and pride in the greatness of their cultural traditions. For many years she fought on behalf of the independence movement of India and was one of the most outspoken British voices defending Indian home rule.

For the 25th anniversary of the Theosophical Society in 1899, Besant delivered four lectures on Avatars in which she interpreted this concept. These lectures addressed four major topics: (1) what is an Avatar? (2) who is the source of Avatars? (3) the types of Avatars, and (4) why Krishna is the greatest of the Avatars. For Besant, the Avatar is the culmination of material and spiritual evolution. The Avatar is on a higher plane in the occult hierarchy than the Mahatma, for the Avatar possesses absolute devotion to

God and great love of humanity. The source of Avatars is always the second aspect of a divine triad, whether it be the Christian Trinity or the Hindu trimurti. According to Besant, 'You will find in the Christian nomenclature the Divine incarnation or *Avatara* is that of the second person of the Trinity . . . and the sign of the second Person of the Trinity is duality.'[29] She 'theosophized' that Vishnu and Krishna are Solar Logoi, while other Avatars are planetary Logoi. Besant regarded Krishna as the greatest Avatar for the following reasons: he was Vishnu's greatest viceroy; he was historical; his milkmaids (*gopis*) were the ancient seers (rishis) reincarnated; and he was the greatest statesman, friend, and teacher. As for the Buddha Avatar, Besant rejected the Hindu Puranic myths of his deceptive mission and interpreted Buddha as an evolving soul or Logos, beginning on Atlantis and ultimately merging with the Solar Logos.[30] Finally Kalki Avatar would come from Shambala, the spiritual world-centre concealed in the heart of Asia, and he would inaugurate the sixth and final root race on earth, a race of occultists, led by a mighty pair working harmoniously together, an ideal king and an ideal priest.

Besant, under the guidance of a Mahatma, continued to receive letters that were 'precipitated' to her through occult means. Her popularity in the 1890s in England and America grew increasingly larger as her oratorical eloquence won her numerous admirers. In 1890 she met Charles W. Leadbeater who had been a curate in the Anglican Church and had joined the Theosophical Society in 1883. In 1885 he was appointed recording secretary of the Theosophical Society in India and went to Ceylon like the others, accepted Buddhism, and looked after the Buddhist schools that Col. Olcott had begun there. In 1906 Leadbeater was forced to resign from the Theosophical Society due to a scandal over his alleged homosexual practices with young boys, to which he replied that in a previous incarnation in ancient Greece his pederastic propensities had been permitted. His detractors suggested that in a previous incarnation he had been Onan. When Olcott died in 1907, the mantle of the Theosophical Twins descended upon the shoulders of Annie Besant, and in this role of authority she virtually built herself a 'Besantine empire'.

Ever since her 1899 lectures on Avatars Besant had been pondering that concept. The idea of the reappearance of a Christ, an Avatar, a World Teacher, had been a common one in esoteric and Theosophical circles, but it was not until 1908 that Besant declared that preparation should be made for the coming of a new Saviour Christ. Moreover, she insisted that Theosophists look for him to come not in the East but in the Western world. At first she said that the second coming would take place in forty years, but the *Theosophic Messenger* announced in 1909 the imminent appearance of the Avatar.[31] In December of 1909, as Besant disembarked in Madras, Leadbeater introduced her to a young large-eyed Indian boy who was destined to become her Avatar, her saviour, and her nemesis.

This new Theosophical divinity was Krishna Jiddu, a Brahmin's son, born in 1895, just four years after the death of Blavatsky. He was called Krishnamurti because, like the Avatar Krishna, he was the eighth son of his parents, and a name meaning 'power of Krishna' was appropriate. His mother died when he was ten, but she believed that he was destined for something extraordinary. He spoke neither English nor Tamil, the two languages used in the school that he attended, resulting in his dreaminess and lack of attention. His father joined the Theosophical Society in 1882 and decorated the walls of his home with pictures of Hindu deities including Annie Besant. Krishnamurti's father brought him to Adyar in 1909 where Leadbeater observed his 'selfless aura' and 'discovered' him. Leadbeater was fascinated by this boy and produced a list of thirty of his previous incarnations based on the belief that the Avatar's soul reincarnates every 700 or 1400 years. This was published as *The Lives of Alcyone*, a pseudonym or 'star name' under which Krishnamurti appeared in the *Lives* and covering the years 22 662 B.C. to A.D. 624. The purpose of *The Lives of Alcyone* was to establish the credentials of Krishnamurti as the Divine Vehicle by tracing his genealogy into prehistory. Like his namesake, the mythological Halcyon, he was expected to become the 'calmer of storms', but little did the theosophists anticipate the storms he would later stir up.

Leadbeater became Krishnamurti's tutor and recommended to Besant that Krishnamurti be sent to England to study. Through occult knowledge, Besant predicted that Krishnamurti was to become a vehicle for the great World Teacher, just as the Christ had used Jesus as a vehicle two millennia before. Another young man, the precocious Hubert Van Hook, who was a leading contender for the position of Theosophical Avatar, was dropped as Krishnamurti ascended in the eyes of Leadbeater and Besant. Besant introduced the astral Krishnamurti to Mars, Mercury, Neptune, Uranus, and Brihaspati (Jesus), as well as other minor astral beings. The World Teacher of the East (Lord Maitreya) informed her that he was sending his star.[32]

Krishnamurti was initiated into the Theosophical Society on 11 January 1910, and this date was celebrated as his occult birthday. His initiation consisted of an astral trip to Tibet where he was led to the throne of Lord Maitreya surrounded by the Masters. In their awesome presence Krishnamurti answered all their questions correctly and a Silver Star flashed overhead. After learning how to form a buddhic body and an astral body he was taken to the Lord of the World who bestowed his blessings upon him.

Now Krishnamurti was attired in silk robes and sandals and was attended by 'Lieutenants of the Lord'[33] who wore purple neckties or purple sashes and yellow symbols of the rising sun. His hair was cut and parted so as to give the Westerner the impression that he was Christ, and the Oriental the impression that he was Buddha.[34] His devotees shaped their hair in the same fashion as a sign of allegiance. When Besant returned to Adyar she proposed to legally adopt Krishnamurti and his brother Nitya, and their father agreed to grant her guardianship provided she educate them in a university in England. Besant first brought Krishnamurti to her Central Hindu College where he spoke to the faculty and students about the ideas he had learned from the Masters. Forming an elite, esoteric group called the Purple Order, faculty and students sat at his feet and marvelled at his purple prose.

On the first anniversary of Krishnamurti's initiation, the Theosophists formed the Order of the Rising Sun to draw together those Indian Theosophists who believed in the imminent coming of the great spiritual teacher, and to prepare for his arrival. A few months later Besant and Leadbeater turned it into an international organization and renamed it The Order of the Star in the East. Krishnamurti was the head of the Order and Besant and Leadbeater were protectors. Each of the members wore a star brooch. A quarterly magazine called the *Herald of the Star* was begun in 1911 with Krishnamurti as editor. However, the Order of the Star in the East was too outlandish for the German Theosophist Rudolf Steiner to accept, so he seceded and took most of the German lodges with him, forming his own group, the Anthroposophical Society.[35]

Besant brought Krishnamurti to England in 1911 and for the first time he forced his feet into shoes. Now Krishnamurti studied

Shakespeare and Sanskrit, and made his first speech in May 1911. Besant attempted to enroll him in an English college while she lectured to overflowing crowds on 'The Coming of the World Teacher'.

On 28 December 1911, while Krishnamurti was conferring certificates of membership in The Order of the Star in the East, Theosophists began prostrating themselves at his feet. Krishnamurti extended his arms in benediction over each prostrate form and all were reminded of a similar scene that had occurred nearly 2000 years before in Palestine at Pentecost. Krishnamurti closed the meeting with the words 'May the blessing of the great Lord rest upon you forever',[36] and it was immediately intuited by those present that Krishnamurti was a vehicle for the Lord and the process of deification was underway.[37]

Meanwhile, Krishnamurti's father brought a lawsuit against Besant in 1912 to regain the custody of his sons, and Besant, who had lost custody of her two natural children years earlier, fought ferociously to keep Krishnamurti and his brother Nitya. Krishnamurti's father charged that Leadbeater had performed immoral acts with his son and that Besant had deified him by announcing that he was to be the Lord Christ. Besant argued that she had Krishnamurti's best interests at heart, but the judge ordered that Krishnamurti be returned to his father. Besant appealed the decision from one court to another, losing time after time in India until finally winning in London in 1914.

On the fourth anniversary of Krishnamurti's initiation he announced unexpectedly that 'The Lord Buddha is here',[38] causing great excitement and rousing high expectancy. A circle of women and girls was forming around this Krishna figure and they referred to themselves as gopis,[39] but Krishnamurti was somewhat frightened by women and strongly influenced by the Theosophical view that sex was something unclean that must be sublimated. Yet he enjoyed the women's affections and learned to play the flute like Krishna. In 1917 it became all too clear that neither Oxford nor Cambridge would accept him and he tried unsuccessfully to enter London University.

In the early 1920s Krishnamurti began experiencing certain mystical 'processes', out-of-body experiences, visions of light, and the awakening of the Kundalini.[40] This was explained through Leadbeater's occult chemistry as Krishnamurti's transformation from the fifth root-race to the sixth via additional spirilae added to the atoms of his brain.[41] In 1924 and 1925 Krishnamurti was leading a select group of twelve Theosophical apostles along the spiritual path, reading to them from *The Gospel According to Buddha* and singing Krishna's songs in Sanskrit. One of these apostles, Annie Besant, interpreted the birth, the transfiguration, the crucifixion, the resurrection and the ascension as stages of the journey of the human spirit through the five Theosophical initiations. Besant and Leadbeater announced that they had passed all five initiations, thus ascribing divinity to themselves. Besant proceeded to announce the founding of a new world religion and a World University with herself as rector and degrees conferred in the name of the Masters.

In 1924 the American branch of the Theosophical Society purchased 118 acres of land in the Ojai Valley of California with the intention of establishing an 'ashram' (holy place) acceptable to 'the Great Ones', to make a training ground for the leaders coming into incarnation, and to establish and maintain a school of Theosophy. The Theosophists believed the valley to be the birthplace of the sixth root-race, especially since it had been consecrated by California Indians as a peace ground. Besant declared the Ojai Valley to be the magnetic centre of the earth and the spot where a new type of humanity would be born. This new type of advanced human being would be marked by a highly developed intuition and great sensitivity. In 1925 she purchased an additional 150 acres at Ojai for the Order of the Star in the East where she planned to build a world religious centre with Krishnamurti at its head.

The year 1924 was the golden jubilee of Besant's public service, for she had laboured since 1874 on behalf of humanitarian causes. Tributes poured in from around the world, including those from G. B. Shaw and Gandhi, who said, 'I wish to express my deep admiration for this long record of service and the amazing energy and courage that lay behind it. I cannot forget, though it is many years ago, the inspiration I drew from her in my boyhood and then again in my experiences of political activity.'[42]

The year 1925 marked the fiftieth anniversary of the Theosophical Society. In this year Krishnamurti's brother Nitya died of influenza. At first Krishnamurti was bereft, but going through great inner turmoil he seemed to absorb the energy of the deceased. On 'Star Day', 28 December 1925, Krishnamurti slipped into the role of the World Teacher, announcing that 'I come to reform and not to tear down, I come not to destroy but to build.'[43] For Besant, the period of preparation was over, the World Teacher and Star of the East had finally arrived. She jubilantly announced that 'The Divine Spirit has descended once more on a man, Krishnamurti, one who in his life is literally perfect, as those who know him can testify . . . The World Teacher is here.'[44]

In 1926, in her lectures on 'How a World Teacher Comes', Besant pointed out that Krishna and Christ are one, that Christ is alive in a physical body in the Himalayas, and that he is omni-conscious. Furthermore she declared that God had spoken through Krishnamurti on 28 December 1925, and that some were able to perceive the Christ in Krishnamurti. Meanwhile some Canadian Theosophists lampooned Krishnamurti's divinity with adverse verse entitled 'The New Theosophy':

It dulls our brains, but entertains, and gives us dreams
    entrancing,
And proves without the slightest doubt the race is sure
    advancing,
Since our new Star, our avatar, was once a moon-chain
    chimpanzee
And arhats good, near Buddhahood, are here as any simp can
    see.

Let zealots rant, intolerant, about our new Theology,
We'll let them see that H.P.B. missed points in sociology.
That we don't lie is proven by our splendid popularity.
Clairvoyantly we always see occasion for hilarity.

In vestments dressed, upon our chest a golden cross we
    dangle.
Poor sinners some; we haw and hum – untwist the ether's
    tangle.
A mystic word, by devas heard – a magic invocation!
And sinners go, as pure as snow, assured to consecration.

Our modern stuff is never rough – we make occultism simple.
To qualify you simply buy a share in our new temple
In Sidney Bay; and watch and pray for Alcy's transformation
From callow youth to Lord of Truth – our Christ by
    acclamation!

So you'll agree, a devotee of up-to-date Theosophy
Is far ahead of one that's fed on H.P.B.'s philosophy,
For he may scan the cosmic plan and sub-divide the Trinity
And may with ease obtain degrees that certify divinity.[45]

Besant's dreams were short-lived, for in 1927 Krishnamurti began to allude to the Masters as 'incidents', and this caused consternation among many Theosophists. He expressed privately a desire to renounce his position and become a forest ascetic. Yet he assured Besant that 'more and more am I certain that I am the Teacher and my mind and consciousness is changed. . . . Oh! mother, the fulfilment of many lives has now come'.[46]

By mid-1927 Krishnamurti seemed to have transcended the Masters, Lord Maitreya, the Buddha, and the World Teacher, and was espousing an independent search for Truth. He had begun to believe in an eternal life-force that was without form. Besant meanwhile went on lecturing on 'The World Teacher is Here', and she was finding it difficult to reconcile what Krishnamurti was advocating with her preconceived Theosophical ideas. Krishnamurti now avoided speaking in the presence of Besant for fear of offending her. To him she was 'the Mother' affectionately called Amma, and he could not bear to hurt her. Gradually, however, Krishnamurti's pronouncements became so utterly revolutionary that the foundations of Besant's world were shaken. It is recorded that Krishnamurti had said that 'he had never been able to read through a Theosophical book in his life – could not understand our Theosophical "jargon", and although he had heard many Theosophical lectures, none of them had convinced him of their knowledge of Truth'.[47] Yet he proceeded to write love letters to Besant, saying 'we two must stick together and nothing else matters'.[48] But Besant was not appeased and the notion that he was a renegade was expressed. Toward the end of 1927 Besant announced in India that Krishnamurti was an amsavatar, a partial Avatar, a fragment of whose consciousness had descended from the Lord and lodged in him. This was glorious news to her Indian audience. Wherever Krishnamurti went in India people acknowledged him as the World Teacher and wanted to know if he was the Christ, the bringer of Truth. This caused him numerous fainting spells. Meanwhile Besant had created a new divine personality, the World Mother. By this time, Krishnamurti was tired of such machinations as Apostles and World Mothers. Furthermore, Besant had declared herself Krishnamurti's 'devoted disciple' in 1927, and the following year Krishnamurti said that he abhorred the idea of anyone calling himself his disciple and even mentioned the possibility of dissolving the Order of the Star. The effect of this was to shatter Annie Besant's magnificent health for the first time. She had to cancel her travels and speaking engagements and was confined to bed. In 1928 in India she closed the Esoteric Section of the Theosophical Society which Blavatsky had founded in 1889. The result was no more Masters and no more Mahatma letters.

Krishnamurti meanwhile was going his own independent way. He warned his listeners that they were to listen only to their own intuition and reject the message of interpreters. By interpreters he meant the leaders of the Theosophical Society. He told a reporter that neither Buddha nor Christ had claimed divinity or wished to found a religion, and that it was their followers who had done so after they were dead.[49] Then he added that he was not divine but rather the 'natural flower of the world'. The reaction of one devoted disciple expressed the general shock and bewilderment that was felt:

> How strange it seems that for seventeen years we have been expecting the World Teacher, and now when He speaks of what is beyond all forms, we are hurt or angry. He is making us do our own work, mentally and emotionally, and that is the last thing we expected of Him. Some people are returning home naked and alone, their foundations shattered, realizing the necessity of reorienting themselves in a world in which every value has changed.[50]

Besant persisted in her attempts to reconcile Krishnamurti's teachings with her own Theosophy by emphasizing that only a fragment of the Lord's consciousness manifested itself through Krishnamurti, and that Krishnamurti did not share in the omniscience of the Lord. However, her contradictory statements must have created more confusion among Theosophists than they cleared up, for she was virtually saying that the World Teacher is here but what He has to say is not necessarily valid. Finally, in 1929, Krishnamurti made a speech in the presence of Annie Besant in which he dissolved the Order of the Star, and asserted that Truth cannot be approached by any religion, sect, or path whatsoever. He insisted upon the human ascent, not the divine descent. After eighteen years of preparing for the coming of the World Teacher, the World Teacher was setting men free. His only concern, he said, was to set men absolutely and unconditionally free to look for the kingdom within themselves. However, Besant declared, 'my fundamental belief in Krishnamurti as the World Teacher makes me more inclined to observe and study rather than express an opinion on one whom I consider far my superior'.[51]

Two months after Krishnamurti dissolved the Order of the Star, Besant reopened the Esoteric Section of the Theosophical Society. Leadbeater turned his back on Krishnamurti and avoided talking with him. Shortly thereafter Krishnamurti resigned from the Theosophical Society saying that he felt sorry for the unfortunate Theosophists. Besant's successor was to bar him from Adyar permanently. And in later years, Krishnamurti developed a 'retroactive amnesia' by which he was to relegate to oblivion everything that had occurred in his life prior to 1929.[52]

Besant was now entering the twilight of her life. As an octogenarian she had attained world-wide recognition and was compared with such notable women as Madame Curie, Jane Addams, Queen Marie of Rumania, Mary Shelley, and Elizabeth Barrett Browning. She was even nominated for a Nobel peace prize on behalf of her work for Indian home rule. In July 1931, at the age of 83, she fell and injured her knee. Her memory and her voice were failing and she was confined to her room. She and Krishnamurti met for the last time in May of 1933. The love of the mother for the divine son, and the son for his divine mother did not abate. She never relinquished her belief in Krishnamurti and insisted to the end that 'Either he is the World Teacher, or I am a liar.' Annie Besant died peacefully at Adyar on 20 September 1933 in the presence of Leadbeater, who died shortly thereafter on his way back to Australia. As her body was being cremated the crowd chanted verses from the *Gita* that she had translated. Her ashes and Leadbeater's are buried in the Garden of Remembrance at Adyar.

Besant's death severed Krishnamurti's ties with Theosophy, and the former World Teacher continued on his path as a spiritual teacher. The death of Annie Besant and Leadbeater silenced the oracles. Since leaving the Theosophical Society at the age of 38, Krishnamurti became somewhat of an oracle himself, preaching fearless courage in religion and calling people away from occultism and mystic rituals to a free and scientific investigation of life. While he tells people that there is no such thing as spiritual authority and that he is not anyone's teacher, people continue to think of him as the World Teacher and Theosophical bookstores proudly display and sell his books, for images concretize themselves and function powerfully long after they have been repudiated intellectually.

Ireland

> I only know that I look everywhere in the face of youth, in the aspect of every new notability, hoping before I die to recognise the broad-browed avatar of my vision.
>
> (George Russell – AE)

The blossoming of the concept of the Avatar in Ireland is based on the imagination of George Russell (1867–1935), widely known by his pseudonym AE. George Russell, seer, mystic, poet, and Theosophist, had a rendezvous with Avatars for 37 years. He was a visionary like William Blake, and began seeing apparitions and having communication with preternatural figures from early childhood. Out of his visions he carved poems, prose, paintings, philosophy, and a panorama of poetic Avatars.

In one of his early visions, AE saw himself as a child in ancient India among happy companions. However, his mind was not with his friends, for he also saw the gods in the sky and longed to be with them. He was grief-stricken because it was revealed to him that the last divine incarnation who would appear for many centuries had died, and the Iron Age (Kali yuga), destined to engulf mankind for more than four hundred millennia, had begun. When the vision ended he understood that what he had seen had taken place five thousand years ago, in 3102 B.C., the traditional date for Krishna's death. The belief that he was living in the Iron Age had a lifelong influence on his thought due to the impact of this vision.

At the age of 21 Russell had painted a series of pictures depicting the development of man from his origin in the Divine Mind to his appearance on earth. While trying to think of a name for the series, Russell heard a voice say, 'Call it the birth of Aeon.' He discovered that Aeon represented an emanation flowing from God, a divine person in whom God was revealed, and the primordial being according to the Gnostics. So he chose AEON for his pen name, but when a proof-reader was unable to decipher it and printed it as AE—?, Russell simply adopted the first two letters as his pseudonym.

Russell's life was dramatically transformed in 1887 when he discovered Theosophy. By 1888 he was in correspondence with Madame Blavatsky in London and began reading *The Secret Doctrine* which he believed was the grandest cosmogony ever conceived and the faith of the future. This book would remain for him one of the most provocative, and he defended it to his countrymen William Butler Yeats and Sean O'Faolain. He joined the Dublin Theosophical Lodge in 1888 and became a member of its Esoteric Section on 8 December 1890. He was recording clerk for the Theosophical Society in Belfast before becoming leader of the Dublin chapter in 1893, and remained a dominant figure in Irish Theosophy for many years. In 1898 he left the society due to a dispute with its leader, but six years later brought many apostates back to the society, before he re-formed them into the Hermetic Society of Dublin in 1909. From 1909 until 1933 Russell reigned as the leader of the Hermetic Society. Its meetings opened with passages from Blavatsky's *The Secret Doctrine* and then moved to discussions of Celtic mythology, literature, and the national and spiritual well-being of Ireland.

Beginning in 1896 Russell began publishing poems that reflected his interest in ancient mysteries. He believed that there was a direct connection between times so ancient that no secular historian knew of them, and a long-awaited apocalyptic event that was about to astonish the world. Russell's messianic expectations were in keeping with Madame Blavatsky's claim during 1888 that the first cycle of the Kali yuga would come to an end in about nine years, or 1897. Another Theosophical leader, William Q. Judge, had also made such prophecies, and he maintained that the spiritual powers that had made Ireland a holy land in the past would soon reawaken. He had written of two classes of Avatars, some like Rama and Krishna who were rulers and lawgivers, others like Buddha and Jesus who were teachers and mystics. A new Avatar, he foretold, would someday appear who would combine the characteristics of both.[53]

Russell was in agreement with William Q. Judge, and he asked the Irish to consider their own land, not Palestine or India, the sacred country. Although he desired to go to India, when he became acquainted with Celtic mythology and adapted it to a Theosophical world view, he gave his spiritual aspirations an Irish setting. He believed that in Europe men's hearts were too heavy to be lifted up by the Avatar, and in America their hearts were too fierce. India had lost its pride in Avatars because it had had so many. Therefore it was Ireland, the new holy land, where the Avatars of the future would touch down, dazzling the Irish imagination and creating a truly spiritual renaissance.

AE was highly influenced by the *Gita*, based much of his thought on it, and wrote poems to Krishna. Like Emerson and Thoreau before him, he was known to exclaim, 'What is the use of reading anything else when all is contained in it. I would rather have that one small book than the varied productions of centuries of European thought and imagination. It is the essence of human wisdom and the mind has not gone beyond it since.'[54] When it came to Krishnamurti, AE wrote,

He has had a claque of charlatans about him since he was a boy, announcing him as an avatar, and it says much for an inherent sweetness and simplicity of character that he has emerged with that sweetness and simplicity from the most horrible chorus of wonder-seekers and devotees who ever encompassed a child with their chattering and folly. Probably driven in upon himself as a refuge he sought for something simple and lovely and sweet in his heart, something altogether different from the church which was being organized for him, and the bishops who were being nominated as his apostles, and the worshippers who waited in expectation of wonders and miracles.[55]

In 1896, AE wrote in his diary: 'I believe profoundly that a new Avatar is about to appear. . . . It will be one of the kingly Avatars, who is at once ruler of men and magic sage. I had a vision of him some months ago and will know him if he appears.'[56] In the early months of 1896 AE experienced a vision of overwhelming power that convinced him that his hopes were about to be fulfilled. It burst into the orderly routine of his life while he was meditating alone in his room. The vision came upon him without warning, and he expressed it in these words:

between heaven and earth over the valley was a vast figure aureoled with light, and it descended from that circle of light and assumed human shape, and stood before me and looked at me. The face of this figure was broad and noble in type, beardless and dark-haired. It was in its breadth akin to the face of the young Napoleon, and I would refer both to a common archetype. This being looked at me and vanished, and was instantly replaced by another vision, and this second vision was of a woman with a blue cloak around her shoulders, who came into a room and lifted a young child upon her lap, and from all Ireland rays of light converged on that child. Then this disappeared and was on the instant followed by another picture in the series; and here I was brought from Ireland to look on the coronation throne at Westminster, and there sat on it a figure of empire which grew weary and let fall the sceptre from its fingers, and itself then drooped and fell and disappeared from the famous seat. And after that in quick succession came another scene and a gigantic figure, wild and distraught, beating a drum, stalked up and down, and wherever its feet fell there were sparks and the swirling of flame and black smoke upward as from burning cities. It was like the Red Swineherd of legend which beat men into an insane frenzy; and when that distraught figure vanished I saw the whole of Ireland lit up from mountain to sea, spreading its rays to the heavens as in the vision which Brigid the seeress saw and told to Patrick. All I could make of that sequence was that some child of destiny, around whom the future of Ireland was to pivot, was born then or to be born, and that it was to be an avatar was symbolised by the descent of the first figure from the sky, and that before that high destiny was to be accomplished the power of empire was to be weakened, and there was to be one more tragic episode in Irish history.[57]

By May or June of 1896 AE and some of his closest associates in the Dublin Lodge of Theosophy saw themselves as a band of disciples waiting to receive the new Celtic Avatar. They believed that a wall of spiritual protection like that which guarded India and Tibet had surrounded Ireland for several centuries, and that now some of the Masters were present in Ireland. In the mountains they continually saw and heard signs of spiritual powers active in preparation for the great coming event. On 10 May AE had a vision of Dactyli, semi-divine beings, followed by a score of

Atlantean Cyclopses whose divine eyes formed a macabre array over the hills.

In April of 1897, the year that Madame Blavatsky had predicted would be the end of the cycle, AE had a vision of an Avatar living in the west of Ireland. AE described this Avatar to his confidant W. B. Yeats in the following words, 'middle-aged, has a grey golden beard and hair, face very delicate and absorbed. Eyes have a curious golden fire in them, broad forehead'.[58]

After his visions of Avatars in 1896 and 1897, AE devoted many years to the writing of a major opus entitled *The Avatars: a Futuristic Fantasy*,[59] published in 1933, two years before his death. In this romance AE sought to recapture the excitement of the summer of 1896 when he and his companions were preparing for the coming of the great Avatar. It is a dream-like vision of two Avatars who come to reveal the spiritual nature of the Irish race to itself. These Avatars are believed to be pivotal figures whose destiny it is hoped will change the course of Ireland's history.

The story that unfolds concerns the development of a dawning spirituality in the west of Ireland, originating in the actions of two Avatars, Aodh, a 14-year old sprite, and Aoife, his young female companion. AE took their names from ancient Celtic mythology.[60] Aodh is a visionary who is at one with nature and makes it vibrate to his fiddle, as Krishna previously did with his flute. Aoife sets the world aglow as Helen of Troy did in the ancient world. Aodh and Aoife communicate without words, are gossamer, and fleeting to the perception of mortals. Although they do not speak or write any scripture, they are spoken of by inspired Irishmen and transform everyone with whom they come into contact. Wherever they go they inspire song and dance, and the people they meet are exalted. Aodh and Aoife are about to lead Ireland to a spiritual renaissance when the monstrous forces of the state appear, and the Avatars disappear, but not before they have revived the creative energies in people and freed them from their bondage. Ultimately a new religion will spring forth from the advent of Aodh and Aoife, and a temple filled with works of art will be constructed on the site where they last appeared.

AE spent many years hoping and waiting for the advent of the Avatar. Aodh and Aoife were his long awaited Celtic–Irish Avatars, and the patron deities of the inspirational arts. AE envisioned Avatars both luminous and impressionistic, Avatars who descend from a divine aesthetic mind. The letters AE stand for George Russell's pseudonym, and remind us of the aesthetic, aethereal aeons, Aodh and Aoife.

THE AVATARS OF THE ARCANE SCHOOL

I would assert here that the great and satisfying reply to all human questioning and human need is to be found in the doctrine of Avatars, and in the continuity of divine Revelations. This is the persistent belief – ineradicable and unalterable – that (at major moments of world need) God reveals Himself through Appearances, through a Coming One. This doctrine is found in all the basic world religions, in every time and age; it appears in the doctrine of the Avatars of the Hindu faith, in the teaching of the return of Maitreya Buddha or the Kalki Avatar, in the belief in the Western world in the return of Christ and His Advent or second Coming, and in the prophesied issuing forth of the divine Adventurer of the Moslem world. All this is tied up with the undying belief of mankind in the loving Heart of God, who ever meets man's need. The witness of history is that always the appearance of man's necessity has been met with a divine Revelation.[61]

(Alice A. Bailey)

The founder and guiding spirit behind the Arcane School was Alice A. Bailey (1880–1949). Born into an upper-class English family, her mother dying when she was six, and her father when she was eight, she was raised by her grandparents. She was a poorly adjusted child who suffered through a miserable adolescence. Accounts of her youth indicate that one morning when she was 15, the door to her room opened and in walked a tall man wearing a turban. He told her that if she could achieve self-control, he had important work for her to do. Alice joined the Theosophical Society at 37 and was admitted into its Esoteric Section. The first time that she entered the shrine room she saw a portrait of her tall turbaned visitor and was informed that it was Master Koot Hoomi. The following year a voice said to her: 'There are some books which it is desirable should be written for the public. You can write them. Will you do so?'[62] Alice referred to this entity as 'The Tibetan' (subsequently identified as Master Djual Khool). Alice reported that Djual Khool 'dropped into her brain parcels sent all the way from India' which she recorded.[63] A 33-year collaboration between them resulted in a voluminous literary outpouring.

Alice Bailey remained a Theosophist for five years, and in 1923 established the Arcane School, proposing her own brand of esotericism, eschatology, salvation and Avatars. Dating the inception of the modern era from 1875, the year in which the Theosophical Society was founded, she derived inspiration from such theosophical notions as the Masters, the Tibetan, the world saviour, and the spiritual hierarchy.

During the last ten years of Alice Bailey's life her thoughts on Avatars unfolded. She understood Avatars to be rays of perfected glory who are able to tap energies transmitted from the solar system or the etheric body of a planet.[64] She placed the Avatars in a hierarchical pattern: human, planetary, interplanetary, solar, and cosmic Avatars. She also described various types of Avatars: 'lesser Avatars', such as Luther, Columbus, Shakespeare, and Leonardo da Vici; 'racial Avatars of the first ray', such as Lincoln and Bismarck; 'teaching Avatars of the second ray' who are Plato, Patanjali, Shankara; 'Ray Avatars' who are connected with the Great White Lodge on the planet Sirius; and 'Transmitting Avatars' such as Buddha and Christ, who are able to link humanity with the hierarchy.[65]

In *The Reappearance of the Christ*, written in 1948, the year before her death, Alice Bailey wove a fabric of world saviours and cosmic Avatars composed of the Avatar of the East and the Avatar of the West. The Eastern Avatar is the Buddha, the Avatar of illumination, called the Light Bearer because of his enlightenment. The Buddha Avatar is regarded as the precursor of the Christ Avatar. The Avatar of the West is Christ, the Avatar of love. The Christ Avatar is the head of the spiritual hierarchy, and His reappearance is inevitable and imminent.[66] Bailey's prophecy is that Christ's new teaching will provide the skeletal structure for the new world religion.[67]

Taking her cue from the incarnational section of the *Gita*, the Avatar is to appear in times of crisis when evil is rampant, and Bailey interprets World War I as the dark period signalling the end of an age and the need for the Avatar's advent. She reports that at the end of World War II Christ made the decision to return in human form. As a result of this decision, God appointed an associate, the silent Avatar of Synthesis, to inaugurate the reign of Avatars and fortify the Christ Avatar.[68] His function is to generate spiritual will-power in the spiritual hierarchy, the General Assembly of the United Nations, and within humanity at large. He works under the laws of synthesis, producing at-one-ment, unification, and fusion.[69]

According to Alice Bailey, the advent of an Avatar is determined astrologically. She uses as an example the Old Testament, explaining that when the Jews worshipped the golden calf they were demonstrating their love for Taurus. She says that they became scapegoats because they forgot the ram in the age of Aries and rejected Christ as the Avatar. For Bailey, Christ being the teacher in the age of Pisces accounts for the fish symbolism in early Christianity. In 1948 she predicted that we are entering a new era called the Age of Aquarius, suggested by the image of the man with a pitcher of water, as found in Luke 22:10.

According to Bailey, Christ is the first Avatar to span two cycles of the zodiac, the Piscean and the Aquarian. Because Jesus was a carpenter in the Piscean age he will be the builder of the Aquarian age and will utilize five divine energies: love, will, wisdom, piscean energy, and aquarian energy.[70] For this monumental task He has been given three associates, the Buddha Avatar with his light energy, the Spirit of Peace with his love energy, and the Avatar of Synthesis with his power energy. In the centre of this divine trinity is the Christ, who will reign for 2500 years and be known as the dispenser of the water of life (Aquarius). In the Aquarian age, the Christ Avatar will absorb the work of the Buddha Avatar and combine within Himself both love and wisdom. This represents the master plan of the Avatars as transmitted by Alice Bailey for her Arcane School.

THE KRIYA AVATARS OF THE SELF-REALIZATION FELLOWSHIP

An avatar is unsubject to the universal economy; his pure body, visible as a light image, is free from any debt to Nature. . . . An avatar lives in the omnipresent Spirit; for him there is no distance inverse to the square.[71]

(Paramahansa Yogananda)

The Kriya Avatars are intimately related to the life and teaching of Paramahansa Yogananda (1893–1952), a yogi of whom it was said that he 'changed the map of American religious life'.[72] His image as a yogi affected many movements, and other holy men from India built upon the legacy that Yogananda began in America in the 1920s. Yogananda attempted to synthesize Eastern yoga with Western science and the result of this mixture caused yet another transformation in the concept of avatarhood. He saw his mission as spreading the message of Kriya yoga, and in order to accomplish this Yogananda created the Yogoda Satsang Society in India, and the Self-Realization Fellowship in America, along with a lineage of Kriya yoga God-men as transmitters of this teaching. The Self-Realization Fellowship claims to have at least 150 centres on four continents. In addition, Yogananda's popular book, *Autobiography of a Yogi*, has gone through more than eight editions, and has been translated into more than a dozen languages.

The message of Yogananda, his spiritual societies and his Avatars are all related to the Kriya yoga. Yogananda was foremost a yogi, and the techniques of Kriya yoga were uppermost in his thought. According to Yogananda, knowledge of the ancient Kriya yoga was mostly lost in antiquity; however, it was uncovered, revived and transmitted by three of Yogananda's predecessors, who, with him, constitute the Kriya yoga lineage. The first of these Kriya Avatars is the eternal Babaji who passed it on to his disciple Lahiri Mahasaya in the 19th century, who in turn transmitted it to his disciple Sri Yukteswar, who conveyed it to Yogananda. These four constitute the lineage of Kriya teachers, and each is designated an Avatar in the *Autobiography of a Yogi*. Yogananda believed that he was responding to a divine 'calling' in his effort to carry the message of Kriya yoga to the West, and he tried to convey it to his Western audience in its own language, which he assumed to be the language of science.

In attempting to assimilate Kriya yoga with science, Yogananda explained the technique as a process of oxygenation that burns out the waste carbon in the venous blood enabling the heart to become calm. Once the heart is tranquil, the mind attains an awareness of inner spiritual forces and subtle life-currents. The blood is then recharged with oxygen and the atoms of this extra oxygen are transmuted into the life-current to rejuvenate the brain and spinal centres.[73] Kriya yoga, he claimed, helps the yogi in attaining power to prevent the decay of his body at the time of death.

Yogananda said that the Kriya yoga speeds up human evolution and can accomplish in three years what it takes nature a million years to accomplish. He wrote that,

The science of *Kriya Yoga* is eternal. It is true like mathematics; like the simple rules of addition and subtraction, the laws of *Kriya* can never be destroyed. Burn to ashes all books on mathematics; the logically minded will always rediscover such truths. Suppress all books on yoga; its fundamentals will be re-revealed whenever there appears a sage with pure devotion and consequently pure knowledge.[74]

Yogananda insisted that the Kriya yoga be taught only to those who chose to be initiated into the Self-Realization Fellowship, and therefore he did not divulge much about it in his autobiography. Furthermore, initiates are required to sign a pledge that they will not divulge the Kriya technique to outsiders.

In introducing the subject of Avatars, Yogananda designates the ancient Indian Avatars to be Krishna, Rama, Buddha, Patanjali, and Agastya. We have described Krishna, Rama, and Buddha as Avatars in chapter one, and we encountered Agastya in the Rama Avatar mythology. While Patanjali is generally regarded as an ancient master of yoga, Agastya, according to Yogananda, is 'a South Indian Avatar who has been alive for over 2000 years'.[75] However, Yogananda is more interested in describing the Kriya Avatars, the first of whom is Babaji. Babaji is the Avatarin, meaning the progenitor of a lineage of Avatars, and this lineage stems from the God Shiva, not Vishnu. However, the descent of Babaji from Shiva is not to be understood to be an aspect of the Shaivite tradition of Hinduism. Among worshippers of Shiva there are no Avatars because Shiva, having no karma, has no need to incarnate.[76] Yet, in the Vaishnava tradition it is believed that Shiva does incarnate, and the *Kurma Purana* names 28 Avatars of Shiva,[77] but ironically Babaji is not among them.

Yogananda relates the following information about Babaji. His name means revered father, and his titles are Shiva Baba, Maha Yogi (the great Yogi), Mahavatar (the great Avatar) and Muhamuni Babaji Maharaj (supreme ecstatic master).[78] We are told that Babaji gave yoga initiation to Shankara and is in constant communion with Christ.[79] He is immortal, requires no food, speaks all languages, travels on the astral plane, and appears with or without a beard or moustache. He has the power to become invisible, but when he does appear it is as a youth with fair skin and of medium height and build. His body casts no shadow and he leaves no footprints.[80] His eyes are dark, his hair is long and copper-coloured, and he glows.[81] He refuses to reveal his birthplace and birthdate, and has lived in seclusion for centuries.[82] He moves with his group from place to place in the Himalayas, and his group supposedly contains two highly advanced American disciples.[83] He has a sister named Mataji who is nearly as spiritually advanced as he.[84]

Yogananda is not the only author to record the existence of Babaji, for he is also the main focus of the book Hariakhan Baba, Known, Unknown[85] by Baba Hari Dass, a teacher of yoga who arrived in America in 1971. Dass reports that the research of Mahendra Brahmachari 'proved that Hariakhan Maharaj and Babaji Maharaj . . . were one and the same person',[86] based upon accounts of Babaji in Yogananda's Autobiography of a Yogi. Hariakhan Baba, Known, Unknown is a book that describes various episodes in the lives of about twenty people, Englishmen, Scandinavians, Sikhs, Parsis, and Hindus, who came into contact with this Avatar from 1861 to 1953. The siddhis and abilities of Hariakhan Baba seem to match those attributed to Babaji in the Autobiography of a Yogi. Both are telepathic, appear in various guises, use astral travel for bilocation (to be in two places simultaneously), and are incarnations of Lord Shiva.[87] Hariakhan Baba has been seen to descend in a divine light and hover above the ground.[88] He was present during the ancient wars described in the Mahabharata epic,[89] and his ashram is called Siddhashram.[90] When Hariakhan Baba does manifest physically, he has brown eyes, smells of musk, but his faeces have no odour.[91] Hariakhan Baba and Babaji are reputed to be one and the same, the Kriya Avatarin.

A reappearance of Babaji was reported in 1980 by Dio Neff of Berkeley, California.[92] She indicates that Babaji has been living in the village of Herakhan, by the Gautam Ganga River in Uttar Pradesh, India, since 1970. Neff explains that Babaji got the name Hariakhan Baba due to his long association with this village.[93] Neff describes Babaji in androgynous terms as a combination of Sioux warrior and madonna,[94] and reports that he has a golden body and a cobra design on the soles of his feet.[95]

The disciple of Babaji is Lahiri Mahasaya who was initiated by Babaji into the Kingdom of God through Kriya Yoga in 1861 at the age of 33 near Ranikhet in the Himalayas.[96] Accounts of his life can be found in both Autobiography of a Yogi and Hariakhan Baba, Known, Unknown.[97] Yogananda bestowed the title of Yogavatar upon Lahiri Mahasaya saying, 'Just as Babaji is among the greatest of Avatars, a Mahavatar . . . so Lahiri Mahasaya was a Yogavatar or Incarnation of Yoga.'[98]

Lahiri Mahasaya was born Shyama Charan Lahiri on 30 September 1828, into the Bengali Brahmin family of Gaur Mahan Lahiri and his wife Muktakashi. Mahasaya means large-minded, a title bestowed upon him late in life.[99] At 18 he married and became a 'householder yogi' raising children and establishing a way of life intended as a model for aspiring yogis. It is said that he reduced the complexities of yoga by stressing Kriya yoga, and was referred to as a 'streamlined' yogi. He said that union with the divine is possible through Kriya yoga, and is not dependent upon theology or the arbitrary will of a 'cosmic dictator'. A significant aspect of Lahiri Mahasaya's mission was to grant Kriya initiation not only to Hindus but to those of any faith, and he could even perform these initiations in people's dreams. It is reported that he was telepathic, performed healings, and used astral travel. Lahiri Mahasaya wrote no books, but is said to have transformed the scriptures into a religious science by stressing Kriya yoga.

Lahiri Mahasaya dropped his body on 26 September 1895. After his body was cremated at the holy Ganges River, he appeared in the flesh to three disciples saying:

> From the disintegrated atoms of my cremated body, I have resurrected a remodeled form. My householder work in the world is done; but I do not leave the earth entirely. Henceforth I shall spend some time with Babaji in the Himalayas, and with Babaji in the cosmos.[100]

The disciple of Lahiri Mahasaya and the third in the lineage of Kriya Avatars is Sri Yukteswar Giri (1855–1936). He was born in Serampore, India, on 10 May 1855, and his birth name was Priya Nath Karada. The title Yukteswar represents one who is united with the Hindu trinity (Ishvara). He is known as the Avatar of wisdom (Jnanavatar), for it was said that he had a command of both Eastern and Western philosophy and spoke five languages. He established the Society of Saints (Sabhu Sabha) to promote the unity of all religious faiths in a scientific spirit.

Sri Yukteswar is Yoganananda's spiritual teacher (*guru*), and Yogananda regards him as both human and divine,[101] referring to him as an Avatar,[102] an Incarnation,[103] and a modern Yogi-Christ.[104] Yogananda spent ten years at Yukteswar's ashram and relates how Yukteswar was never sick, cured people of various ailments, 'magnetized' a cobra that was about to strike him,[105] was telepathic, could travel astrally, and prescribed Kriya yoga.

Yukteswar elevated Yogananda into the monastic order of swamis in 1914, initiated him into the Kriya yoga,[106] and bestowed the title of Paramahansa upon him in 1935.[107] It is significant that Yogananda attributed everything that he knew about Avatars and Babaji to Yukteswar. Shortly before Yukteswar's death he appointed Yogananda as his successor as the president of the Society of Saints. He died on 9 March 1936, and three months later was said to be resurrected on the astral plane where he conveyed messages to Yogananda via 'idea-tabloids'.[108] Yogananda reports that Yukteswar lives on the planet Hiranyaloka[109] (the golden world), from which he conveyed the information that astral beings composed of lifetrons watch astral television, eat astral vegetables, drink nectar, and live from five hundred to one thousand years. Meanwhile, fallen angels living on lower astral planes engage in wars in which they use 'lifetronic bombs or mental mantric vibratory rays'.[110]

Sri Yukteswar's chief disciple was Paramahansa Yogananda (1893–1952), the fourth Kriya Avatar, a Premavatar, or Avatar of love. Born in Gorakhput in Northern India near the Himalayan mountains on 5 January 1893, his given name was Mukunda Lal Ghosh. His parents were disciples of Lahiri Mahasaya who initiated them into the Kriya yoga. When he was a baby in his mother's arms, Yogananda was spiritually baptized by Lahiri Mahasaya, who prophesized that he would carry many souls to God's kingdom. Although Lahiri Mahasaya died when Yogananda was two years old, Yogananda said that at the age of eight he was healed of cholera by 'bowing mentally' to Lahiri's picture.[111]

In his youth Yogananda manifested an unusual spiritual drive and remarkable psychic powers, and he visited many Hindu holy men observing their disciplines, powers, and miracles. He was evolving the potential for a cosmic consciousness in which psychic feats, miracles, and control over the body during life and death could occur. Yogananda's search for a guru was fulfilled when he was initiated into the Kriya yoga by Sri Yukteswar.

Yogananda left India at the age of 27 on a divine mission. He heard the voice of Babaji, received the call, and arrived in America in 1920 where he remained for more than thirty years. He was the first Hindu holy-man to teach in the West for such an extended period. In America Yogananda founded the Self-Realization Fellowship, whose aim it is to spread the knowledge of the technique for attaining direct personal experience of God through Kriya yoga. Yogananda lectured extensively and wrote books entitled *Cosmic Chants*, *Metaphysical Meditations*, *Whispers From Eternity*, and *The Science of Religion*. In 1946, six years before his death, he published his magnum opus, the *Autobiography of a Yogi*, in which he attempted to set forth evidence for the authenticity and scientific validity of Kriya yoga.[112]

One of Yogananda's major tenets was that the philosophy and technique of yoga underlie all the major religions and scriptures of mankind. The myths and symbols of world religions are viewed as misconstrued expressions of the goals of yoga and the stages by which it is attained. Furthermore, Yogananda was convinced that Jesus and spiritual masters from other times and places were in fact yoga masters. He attempted to show that the true religion of Jesus and the original yoga were in complete harmony, and that Jesus was a master of the Kriya yoga, enabling him to voluntarily materialize or dematerialize his body,[113] thus accounting for the resurrection. Yogananda connects Jesus with Babaji by citing numerous passages from the gospels. Both are referred to as a 'Son of God',[114] both practice the washing of the feet, both resurrect people who have died,[115] and both are regarded as knowing the sequence of their lives from start to finish.[116] All of these parallels are meant to demonstrate that the Kriya Avatars are on a par with Christ and all divine. Yogananda relates how

> Babaji is ever in communion with Christ; together they send out vibrations of redemption and have planned the spiritual technique of salvation for this age. The work of these two fully illuminated masters – one with a body, and one without a body – is to inspire the nations to foresake wars, race hatreds, religious sectarianism, and the boomerang evils of materialism.[117]

Paramahansa Yogananda died at the age of 59, on 7 March 1952. During the twenty days immediately following his death his body revealed no sign of decay or decomposition and this was certified by the mortician of Forest Lawn Cemetery in California.[118] As an accomplished Kriya yogi, Yogananda was demonstrating the ability of the Kriya yoga to conquer and overcome death. Shortly after

Yogananda's passing his chief disciple bestowed upon him the title of Premavatar, the Avatar of love.[119]

In summation, Yogananda was the first Hindu holy-man to settle in the West and accept his avatarhood. In his 32 years in America Yogananda became partially Westernised, and tried to accommodate the avatar concept to Western modes of thinking as he perceived them. From Yogananda's interpretation of Avatars, four peculiarites can be noted: (1) the Kriya Avatars descend from Shiva, not from Vishnu; (2) the Kriya Avatars have replaced reincarnation with resurrection of the dead; (3) yoga underlies all religions, scriptures, and God-men including Jesus; and (4) the transplanting of the Indian concept of Avatar to the West resulted in a Kriya Avatar lineage existing more in the astral sphere than on the earth.

THE AVATAR OF THE HARE KRISHNA MOVEMENT

> I offer my humble obeisances unto His Divine Grace
>   Prabhupada A. C. Bhaktivedanta Swami . . .
> who, always engaged in chanting and celebrating the
>   message of Lord Caitanya, sometimes dances in ecstasy
>   and trembles and quivers in his trance,
> who sat quietly beneath a persimmon tree reading
>   Srimad-Bhagavatam and musing over the Appalachians
> Who composed Sanskrit odes to the Primeval Spirit whose
>   eternal teenage lips play a flute.[120]
>
> (Hayagriva dasa Adhikari)

Hardly a reader of these pages will not have seen on the streets of the major cities of the United States the exotic appearance of a Hare Krishna disciple with shaven head and saffron *dhoti* or *sari*. These Hare Krishna disciples belong to the Society for Krishna Consciousness which dates from 1965 in the United States and has had a rapid growth and geographical expansion in America as well as in much of the world. Here is an account of the Hare Krishna Avatar.

The spiritual leader of the International Society for Krishna Consciousness is A. C. Bhaktivedanta Swami Prabhupada, and within the society he is regarded as an Avatar. His given name was Abhay Charan De, and he was born in Calcutta on 1 September 1896, to a middle-class Vaishnava family. While he was an undergraduate at the University of Calcutta, De became an ardent nationalist and follower of Gandhi. After graduation, he married and took a position managing a chemical company. In 1922, he met Swami Bhaktisiddhanta Sarasvati, whose father Swami Bhaktivinoda Thakur, was the leader of a revivalist movement in Bengal among Vaishnava Krishna worshippers inspired by Chaitanya. Swami Bhaktisiddhanta was the founder of the Gaudiya Vaishnava temples and in 1933 De became his disciple.

Bhaktisiddhanta Sarasvati, shortly before his death in 1936, is said to have commissioned De and other disciples to propagate the teachings of Krishna Consciousness in English, and De began to fulfil his vow in 1944 with the publication of an English language magazine called *Back to Godhead*, which he wrote, edited, published, and distributed himself. When he began to hold devotional meetings at home his wife objected, and she also refused to allow their children to be instructed in Vaishnavism. De's domestic difficulties were compounded by business reverses and in 1950 he left home and assumed the name Swami Bhaktivedanta. For more than five years Swami Bhaktivedanta lived and worked alone at the historic Radha-Damodara temple in Vrindavana which was established by the followers of Chaitanya, and in 1959 he became a renunciate of this world (*sannyasin*) and accepted the monastic order. At Vrindavana he began his major life's work, a multi-volume translation of, and commentary on, the 18,000 verse *Srimad-Bhagavatam*, the *Bhagavata Purana*. In his lifetime he wrote approximately fifty books including a translation of the *Bhagavad Gita*.

After publishing three volumes of the *Bhagavata Purana*, Swami Bhaktivedanta came to the United States in 1965 to fulfil the mission of his spiritual master. When he arrived in New York City he was 70 years old and practically penniless. In September of 1965 he first attracted attention by chanting the Krishna mantra in New York City. It was after a year of great difficulty that he established the International Society for Krishna Consciousness (ISKCON), in July of 1966.

The biographies of Swami Bhaktivedanta emphasize that the swami's vow to spread Krishna Consciousness in the English-speaking world is the pivotal event of his life. Bhaktivinoda Thakur, it is claimed, was referring to Swami Bhaktivedanta when, in 1896, he predicted that a person would soon appear to preach the teachings of Lord Chaitanya and fill the whole world with his message.[121] The Krishna Consciousness movement itself is seen as the fulfilment of a prophecy made by Chaitanya that the chanting of the holy names of God, Hare Krishna, would be carried to every town and village of the world.

During the first two years of the Krishna Consciousness movement in America, 1966 and 1967, Swami Bhaktivedanta functioned as missionary–parent–therapist–friend–swami to a score of young Americans disillusioned with 'the system' and searching for ultimate experience. Swami Bhaktivedanta was an excellent therapist. He seemed to have an infinite store of patience and never rebuked the devotees. It was largely due to Swami Bhaktivedanta's example and sense of mission that many of the early followers were gradually weaned from drugs. The early devotees were greatly impressed by the swami as *acarya*, that is, one who teaches by example and whose life reflects peace, self-discipline, and truth. Through an intimate and personal encounter with the swami there often followed a conversion to Krishna Consciousness.

In August of 1968 the Krishna Consciousness movement purchased 133 acres of land near Wheeling, West Virginia, and founded New Vrindavana. The creation of New Vrindavana represented a disciplined and formal Vaishnava monastic community in which Vaishnava ritual, Krishna mythology, and certain Bengali cultural mores of food, dress, and personal conduct became essential. Other aspects of the process of Hinduization included the exclusive use of assumed names as well as Sanskritization. The hippie convert of the earlier years now became the novice-devotee. No longer was Swami Bhaktivedanta addressed familiarly. He now assumed the honourific Srila Prabhupada, reflecting his new formal role as guru. Srila purports to refer to the Lord, while Prabhupada indicates the person at whose feet many masters sit.

The transformation of the movement at this time is best seen in the swami's vision of New Vrindavana as a model 'transcendental' community where devotees could live completely divorced from any contact with corruptive, materialistic American society. Swami Bhaktivedanta described New Vrindavana as 'the first community in the West dedicated to Krishna consciousness living', and envisioned the emergence of a new people:

There will be a new growth of superior population. They will not be like cats and dogs, but will actually be demi-gods. 'Demigod' means devotee of Krsna, that's all. And 'asura' (demons) means non-devotee. . . . This demonic civilization is actually killing the human race. . . . So one of the major advantages of the New Vrindaban is that it is out of contact with the asuric civilization.[122]

Separation from the demonic civilization even extended to a prohibition against taking outside jobs, as well as employing modern, industrial machinery. 'The Vrindavana conception', explained the swami, 'is that of a transcendental village, without any of the botheration of the modern industrial atmosphere.'[123]

It was intended that New Vrindavana would be 'transcendental' in that it would recreate the ancient 'vedic' village where Krishna sported with the gopis. People in the various stages of life, namely *brahmacarins* (celibate students), *grhasthas* (householders), *vanaprasthas* (the retired), and *sannyasins* (detached holy men) would live independently and self-sufficiently, completely sustained by agricultural produce and milk from the cows. One of the objectives of New Vrindavana would be the protection of the cow primarily as a symbol of man's yearning for God. In the new Vedic community, work roles would be assigned according to traditional Vedic injunctions. 'The women's business will be to take care of the children, to cook, to clean, and to churn butter, and, for those who have the knowledge, to help in typing',[124] Bhaktivedanta said.

The role of Swami Bhaktivedanta in the new society is clearly stated in the *Krsna Consciousness Handbook* of 1970. Swami Bhaktivedanta is spiritual master and 'guru':

As spiritual master, Bhaktivedanta Swami is the last recourse and the ultimate standard of Krsna consciousness. . . . He himself resides in no one place, but travels from center to center and regularly lectures. The spiritual master is responsible for his devotees . . . his order is to be taken as one's life and soul . . . therefore honor the spiritual master with the honor due to God because the 'guru' is the transparent via media (sic) or representative of God.[125]

Here and throughout the literature of this period, Swami Bhaktivedanta is viewed within the context of the guru-disciple relationship.

Since 1971, the International Society for Krshna Consciousness has gradually shifted away from the isolationist position symbolized by New Vrindavana to one of engagement and confrontation with the traditional values of American society. Far from replacing the demonic civilization, there is a growing tendency to work within the system. The world view which characterized New Vrindavana, namely, the separation of the spiritual few from the demonic culture, is now seen with a more optimistic view of society's chances. The new approach suggests the possibility of peace and prosperity for the whole world, if all men become conscious of Krishna. In more recent literature of ISKCON, New Vrindavana is no longer referred to as the transcendental Vedic model, but rather more modestly as the movement's model agricultural community established to show how one can live simply with a cow and some land.

The focus gradually shifted in the mid-1970s to the city temples, which became increasingly involved with the social, political, and economic concerns of society at large. Significantly, this period witnessed the development within ISKCON of specific social programs and business ventures as well as a political party, which was short-lived. Additional indications of such involvement has been the tendency within ISKCON to employ given as well as assumed names, the demythologization of sacred language in favour of current, socio-political rhetoric, and recently a modification of traditional Indian garb in favour of more modern Western clothing.

As ISKCON became cosmopolitan the role of Swami Bhaktivedanta expanded to cosmic proportions. No longer was he simply another guru with a mission restricted to the English-speaking world. Now he was regarded as the sole, perfect manifestation of Lord Krishna alive today. This transpired through Bhaktivedanta's interpretation of Chaitanya's teachings and the 'Vedic literature' that he frequently alluded to as the source of his esoteric knowledge. The Avatarin, or Supreme Personality of Godhead, is Krishna. Krishna is the original Avatar because He originally gave the Vedic instructions to Brahma, and later the *Gita* to Arjuna. In the Krishna Consciousness movement the genuine Avatar must be in the line of disciplic succession stemming from Krishna, and a representative of Krishna. The Avatar is empowered by Krishna. He is the personification of the Vedas, is dedicated to service in Krishna, knows the 'science of Krishna', and must be a Vaishnava.[126]

The science of Krishna is described in *The Teachings of Lord Chaitanya*, written by Bhaktivedanta. From Krishna six types of Avatars descend: (1) the Purusa Avatar, who is Vishnu; (2) the 'Pastime (Lila) Avatars such as Matsya, Kurma, and Vamana; (3) the Guna Avatars; (4) the Manvantara Avatars; (5) the Yuga Avatars; and (6) the avesa Avatars, of which there are two varieties – direct and indirect. The direct avesavatar is the Lord Krishna, and the indirect avesavatar is an empowered being who represents Krishna. A. C. Bhaktivedanta Swami Prabhupada is clearly regarded by ISKCON devotees as an indirect avesavatar, possessed or empowered by Krishna and representing Him.

According to ISKCON's religious thinkers the salvific message, revealed by Krishna, has been faithfully transmitted by disciplic succession through Chaitanya to Swami Bhaktivedanta. In effect, there is but one teacher, Krishna, and a line of 32 faithful transmitters, the latest representative being Swami Bhaktivedanta.[127] While Krishna speaks directly through the *Gita*, such teaching can be correctly interpreted only by his disciples, and by Swami Bhaktivedanta as the modern successor. Nor is it possible to speak directly to Krishna, for the process requires that one surrenders to Krishna's representative before one surrenders to Krishna. 'There is no difference', explains the Swami, 'between Krishna's instruction and our instruction.'[128]

It is imprecise and possibly misleading to speak of surrender to Swami Bhaktivedanta, for in the last analysis, one does not surrender to the swami but rather one surrenders to Krishna through the swami. In ISKCON belief, Swami Bhaktivedanta is no longer an individual entity, but rather, 'Prabhupada', that is, 'he who has taken the position of the Lord'.[129] He is a window, an instrument, a pure medium, and Krishna lives through him. Hence, for the ISKCON devotee, to see Swami Bhaktivedanta is to see Krishna, to hear Swami Bhaktivedanta is to hear Krishna, to please Swami Bhaktivedanta is to please Krishna, and to worship Swami Bhaktivedanta is to worship Krishna. In short, 'the disciple should accept the spiritual master as God because he is the external manifestation of Krishna'.[130] Thus, Swami Bhaktivedanta is the medium of God's presence and the source of God's salvific grace for our world. Swami Bhaktivedanta may not be God, but he is the way to God, and the way back to Godhead.

Swami Bhaktivedanta explained that the word *Christos* is the Greek version of the word Krsna, and that Christ is the same as Krishna.[131] He said that when a Hindu calls upon Krsna he often says Krsta, a Sanskrit word meaning attraction. Furthermore, the sound of Krsta and Christ are so alike that they must be the same, for 'when we address God as "Christ", "Krsta", or "Krsna", we indicate the same all-attractive Supreme Personality of Godhead. When Jesus said, 'Our Father, who are in heaven, sanctified by thy name,' that name of God was Krsta or Krsna'.[132] ISKCON regards the teachings of the Bible and the *Gita* as essentially the same, saying, 'worship the Lord of creation and do everything as an offering to Him'.[133]

In 1971 Swami Bhaktivedanta returned to India. He arranged for the world headquarters of the ISKCON movement to be built at Mayapur, India. Shortly before his death he designated eleven ISKCON devotees to act as spiritual masters and to be gurus. On 14 November 1977 at the age of 81, A. C. Bhaktivedanta died at his temple in Vrindavana. Twenty-four hours of continuous chanting followed his passing.

After the death of A. C. Bhaktivedanta in 1977, a memorial was begun at New Vrindavana in West Virginia worthy of a God-man. It is called Prabhupada's palace of gold and has been labelled 'The Taj Mahal of the West'.[134] It is indeed a palace, for it covers 35 000 square feet and consists of 254 tons of marble. Its 300-ton dome, which is 8000 square feet, is covered with 22 Carat gold-leaf, making it sparkle like the sun. Inside the palace one can see a replica of A. C. Bhaktivedanta seated in his study appearing to be translating scriptures of Krishna Consciousness into English. But the *pièce de résistance* is the life-size replica of His Divine Grace A. C. Bhaktivedanta Swami Prabhupada that reigns over the main temple. Here he is preserved for eternity upon a throne of gold and marble, and every day his devotees prepare vegetarian food according to ancient Hindu recipes and offer it up to him as an act of devotion.[135]

THE AVATAR OF THE BAHA'I FAITH

The Revelation which, from time immemorial, hath been acclaimed as the Purpose and Promise of all the Prophets of God, and the most cherished Desire of His Messengers, hath now . . . been revealed unto men. The advent of such a Revelation hath been heralded in all the sacred Scriptures.[136]

(Baha'u'llah)

This section focuses upon the Baha'i Faith, a religion which derives from Islam in the 19th century in Persia, and has an Avatar named Baha'u'llah.

From a sect of Islam known as the Twelvers (believers in twelve Imams), there arose in Persia in the 19th century two groups, the Babis and the Bahais. The Babis were followers of Ali Muhammad Shirazi, known as the Bab, meaning the gate, who functioned like John the Baptist, as a forerunner proclaiming that 'One Greater than He' would soon arrive. One of his followers, Mirza Husayn Ali (1817–92), proclaimed himself 'Him who God Shall Make Manifest', as foretold by the Bab, and assumed the name Baha'u'llah, meaning The Glory of God. The Baha'i Faith is rooted in the spiritual message of Baha'u'llah who is regarded by Bahais as a Manifestation of God. We shall trace how Baha'u'llah has been transformed from a Manifestation into an Avatar.

The closest approach to incarnational theory among the Bahais adopts the form of progressive revelation via the Manifestation of God. Manifestations differ slightly from Avatars and Incarnation in that they are not composed of the same essence as God. Rather, they are mirrors or reflections of God's glory, just as a ray of the sun is a reflection of the sun. Manifestations are those individuals who know God best, are most sensitive to His Will, and who deliver a spiritual message for an age, inaugurating a new era. An approximate list of Baha'i Manifestations are (1) Adam, (2) Noah, (3) Hud, (4) Salih, (5) Rama, (6), Krishna, (7) Abraham, (8) Moses, (9) Zoroaster, (10) Buddha, (11) Christ, (12) Muhammad, (13) the Bab, and (14) Baha'u'llah. This list is approximate because Bahais are reluctant to make the list definitive, as only a Manifestation would have the ability to really know the divine lineage. This list includes founders of such religions as Judaism, Christianity, Islam, Baha'i, Hinduism, Buddhism, Zoroastrianism, and the

Sabean religion. We may recall that Meher Baba, in Chapter 2, accepted six of these fourteen Manifestations as Avatars.

A basic principle of the Baha'i Faith is a recognition of the divine foundation of all religions, and the working toward the unification of them into one universal faith. With this aim in mind, one can comprehend a recent tendency among a group of Bahais, especially in India, to attempt to subsume the Hindu religion within the Baha'i Faith. The link by which Hinduism is brought into convergence with the Baha'i Faith is through the similarity between Avatars and Manifestations. Bahais acknowledge the Hindu Avatars Rama and Krishna as Manifestations, thus establishing a connection. Furthermore, in discussing the periodic appearance of the Manifestation, Bahais cite the incarnational passage of the *Gita* (chapter 4, verses 6 and 7) as their guide.[137]

Recently, tracts promulgated by the American Baha'i headquarters declare that 'If you are a Hindu, whose faith began several thousand years B.C., your prophecy concerning the return of Krishna has at last been fulfilled by the same new Prophet Baha'u'llah.'[138] And the Baha'i Publishing Trust of New Delhi, published the writings of Professor Pritam Singh, entitled *The Second Coming of Shri Krishna*, showing that Krishna has returned in the Manifestation of Baha'u'llah.

Baha'u'llah is not only recognized as the second coming of Krishna, but he is also considered by some Bahais to be the realization of the Kalki Avatar. Baha'u'llah's son, Abdul-Baha, approved of Baha'u'llah's identification with Kalki,[139] and in his article 'My Quest for the Fulfilment of Hinduism',[140] S. P. Raman proclaimed that the Kalki Avatar is fulfilled in the Manifestation of Baha'u'llah. Another Baha'i, Prakash Narayan Mishra, in his book *Kalki Avatar Ki Khoj (The Quest for Kalki Avatar)*, has identified the long-awaited tenth Avatar, Kalki, with Baha'u'llah.

In 1976 the Baha'i Publishing Trust of New Delhi published Jamshed Fozdar's *Buddha Maitrya-Amitabha Has Appeared*.[141] Here is a meticulous attempt to prove that Baha'u'llah is the long-awaited Maitreya Buddha and Kalki Avatar. In his search for the fulfilment of the Kalki prophecy, Fozdar eliminates Kalki's mythic components such as white horse and sword. He attempts to demonstrate that the Avatar of the future, Kalki, is also the Buddha of the future, Maitreya, both of whom are truly Baha'u'llah. The logic of this is based upon the notion that

since Buddha is Vishnu's ninth Avatar and Kalki is the tenth
and final Avatar, then Maitreya, the Buddha of the future, must be
the same as the Kalki Avatar. Through laborious chronological
calculation and evidence of the wickedness and immorality of
modern man in the Kali Yuga, Fozdar finds Baha'u'llah to be
the fulfilment of both the Hindu and the Buddhist prophecies.
Baha'u'llah is shown to be the 'eon-ender', the Kalki Avatar,
the one who ends the Kali Yuga and establishes the new age of
Baha'i.

One can observe a tendency among some Indian Bahais to view
Baha'u'llah as the modern Manifestation of the Krishna Avatar or
the Kalki Avatar according to the prophecy in the *Gita*. The Hindu
mythological features of the Krishna and Kalki myth are replaced
by an historical person, Baha'u'llah, who fulfils eschatological
expectations. A contemporary Bahai devotional song *(Bhajan)*
integrates the themes:

The Kalkin Avatar

Arise O children of India, the kalkin avatar has come;
Vishnu's avatar has come with the name Baha'u'llah
Nowhere in the entire world can the influence of religion be
    seen.
The wicked have obtained everything; the truthful have lost
    all;
According to the Gita the time of Vishnu's avatar has come.
The Gita has said when circumstances are such, religion is
    again established just as it has happened today.
In order to save the righteous the kalkin avatar has come.
Foolish people have not realized that Vishnu's avatar has
    come again.
Radha and Arjuna knew that the Lord had taken a new abode.
The eternal has once again manifested himself, the avatar of
    God.[142]

THE ENGLISH AVATAR MOVEMENT

And his philosophy will stand the test of all time, for it is the
one-and-only, age-old wisdom re-presented and clarified in
terms best suited to answer the special needs of our own day.[143]

(Avatar Imperium Internum)

The embodiment of English Avatarhood is John van Ryswyk, the 'Imperator-Pontifex' of Avatar Imperium Internum. Born Jocabus Johannes van Ryswyk on 16 July 1898, in Holland, he was interested in various churches and religions in his youth. As a member of the Dutch Royal Navy he sailed to India and studied Sanskrit. Becoming a British subject in 1936, he formed a spiritual movement known as the Temple of Service, and gave lectures and healing services. In 1938 he reshaped his spiritual movement along chivalric lines and changed its name to 'Avatar, Defenders of Civilization'. This evolved into Avatar Imperium Internum, with knights of Avatar (Ordo Equestris Militaris Avatar), and ladies of Avatar (Ordo Dominarum Nobilium Avatar). Its motto is *Veritas, Caritas, Libertas*, (truth, charity, and liberty), and its declaration of faith is in one supreme God, one eternal truth, and one divine purpose.

At the beginning of World War II van Ryswyk established a political plan called the New Constitutional Order as an alternative to Hitler's 'New Order'. Its aims were to challenge atheism and tyranny, eliminate communism, defend the sacredness of the individual, and affirm the spiritual foundation of human existence. During World War II van Ryswyk also turned his energies to establishing the Avatar International University for the Advancement of Learning and the Rewarding of Outstanding Merit, and the Avatar College of Chivalry for the Study of Heraldry and the Recording of Arms and Titles. These schools were intended to lead civilization to a new level called Christocracy, which was, at one time, the name of their magazine.

In 1942 van Ryswyk founded his church and consecrated it in both the Roman and Eastern rites. He called it 'The Apostolic Church of St. Peter (autocephalic)', in an attempt to return to Christian doctrine prior to the Council of Nicea. He was consecrated Bishop Johannes van Ryswyk with Apostolic Rites after which he became the 'Imperator-Pontifex' of Avatar Imperium Internum. In 1951 he was received by Pope Pius XII at the Vatican. On 24 February 1963 John van Ryswyk died, and this resulted in the closing of the Avatar College and University. His spiritual movement, however, continues with headquarters in London.

The philosophy of John van Ryswyk is embedded in the 116 lectures that he delivered between 1942 and 1947, which constitute the Avatar School of Philosophy. This message is an attempt at reconciling philosophy, science, and religion. It offers an esoteric interpretation of Christianity, Islam, Buddhism, Taoism, Gnosticism, the Bible, and the Akoshic records, based upon contrasting such polarities as God–Satan, love–hate, good–evil, light–dark, potentiality–actuality, soul–mind, and involution–evolution. It incorporates a belief in reincarnation of the soul and professes that all the Avatars are Christ, and Jesus but one incarnation of the recurring Christ.

According to the philosophy of John van Ryswyk the word 'Avatar' derives from three Sanskrit words, Av, At, Ar, each referring to an aspect of the Trinity.[144] He translates the word 'avatar' as bringer of light or the highest good. An incarnation enters the world when the necessity for a great enlightenment arises, and when the magnetic field of the planet is properly aligned. When He ascends into heaven He dematerializes His physical body and distributes His atoms within this planet and the surrounding atmosphere.[145] Van Ryswyk explains that Krishna gave us the power, Zoroaster endowed us with the light, Buddha bestowed us with the middle way, and Jesus Christ blessed us with the knowledge that God is love which is the key to salvation. Presumably he should know for it is believed that John van Ryswyk was either a servant or apostle of Jesus, and remembered Him as

outstanding tall compared to the people of that time; He was not handsome, as we think of handsomeness, but He had a fine, upstanding Guardsmanlike figure. His hair was always windblown; He preferred to be out of doors, for He felt constricted within walls. He always slept out of doors, in the garden. His eyes were a beautiful hazel, which could change to any colour – and black when He was angry! When He walked alone in meditation, on the shores of the Sea of Galilee, the Light that spread out from Him extended many miles.[146]

Van Ryswyk's Christology is based on the idea that for each level of being there is a perfect prototype, and for the human level it is Christhood. According to van Ryswyk the crown of all philosophy is Christ. Christ is 'the first undulating, moving vibration, that Divine Ground whom we call God'.[147] Those who are spiritually advanced carry the image of Christ within, for the soul is Christ, which reincarnates repeatedly to remove the sins of the world and destroy evil.[148] When we are fully aware that we are the highest electrical phenomenon in existence, we shall share the consciousness of Christ, the instantaneous Conductor, for the universe is one creation, one circuit.[149]

John van Ryswyk's new order of Avatar Imperium Internum is a mixture of spiritual chivalry, electromagnetism, and esoteric interpretations. Its goal is the attainment of Christocracy through avatarhood.

MAGICAL AVATARS OF THE OCCULT

I call on Thee, Mighty Arzel, who stands in the East, to assist me in this and all my ventures. I know now that my New Avatar Power is flooding to the surface.[150]

(Geof Gray-Cobb)

The avatar concept has gone through a great transformation since leaving its Indian homeland, and now it is given a do-it-yourself treatment. One can discover how to become an Avatar by following the instructions found in *The Miracle of New Avatar Power* written by Geof Gray-Cobb in 1974. Mr Gray-Cobb has studied magic for many years and has been an occult research editor for such periodicals as *The National Examiner*, *Midnight*, and *Fate*. *The Miracle of New Avatar Power* comprises the essentials of a course that Gray-Cobb has taught for four years and that reveals the magical ways of acquiring the power that the Avatars once possessed.

According to Gray-Cobb, about 10 000 years ago many people knew the secrets of the universe called the 'Old Wisdom'. These people were ordinary folk, yet through knowledge of the Old Wisdom they seemed special and legends developed in which they became known as 'Avatars'. The Old Wisdom enabled them to do anything they wished, including make gold, produce food out of thin air, win the love of a mate, etc. Their secrets were sought by envious rulers, so the Avatars sought refuge in such remote places as Tibet and the Himalayas. They grew older and older and some chose to vacate their ageing physical bodies, but a few ancient ones still survive in Tibet. Gradually all but a few Avatars left the earth, but they left behind some clues of their work which can be found in the *Cabala*, the Egyptian pyramids, the Tarot, and ancient scrolls. After years of research into the occult,

Gray-Cobb uncovered the old spells and rituals and offers them to anyone wishing to acquire Avatar power.

According to Gray-Cobb, everyone has Avatar power but some utilize it and others do not. Deep inside us there lie 'ancestral memories of the time when these miracles were free to every man and woman who used his or her Avatar power'.[151] Anyone who wishes can be an Avatar and anyone you meet may be one. An Avatar appears to be no different from anyone else, but he possesses Avatar power, and knows that if he needs assistance he can invoke a spirit by using the secret word AUM.[152]

The trick is to learn the proper way to become an Avatar. A person may become an Avatar by awakening and developing his New Avatar Power (abbreviated NAP). As bodily tensions keep NAP in check, physical relaxation is essential to bringing Avatar power to the surface. One must allow the 'inner mind' to help the NAP to flow and by-pass the conscious mind where disbelief may exist. Gray-Cobb makes it clear that NAP can be awakened by reading his book, and whether or not the words are believed, the thoughts may slip past conscious awareness into the inner mind. Once the inner mind perceives the meaning behind these thoughts, a process is set in motion by which NAP is awakened and available for use.

The novice Avatar must learn numerous invocations and rituals. Only then will he acquire the 'Power of the Mysteries', which the ancient Egyptians and Essenes possessed, enabling him to perform astral travel.[153] He must also keep a diary of his daily experiences, known as a Book of Shadows, or grimoire. A dozen special invocations are offered for obtaining money, love, success, health and power. The efficacy of these invocations seems to be their relation to the Hebrew language. The New Avatar Power formula is Ankar Yod Hay Vaw Hay, approximating the Hebrew letters that represent God (Tetragrammaton). The invocation for money is Yeh-ho-vo-eloh-heem,[154] a combination of Jehovah and Elohim, two Hebrew names for God. Other invocations use references to deity such as Emanuel and Adonai. The invocation for winning contests is Ski-ma-ah-mathee-uh, supposedly used by Joshua when he made the sun stand still.[155] Learning New Avatar Power also includes numerous rituals, such as the defense armour ritual, the astral bomb attack ritual, the etheric shrapnel ritual, the occult judo ritual, and the theurgic booby-trap ritual. A good avatar must know how to perform all the rituals as well as recite the invocations.

There are five NAP spirit gates that are energy centres located in the throat, the heart, the pelvis, the feet, and over one's head. This energy is raw Avatar power and needs to be circulated around one's body. Arcane invocations are used to open these gates. If one feels a small insect crawling under one's skin slightly above the brow (Ajna Chakra), this is called 'the tickling of the ant', and is a sign of success and an indication that NAP is awakening.[156] Here is a tenuous link between NAP and esoteric Kundalini yoga.

Gray-Cobb suggests that his technique be treated as a New Avatar Power driving course. Use it as you would manipulate a car, he advises. 'Why it works is unimportant: you are looking for concrete results, not reasons.'[157] This thaumaturgist would have us recognize that 'mind power is more powerful than atomic fission, and that Avatar power is the most powerful force in the cosmos'.[158]

ASTRAL AVATARS OF SCIENCE FICTION

He has no material power as the god-emperors had; he has only a following of desert people and fishermen. They tell him he is a god; he believes them. The followers of Alexander said, 'He is unconquerable, therefore he is a god.' The followers of this man do not think at all; he was their act of spontaneous creation. Now he leads them, this madman called Jesus of Nazareth.

And he spoke, saying unto them, 'Yea, verily, I was Karl Glogauer and now I am Jesus the Messiah, the Christ.'

And it was so.

(Introduction to *Behold The Man*[159])

Science fiction is mythic literature involving the hopes, dreams and fears of a people. While it is clearly imaginative, it offers a vision pointing to what may become reality. It voices a belief in transcendence, omniscience, perfection, and redemption, and deals with future history and ultimate salvation.

The literary conventions of science fiction relevant to the Avatar are the themes of descent and ascent; the dream of an achievable perfect human society (utopia, Zion); the longing to make contact with other beings, especially those of a higher order; and the apocalypse.[160] Science fiction provides a launching pad for the exploration of universes where Avatars may exist. For science fiction writers, 'myths are not fiction, but history seen with a poet's eyes, and recounted in a poet's terms'.[161] In the intellect and imagination 'we melt into ONE at the touch of infinity', the astral region where Avatars are sought.[162]

In *The Avatars*,[163] science fiction writer Poul Anderson introduces two Avatars, Aengus mac Og, the Avatar of love, and his sister Brigit, the Avatar of poesy. The Avatars exist on the planet of 'the Others', where they are concerned with exploring, understanding, and celebrating existence. Being an 'Other' is to be in a higher mental state than anything experienced by humans. The advanced technology of 'the Others' is able to map out a pattern of personality, to resurrect a body at death, and to possess the highest level of mental telepathy. But the most subtle achievement of 'the Others' is 'to summon' an Avatar who is God-like yet human. The Avatar's main preoccupation is to make 'oneness' possible through mental telepathy, soul transference, and immortality. Anderson's *The Avatars* suggests the possibility that humans may evolve into a civilization like 'the Others' and ultimately summon avatars.

Science fiction often seeks for salvation and deliverance at the apocalypse from someone more-than-human, and no one could be better suited than the Kalki Avatar as found in *Lord of Light* by Roger Zelazny.[164] This story takes place on a Hindu–Buddhist planet where Avatar Mahasamatman is a combination of Kalki, Buddha, and the Lord of Light. Zelazny's narrator recounts:

> His followers called him Mahasamatman and said he was a god. He preferred to drop the Maha- and the -atman, however, and called himself Sam. He never claimed to be a god. But then, he never claimed not to be a god. Circumstances being what they were, neither admission could be of any benefit. . . . Therefore, there was mystery about him.[165]

Like one of Vishnu's Avatars, Mahasamatman fights for the restoration of the balance between the forces of good and evil. He appears with blazing sword upon a white horse as Kalki, the Avatar who will inaugurate the end of the age of darkness (Kali Yuga). The evil powers are defeated when Mahasamatman kills Brahma and Shiva. Mahasamatman acts out of love in the Celestial City knowing that his actions are cosmic necessities.

In science fiction one can travel via a time machine of mythic imagination to Godmen of the future, or to the Godman of the past, namely Jesus Christ. Two examples of travelling back to the time of Jesus are found in *The Jesus Incident* by Frank Herbert and *Behold The Man* by Michael Moorcock.[166] Both of these stories end with a reenactment of the crucifixion of Jesus Christ. In science fiction, whether one travels back to the future or forward to the past, the great expectation is to have a 'close encounter of the third kind' with a God-man.

CONCLUSION: WESTERN AVATARS AND CHRIST

Chapter three reveals the avatar concept gradually separating from its Hindu heritage and finding itself a new home in the West. There is a gradual loosening of the ties that the Western Avatar has with the Vaishnava tradition and the Hindu scripture, the *Bhagavad Gita*. In the Theosophical Society, the Self-Realization Fellowship, and the International Society for Krishna Consciousness, the Avatars still are predominantly Indian and in these movements the *Gita* remains an important text, demonstrated by the fact that Annie Besant, Yogananda, and A. C. Bhaktivedanta each translated it into English. The Bahais of India retain a connection with the *Gita*, citing it as the scriptural source for the coming of God's Manifestations. In its cross-cultural context the *Gita* has become a neo-Hindu 'New Testament', announcing the advent of the God-man. Kenneth Rexroth may be correct in his assessment of the *Gita* as 'one of the three or four most influential writings in the history of man'.[167]

Concerning the Western adaptation of the Avatar concept, the ten mythological Avatars of Vishnu are all but forgotten, and Krishna and Buddha are regarded as founders of religions rather than as Avatars. Modern Indian Avatars from Chaitanya to Satya Sai Baba are out of the picture. Little is made of such mythemes as yoga, yugas, cobras, or shakti. When yoga is used by Western Avatars it appears in such unorthodox forms as Kriya yoga. The cobra, which is integral to the Indian Avatar, is now found internalized in Kundalini imagery, or alchemized as in magical Avatar power. And the Sanskrit language has been replaced by ancient Western languages such as Hebrew, Latin, and Greek. Only golden imagery remains.

A new mythology surrounding the Western Avatars emerges.

The mystery is enhanced by their reputed location in the Himalayan Mountains of India and Tibet. Blavatsky, Besant, Bailey and Babaji connected Avatars with Tibet. It is reported by some of the spiritual movements in this chapter that the Avatars dwell around the Himalayan Mountains, the world's most remote and inaccessible mountain range, making them mysterious and full of mystique. Since the Himalayas are the world's highest mountains the Avatars are placed in close proximity to their heavenly home. In this rarified atmosphere Avatars are said to have non-physical bodies and require no food (Babaji), or eat astral food while watching astral television (Yukteswar). Astrology and the astral plane form part of the new mythology of the Western Avatars.

A new Avatar emerges prominently in the West, the God-man Jesus Christ. For the Theosophists, the World Teacher embodies the Solar Logos and appears as Krishna, Buddha, and Christ. Theosophical Mahatmas dwell in the Himalayas, so Christ is said to be there too. In Alice Bailey's Arcane School, Christ is the transmitting Avatar who links humanity with the spiritual hierarchy. Christ will surpass the work of the Buddha Avatar and build the Aquarian age. Paramahansa Yogananda views Jesus as a master of Kriya yoga, and claims that all four Kriya Avatars are on a par with Jesus. The Krishna Consciousness Avatar, A. C. Bhaktivedanta, believed that the Father in heaven about whom Jesus spoke was none other than Krishna, and that Jesus pointed back to Godhead in the direction of Krishna. The Baha'i Faith regards Jesus Christ as a Manifestation rather than as an Avatar. In accordance with its Islamic background, the Baha'i Faith does not adhere to an incarnational theory whereby God can bear a son. Jesus is viewed as a Manifestation, a ray of the solar splendour. The English Avatar movement teaches that the key to avatarhood is found in Jesus' message of love. John van Ryswyk taught that all people will be reunited in Christ through reincarnation, and that civilization's progress based on love will eventually lead to Christocracy.

While the connection with the Hindu tradition has dwindled, the concept of the avatar has permeated Western culture in such a way as to attract attention among various popular spiritual movements. The avatar concept, born and bred in India, has become a radically transformed cross-cultural phenomenon. The supreme position of Krishna has been replaced in the West by Christ, who is regarded as the full and complete Avatar, an Avatar of love, a saviour figure, and a Son of God. The Avatar has been transmogrified and its image has become inextricably interwoven with the cultural horizon in which it is found.

Now let us turn to Jesus Christ as a God-man within the context of the Christian religion and the environment in which it developed, to see if Jesus Christ is really an Avatar as the Hindus claim, and how there may be similarities and differences between the Hindu God-men and the Christian God-man.

4

Avatars and Christ

INTRODUCTION: JESUS CHRIST A WESTERN AVATAR

Jesus was the avatar to end all avatars. If we take his life message seriously, we need not rack our brains to figure out which of the current contenders is an avatar of the divine. All are, and none is; and the avatar we are seeking is already in the midst of us, in us and in those closest to us and farthest away.[1]

(Harvey Cox)

That Jesus Christ is a God-man is generally acknowledged. That he is the Incarnation of God is dogma in the Christian religion; that he is an Avatar is to view him through Hindu eyes. In the West there has emerged a gradual recognition of Jesus Christ as an Avatar, and it developed circuitously, partly through secret societies, mystery schools, esoteric groups, and non-Christian religions such as Islam. It has already been shown how in the 1870s, Ramakrishna embraced Jesus as an Avatar and placed him within the Hindu pantheon. Half a century later a Hindu convert to Christianity, V. Chakkarai, in his book *Jesus the Avatar*,[2] stated that according to the Christian view Jesus Christ was 'the Avatar of God'.[3] And it has been shown in Chapter 3 how Christ replaced Krishna as a Western Avatar.

The association of Jesus with India has been a longstanding one. A major Western influence connecting Jesus with India has been the Islamic religion. According to Islamic belief based upon its scripture, the Koran, a prophet cannot die ignominiously upon a cross, and therefore Jesus, being a prophet, did not die when he was crucified. Islamic legends tell of Jesus being revived in a cave, smuggled out of Palestine, and making his way to India. Islamic

157

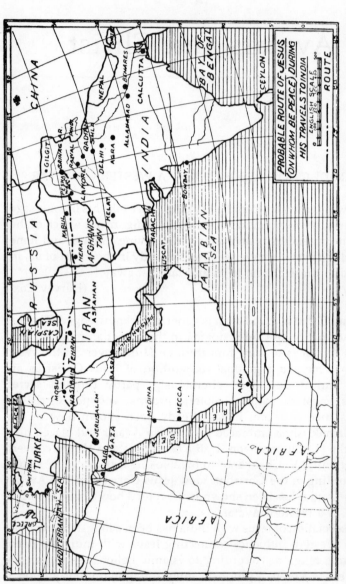

SOURCE   Hazrat Mirza Ghulam Ahmad, *Jesus in India* (Rabwah, Pakistan: The Ahmadiyya Muslim Foreign Missions Department, 1962).

MAP   *Probable route of Jesus during his travel to India*

books such as the *Rauzat-us-Safa*[4] recount tales of Jesus' travels to Kashmir (see Map). Jesus is reported to have walked with some of his disciples to Nasibain (450 miles from Jerusalem) where he performed miracles and healings. His journey took him through Persia and Afghanistan to Srinagar in Kashmir where he tried to locate the lost tribes of Israel in order to preach his message to them. The lost tribes that he found were the Afghans and Kashmiris.[5] They say that he was given the name 'Messiah' because he was a great traveller, for to them messiah means the travelling prophet.

Another Islamic legend tells how Jesus came to Kashmir in his youth and learned the practice of yoga, accounting for his ability to perform miracles later in Palestine. He did not die when he was crucified but was cared for by some Essenes who restored his health. They sent him back to Kashmir where he lived with his masters until his natural death.[6] A tomb in Sringar is reputed to be the tomb of Yousa-Asaf, which is the name by which Jesus Christ is known there.[7]

Yet another Islamic legend asserts that the lost years of Jesus are accounted for in the *Nath Namavali* manuscript kept in Tibet. A part of this text is regarded as having been written by Jesus himself. Jesus, known as Ishai Nath, came to India at age 14, and for 16 years focused his attention on the Hindu deity Shiva. Returning to Israel, he preached, was crucified, passed into a yogic state which looked like death, and was hidden in a tomb. His guru, the great Chetan Nath, saw Jesus' suffering in a vision, travelled astrally to him, revived him from the yogic state and led him to India. Ishai Nath (Jesus) established an ashram in Kashmir and at the age of 49 voluntarily surrendered his body, having gained control over it through yoga.[8]

In the last century a spate of esoteric and occult literature has sprung up dealing with Jesus Christ in various 'mystical' modes. Numerous attempts have been made to herald a 'New Age of Truth' by tapping sources from the deep unknown, secret societies, mystery schools, and hidden masters, and relating it to Jesus Christ the Avatar. A few samples of this genre are now offered.

The Aquarian Gospel of Jesus the Christ, written around the turn of the century by Levi Dowling (1844–1911), is a so-called transcription 'from the Akashic records'. It accounts for the 'lost years' of Jesus in India. According to this Gospel, Rabbi Hillel introduced

Jesus to Prince Ravanna of Orissa. Ravanna recognised Jesus as the son of heaven and son of God (21:8, 12) and took Jesus to India to learn the religion of the 'Brahms'. Jesus learned the Vedas and taught that salvation is attaining 'deific life' where man and God are one (22:31). Jesus taught that God is One, but that His name is known to the Hebrews as Jehovah, to the Hindus as Parabrahm, and to the Greeks as Zeus (28:19). In Benares, Udraka, the greatest of the Brahmic healers, taught Jesus how to avoid sickness, a sign of sin. Jesus repudiated the caste system thus offending the Brahmic priests who drove him from their temple. The priests of Benares conspired to kill Jesus, but he fled to Nepal foiling their plans. *The Aquarian Gospel of Jesus the Christ* regards Christ as 'the God-man of the ages . . . qualified to be an Avatar'.[9]

Edgar Cayce (1877–1945), known as the 'sleeping prophet', was a psychic who inspired a large following in the first half of the 20th century. From 1901 to 1945 Cayce made thousands of psychic readings. His revelations, known as 'readings', included peoples' previous lives, medical diagnoses, future events, earth changes, presidential assassinations, and the emergence of the lost continent of Atlantis. Especially interesting are his readings concerning Jesus Christ. Cayce believed that Proverbs 8:22–31 offered evidence within the Bible for reincarnation, and he connected Jesus with a reincarnating soul that appeared as Amelius, Adam, Enoch, Melchizedek, and Zoroaster's father, and finally assumed the body of Jesus. According to Cayce, Jesus was sent to India from his thirteenth to his sixteenth year by the leader of the Essenes, Judy. In India he studied under Kahjian and learned 'those cleansings of the body as related to preparation for strength in the physical, as well as in the mental man'.[10] According to Cayce, Jesus submitted to the crucifixion in order to show 'the total unimportance of the body after it ceases to house the soul'.[11] Jesus resurrected his body 'from the ether waves that were already within the room'.[12] Cayce's readings about Jesus Christ were to have come from 'a universal storehouse of knowledge' which Cayce reputedly could penetrate. In *Cayce, Karma, and Reincarnation*, I. C. Sharma writes that Edgar Cayce's readings reveal that 'the last great Avatara, or Divine Descent, was in the person of Jesus Christ'.[13]

The Mystical Life of Jesus (1929) by H. Spencer Lewis,[14] presents the Rosicrucian doctrine of Jesus Christ taken from archives of the Great White Brotherhood reputed to be in Tibet, India, and Egypt. Herein one finds that Joseph, Mary, and the Apostles were

Essenes who accepted reincarnation. Jesus was one Avatar among many including Akhnaton, Zoroaster, Adonis, Buddha, and Krishna, and they were all members of the Great White Brotherhood that had its headquarters at Heliopolis in Egypt. As part of Jesus's training for Avatarhood he had to study various 'heathen religions'[15] and he travelled with two Persian Magi to India. In Benares Jesus learned the Hindu principles of healing from guru Udraka. He learned the Hindu and Buddhist teachings before delivering his own system entitled 'Entering the Silence' which became an important feature of later mystical methods.[16] Jesus became a Master, an Avatar, and a Son of God at Heliopolis and attained attunement with the consciousness of God. The title 'Christ' was bestowed upon him in a mystical initiation of the Great White Brotherhood in a secret chamber of the Egyptian pyramid of Cheops. The apostles organised 'the Christine Church'[17] and adopted the cross with a rose upon it as the symbol for Rosicrucianism.

Two more of these apocrypha are noteworthy. In a letter allegedly written by Benan, a priest at Memphis (*Der Benan-Brief* by Ernst von der Planitz, 1910),[18] Jesus attained his reputation as a great healer after studying medicine in Egypt, where he made contact with the Therapeutae, a group of Essenes who practiced healing. It was the High Priest of the temple in Egypt who sent Jesus to teach and heal people in Jerusalem. And in George Williamson's *Secret Places of the Lion*,[19] the 'hidden history and mysterious origins of the wise men reincarnated'[20] are supposedly unsealed. Based upon ancient manuscripts preserved in a mystery school of Peru, Jesus spoke the language of the angels, the original solar tongue.[21] Williamson discloses that Jesus the Christ had previously been Melchizedek, Zoroaster, and Buddha.[22] Jesus' so-called missing years before his baptism are found to have been spent in Britain, Egypt, and Tibet.[23]

These examples of a 'New Age Christianity' with its 'Aquarian' Christ and its 'decoded' versions of the Christ Avatar are recent imagings of Jesus. How it became possible for Jesus to be 'Avatarized' is based upon how Jesus became divinized, i.e. how the historical Jesus became the divine Christ. This shall be described in what follows.

MYTHS OF INCARNATION IN THE ANCIENT NEAR EAST

Man knows nothing more sacred than heroes and reverence for
heroes.

(Thomas Carlyle)

In previous chapters we observed how Avatars become the
embodiment of a mythic awareness of the divine on earth, and
how after many centuries in India the idea of the Avatar spread to
the West. Now let us go back in history to the ancient Near Eastern
world to the times that both preceded Jesus Christ and were
contemporary with him, in order to understand incarnationism in
those periods.

In the ancient Near East the kinship of men with gods was
mythologically commonplace. The myths of the 'immortals' were
utilized to express a sense that they belonged to a superior race and
another realm. The titles 'son of Zeus' or 'son of Helios' were very
common and had their origins in ancient mythology, especially in
the myth of Heracles. Early Christian apologists had to reckon
with Heracles, Asclepius, and Dionysius as potential rivals to
Christ. In the second century of our era, Justin Martyr dismissed
these rivals as deceitful fabrications designed to reduce the Christian account to a mere tale of wonders like the stories told by the
poets. [24]

In the pre-Christian era the notion of divine parentage was not
uncommon. Myths of descent of deities and deification of humans
in ancient Greece clustered around two pre-Socratic Greek
philosophers, Pythagoras and Empedocles. Pythagoras was
thought to be the incarnate son of Hermes who possessed the
facility of remembering a series of reincarnations. His disciples
claimed that he was the Hyperborean Apollo, a fact mentioned by
both Diogenes and Aristotle. [25] As for Empedocles, he is known to
have said, 'All hail! I go about among you an immortal god, no
more a mortal', [26] and the people responded by 'worshipping and
praying to him as to a god'. [27]

The account of Plato's divine parentage goes back well before
New Testament times. Diogenes Laertius mentions it and cites as
his authorities Plato's nephew Speusippus, Aristotle's pupil
Clearchus, and Anaxilaides. The story of Plato's miraculous birth
is also found in Plutarch, who, after reporting Plato's divine birth,
offers this explanation:

I do not find it strange if it is not by a physical approach, like a man's, but by some other kind of contact or touch, by other agencies, that a god alters mortal nature and makes it pregnant with a more divine offspring. . . . In general (the Egyptians) allow sexual intercourse with a mortal woman to a male god . . .[28]

Plutarch, who lived in the latter half of the first century A.D., was contemporary with New Testament times. In Plutarch's most famous work, *Lives*, we find genealogies and stories of the supernatural begetting of outstanding rulers and founders of cities. One such ruler was Alexander the Great. Plutarch regards it as beyond question that Alexander was a descendant of the god Heracles on his father's side, and descended from mythical heroes of Troy on his mother's side.[29] Plutarch relates various versions of Alexander's birth, one of which attributes Alexander's conception to a god who took the form of a serpent and slept with his mother Olympias. An oracle declared that the serpent was Zeus Ammon, and Alexander claimed this to be his true paternity.[30]

The deification of Alexander the Great brought about something entirely new to the concept of incarnationism in the ancient Near Eastern world. While the divinization of a king was nothing new in ancient Egypt where Pharaohs upon attaining the throne were regarded as the living form of the sun-god Horus, it was shocking for the Greeks to deify a man who was still alive. The distinguishing attributes of the Greek gods were their immortality, incorruptibility (i.e. not being subject to physical decay), and divine paternity. Alexander, meanwhile, demanded from the Greeks and some of his other subjects divine worship during his lifetime and this was accorded him by Athens, Sparta, and other Greek city-states. Thus, Alexander was the first Greek king to demand worship as for a god, and to receive it during his lifetime.[31]

What began with Alexander mushroomed with his successors. Ptolemy and Arsinoe were proclaimed 'Saviour-gods' by their Greek and Egyptian subjects quite apart from any identification of themselves with any Egyptian deity. The barrier between divine and human became so thin that the Greeks not only thought that men might become gods but declared that the gods were only deified humans. Within a few years after Alexander's death, Euhemerus advocated a theory that bears his name, that all the gods had either been kings or heroic people. After Alexander the

Great the Greco-Roman world became accustomed to deifying its monarchs. Greek kings represented themselves on coins as the god Zeus or Apollo, and it was common for rulers in Greece and Rome to have their statues erected in temples alongside the gods. It is not uncommon to find the Greek words for god (*Theos*), son of God (*hyios tou Theou*), saviour (*Soter*), and Lord (*Kyrios*) referring to Greek and Roman emperors such as Augustus, Caesar, and Nero.[32] An inscription dated 48 B.C. speaks of Julius Caesar as 'god manifest, offspring of Ares and Aphrodite, and common saviour of human life'.[33] The Roman emperor, Claudius Caesar, who is contemporary with Jesus, while declining to become a God was nevertheless deified by his British subjects and worshipped in a temple with awe. The poet Seneca satirized his deification calling it 'The Pumpkinification of Claudius'.[34]

The association of men with divine appearances was particularly marked in the case of rulers. Just prior to the time that Jesus lived, Cicero in 60 B.C. wrote that the Greeks in Asia were so impressed by the incorruptibility of their governor that they thought some divine man from heaven had dropped down into their province;[35] Virgil in 40 B.C. associated the arrival of a Golden Age with the birth of a child whom he addressed as 'dear offspring of the gods';[36] and Horace in 30 B.C. regarded the emperor Augustus as an incarnation of the god Mercury.[37] (It was during the reign of this Augustus that Jesus was born.) The Roman poet Ovid in his *Metamorphoses*, written about 7 A.D., tells of the visit of the gods Jupiter and Mercury in the guise of mortals seeking respite and finding it in the humble home of Baucis and Philemon.[38] The appearance of gods to men on earth was the stock-in-trade of mythology and poetry in Greece and Rome from Homer onwards. The theme of the visit of the gods in human form goes all the way back to the earliest Greek epic where one finds 'you are doomed, if he is some god come down from heaven. Yes, and the gods in the guise of strangers from afar put on all manner of shapes and visit the cities' (*Odyssey*, 17, 484). Just how seriously these mythological stories were taken is difficult to determine, but that many people really believed in them is evident from the story told in Acts 14:8–18 where Paul and Barnabus are recognised by the Lycaonians as appearances of Hermes and Zeus, the Greek gods with whom Ovid's Jupiter and Mercury are equated.

Although it may be argued that these allusions to divinity are literary conceits, they serve to remind us that such ideas were current in the time of Jesus and were frequently applied to rulers. From these few examples it is clear that a Greco-Roman mythology of descending gods who appear on earth had already been used to interpret the lives of historical figures and existed early enough to be available for Christian appropriation.

In the second century A.D. two pagan authors, Celsus and Lucian of Samosata, wrote important documents dealing with incarnation. The Platonist, Celsus, rejected Christianity and regarded Jesus as but one of many claimants to divinity, pointing to the many prophets in Palestine who wandered about claiming to be God, or a Son of God, or a divine spirit.[39] Celsus' arguments imply a cultural climate in which incarnational claims were acceptable. He insisted that Apollo and Asclepius 'came down' with oracles and miracles, and cited witnesses to this fact. He objected to the claims for Jesus made by Christians, saying that Jesus was not what one would expect a God to be. Origen, a third century Christian Church Father, undertook to reply to Celsus' attack on Christianity, and one of the things he defended was the notion of the virgin birth, which he did by appealing to parallel pagan stories. Thus, Origen lived at a time when such stories were current, and the notion of divine paternity was common.

The other second century pagan author, Lucian of Samosata, attempts to expose the fraudulent claims of divinity of Alexander of Abonuteichos and Peregrinus. Lucian reports that Peregrinus went to Palestine, joined up with the Christians, became a prophet and cult-leader, and 'they revered him as a god . . . next after that other whom they still worship, the man crucified in Palestine . . .'.[40] Lucian's other divine impostor was Alexander of Abonuteichos. Lucian reports that Alexander, using a tame serpent known as Glycon, contrived to be the incarnation of Asclepius, the god of healing. That many believed him and that the cult of Glycon was a long-standing success is well documented.[41]

Mention needs to be made of a book by Philostratus called *The Life of Apollonius*, written in the early third century A.D. The subject of this work is Apollonius of Tyana, a neo-Pythagorean philosopher admired for his asceticism, his remarkable cures and miracles, and his visits to the Hindus of India. *The Life of Apollonius* is thought by many to be the closest parallel of any ancient book to the life of Jesus as found in the synoptic Gospels for the following reasons: his miraculous birth, his divine paternity, his supernatural attributes, his disappearance at death, and his resurrection. However, there is a major difficulty here. What we know of Apollonius of Tyana comes to us mainly from Philostratus, and scholars regard his biography as 'a highly romantic and extremely untrustworthy work', written primarily to counteract the effect of the Christian Gospel by producing a parallel pagan one.[42]

Additional accounts of incarnational myths in the ancient Near East exist, many of which pre-date the Christian era. Recent scholarship suggests that Jewish sources as found in intertestamental literature also dealt with divine paternity, angelic beings, and 'sons of God'. Within Judaism itself the notion of a man being called 'son of God' had a long tradition. King David, King Solomon, even all of Israel were designated sons of God in the Old Testament. Anyone who was obedient to the divine will was a son of God, for the people of Israel thought of themselves as the children of God. Thus the Messiah, the agent through whom God's kingdom would finally be established, would be the preeminent son of God. The Messiah was to be an earthly king and descendant of David, and the ancient kings of David's line, when anointed during the coronation ceremony, were adopted as 'Sons of God'. The words of Psalm 2:7, 'He said to me, You are my son, today I have begotten you', may have been spoken at the coronation ceremony of the king. According to the scholar Sigmund Mowinckel, 'The king stands in a closer relation to Yahweh than anyone else. He is His "son" (Ps. 2:7). In mythological language it is said that Yahweh has "begotten" him, or that he was born of the dawn-goddess on the holy mountain (Ps. 60:3).'[43] According to Psalms 2:7 and 100:3 the enthronement of the Davidic King on Zion is understood as birth and creation through God. It is no coincidence that these two Psalms became important pillars in the early church's christological argument from scripture.

By the time of the Book of Daniel and the first Book of Enoch, i.e. in the apocalyptic and apocryphal literature, an elaborate system of angels and archangels had evolved, and a number of passages refer to these beings as 'sons of God'. Jewish apocalyptic speculation envisioned these supernatural figures as coming down to earth often disguised as men. It is said in Hebrews 13:2 'Do not neglect to show hospitality to strangers, for thereby some have entertained angels unawares.' And in the apocryphal book of Tobit, written in the second century B.C., Azarius declares,

God sent me to heal you and your daughter-in-law, Sarah. I am
Raphael, one of the seven holy angels who present the prayers of
the saints and enter into the presence of the glory of the Holy
One. . . . All these days I merely appeared to you and did not eat
or drink but you were seeing a vision. And now give thanks to
God, for I am ascending to him who sent me.'[44]

Here in an earthly context we meet an angelic redemption figure
who descends and ascends and who, while on earth, appears to be
a man.

In the Hebrew Wisdom literature which shortly preceeded the
New Testament, heavenly Wisdom descends to earth and lives
among men. In the first Book of Enoch (42:1–2), Wisdom comes
down from heaven (descends), but finding no dwelling place
returns to heaven (ascends), and takes her seat among the angels.
Other apocryphal-pseudepigraphal texts such as the Testament of
Job, the Apocalypse of Moses, and the Testament of Abraham, all
written in approximately the first century A.D., present descending angelic redeemer figures.

Philo Judaeus (20 B.C.–A.D. 50) an Alexandrian Jew and contemporary of Paul, was well versed in Greek philosophy and his own
Jewish traditions. He contended that the three visitors to Abraham
in Genesis 18:2 were divine beings incarnated as men. Philo
linked the Logos, the firstborn Son, and the angel of God. He
developed the doctrine of a heavenly Logos–Man, an inter-
mediary-being of the kind Christians were to identify with
Christ. Indeed, while Philo sometimes spoke of this heavenly
figure in personal terms, for him the Logos was not truly personal.
He did not identify his heavenly Logos–Man with any particular
figure. While it is impossible to establish conclusively whether
Philo's writings were known to have influenced the authors of the
New Testament books, it is reasonable to assume that Philo was
but one voice within a culture of Hellenistic Judaism, and that
New Testament writers such as Paul and John may have come
under similar influence. The apocryphal book, *The Wisdom of
Solomon*, which existed prior to Philo, brought together various
concepts. The resulting configuration yielded a divine redeemer
figure who is alternately identified as wisdom–logos–angel–Holy
Spirit (ch. 9:18). In this mythology the redeemer figure is personal,

and she is sent from the heavens as a saviour figure for this world (ch. 7:27; 8:10) and for the next (ch. 6:18–20).

Another example of incarnationism may have arisen in Samaria, the ancient northern kingdom of Palestine. The Samaritans were an established heterodox Jewish community centuries before Jesus, and a powerful influence in the first century of the Christian era. The doctrine of incarnation was an accepted belief among the Samaritans in the first decade of the Christian era. One of their religious leaders, Simon Magus, the Samaritan messiah, established himself as an incarnation of one facet of God, and in the New Testament we find him asking Peter and John to bestow the Holy Spirit upon him (Acts, 8:18–19). Between the years 30 and 40 of our era, Simon Magus referred to himself as 'the Standing One', an enigmatic title representing his claim to divinity. The Church father, Justin, wrote:

> There was a Samaritan, Simon, a native of the village of Gitto, who in the reign of Claudius Caesar, and in your royal city of Rome, did mighty acts of magic. He was considered a god . . . and almost all the Samaritans, and a few even of other nations, worship him, and acknowledge him as the first God.[45]

Michael Goulder, a British scholar, contends that Paul appropriated the idea of Jesus' incarnation in the course of discussion with the Samaritan missionaries in Corinth and Ephesus between A.D. 50 and 55.[46] Goulder believes that this is one of the most significant influences upon the incarnation concept in Christianity.

There is also the notion that the Christian concept of incarnation may have been influenced by Greek mystery cults and mystery language. The figures of Osiris, Isis, Adonis, and Attis, as well as the Eleusinian and Dionysian mysteries utilising dying and rising gods, are frequently thought to have influenced early Christian thinking. Yet these deities were born on this earth and began their existence at that point in time; they might descend into death and the underworld, but they had not descended into life and were not sent by a heavenly father. The cult of Mithras, which is a survival from Persia, had little if anything to do with the later mystery cults. The scholar Martin Hengel has quite clearly distinguished between the mystery cults and early Christianity.[47]

Certain biblical scholars, such as the renowned Rudolf Bultmann, have suggested that a Gnostic redeemer-myth influenced ideas of Christ's incarnation. Some of the so-called Gnostic sects which flourished in the early centuries of the Christian era believed in an archetypal, heavenly figure who descended into the world to reveal the secrets of the universe and the destiny of man. They believed that Jesus was the son of Joseph and Mary into which the Holy Spirit was poured. The Holy Spirit was called 'virgin spirit'. It was feminine and it descended into Jesus, not Mary.[48] Most Gnostic sects believed in the doctrine of emanations called 'eons', which were actual forces, flowing from God and in whom God was revealed. They believed that the greatest of these emanations was Christ.[49] However, these Gnostic sects may have existed before, during, or after the early Christian community. So who influenced whom? Was there any influence at all? It is difficult to establish.

All of the aforementioned sources form a rather large and complex configuration of elements that existed prior to, or around the time of Jesus. In summary, they are: (a) The use of titles such as 'son of God', used with a wide range of implications and applied to both human and superhuman beings; (b) The apotheosis or ascent of an exceptional man to the heavenly realm; (c) Belief in heavenly beings or intermediaries, the first of whom might have been God's instrument in creation, others who might descend to assist man, and one who might act as God's viceregent in judgement at the end of time; (d) Salvation imparted to initiates through mystical identification with a dying and rising god as practiced by certain mystery-religions; (e) The coming of an archetypal, heavenly figure into the world to reveal the secrets of the universe and the destiny of spiritual man, as portrayed in certain Gnostic redeemer myths; and (f) The manifestation of the chief of these heavenly beings on earth in a genuine incarnation.

While full-scale redeemer-myths are found after Jesus and not before, there does not seem to be an exact analogy to the fully developed Christian claims about Jesus in any literature that is definitely pre-Christian. However, as the scholar A. D. Nock stated, 'the impact of the figure of Jesus crystallised elements which were already there'.[50] The incarnational mythology current at the time of Jesus allows for the possibility that the early Christians produced accounts with parallel motifs to explain their perception of Jesus the Christ.

If one were to apply the general pattern for the mythic hero to

the life of Jesus, one would find that of the twenty-two characteristics developed by Lord Raglan that comprise this pattern,
seventeen clearly apply to Jesus. They are: (1) virgin mother, (4)
unusual conception, (5) hero reputed to be son of god, (6) attempt
to kill hero, (7) hero spirited away [flight into Egypt], (8) reared by
foster parents [Joseph], (9) no details of childhood, (10) goes to
future kingdom, (13) becomes 'king' (cf. the mock title of king of
the Jews: INRI), (14) 'reigns' uneventfully for a time, (15) pre-
scribes laws, (16) loses favour with some of his 'subjects' (e.g.
Judas), (17) driven from throne and city, (18) meets with mysterious death, (19) at the top of a hill, (21) body is not buried, and (22)
he has a holy sepulcher. According to Professor Alan Dundes,
these seventeen characteristics indicate that the life of Jesus con-
forms more closely with the mythic hero pattern than does the life
of Apollo, Asclepius, Zeus, Joseph, Elijah, and Siegfried, and he
concludes that Lord Raglan's hero pattern 'provides a new vantage
point for those who seek to understand the life of Jesus as it is
reported in the Gospels'.[51] The fifth characteristic of Raglan's hero
pattern, 'hero reputed to be son of god' is the incarnational motif
and the focus of our concern. We have already investigated this
motif in India and have seen how it was applied to Vishnu's
Avatars. How this theme came to be applied to Jesus in the
religion of Christianity is the subject of the next sub-heading.

THE INCARNATION MYTH IN CHRISTIANITY

In proclaiming the Incarnation, Resurrection, and Ascension of
the Word, the Christian Fathers were sure that they were not
putting forth a new myth. Actually, they were employing the
categories of mythical thought. Obviously they could not recognize this mythical thought in the desacralized mythologies of
the pagan scholars who were their contemporaries. But it is clear
that for Christians of all creeds the center of religious life is
constituted by the drama of Jesus Christ. Although played out in
History, this drama first established the possibility of salvation;
hence there is only one way to gain salvation – to reiterate this
exemplary drama ritually and to imitate the supreme model
revealed by the life and teaching of Jesus. Now, this type of

religious behavior is bound up with genuine mythical thought.[52]

(Mircea Eliade)

In approaching the subject of incarnation in the Christian tradition, we should note that the Word of God speaks through or with the words of man and uses the language of man. The Word of God communicated through language often necessitates a mythical context, and the language of myth is prominent among the ways human beings speak. In dealing with as momentous a figure as Jesus Christ it is well to remember that when something is extraordinary there is a human impulse to ascribe to it a miraculous character. This is the way that man evokes wonder at what may indeed deserve wonder. A narrative miraculous in character is often the very best way to convey a mystery that may or may not be miraculous.

The early Christian vision of reality as revealed in the Christian scriptures had a dynamic character rich in both history and myth. Myth is not meant here in a pejorative sense, but rather as a rich, meaningful and significant interpretation of reality. Mythology was pervasive in the New Testament as it was in the Old Testament and throughout the ancient Near East. The New Testament scholarship of Rudolf Bultmann has elucidated much of the mythic dimension of the Christian scriptures. He has shown that in New Testament times people believed that the world consisted of three levels – heaven, earth, and hell – and that they believed that supernatural beings could ascend and descend as on a 'celestial elevator',[53] thus making the intervention by supernatural beings, the resurrection–ascension, and the second coming of Christ, credible.

The early Christian community expected Jesus to return as the Son of Man on the clouds of heaven, bringing salvation to some and damnation to others as judge of the world, and inaugurating the Kingdom of God on earth. This eschatological vision is a mythic image. In addition, Jesus is set in a mythological context when he is said to have been begotten of the Holy Spirit and born of a virgin. Furthermore, the conception of the pre-existent Son of God who descends into human form to redeem mankind is analogous to certain ancient redeemer myths. The New Testament phrases, 'He descended from heaven', or simply 'He descended', are terms indicating movement in space that do not describe the nature of God's redeeming activity, but are mythological in form.[54]

What is paradoxical is that the Christian scriptures, like the Jewish scriptures before them, are demonstratively mythoclastic, i.e. they adamantly reject pagan myth. However, both Testaments substitute one type of myth for another, and, as Amos Wilder suggests, in both Testaments myth is overcome with the help of myth.[55] Furthermore, both Testaments consist of a complex inter-relationship between the historical and the mythical.

Myths take place in mythical time like the forty days of the flood or the seven days of creation, and they usually do not involve the element of historical time. However, the New Testament blends the mythical with the historical. The New Testament scholar, Norman Perrin, suggests that this commingling developed in three ways: (a) a correlation between the factual data of history and the claims of the myth; (b) the use of myth to interpret and give meaning to history; and (c) the history itself as remembered and retold becoming the bearer of the myth.[56] The New Testament account of God incarnate consists of all three of these develop-ments. As for the correlation between myth and history, while Jesus may or may not have made personal claims to be divine, the New Testament writers did make extensive claims for him, one of which was that he exemplified an incarnate deity. As for the second development, the myth offering meaning to history, Jesus as the Incarnation of God is represented as fulfilling the Old Testament prophecies of a redeemer–saviour sent by God as a redemption for sin. Here the myth is a vivid, pictorial way of interpreting the history. As for the last, history itself functioning as myth, the narration of events in the New Testament helps to bring out the significance of those events for future generations. The story of Jesus becomes a new covenant with the focal point being God's self-revelation to humankind. The history itself, mythicized as that historical time when Jesus walked upon the earth, has become a mythic sacred time.

The New Testament presents a dual vision of Jesus: historical and mythical. Jesus of Nazareth is a man of history occupying time and space, while 'Jesus the Christ' is a mythical–theological ex-pression of the community's faith in an extraordinary charismatic being. The view of Jesus modulates between history and myth and is a sharing of what the early writers both understood and felt. It is

extremely difficult in the New Testament to penetrate to the actual
Jesus of history and to reconstruct the historical Jesus, partially
because the reports of his teachings and conversations began to be
written down after the lapse of at least a full generation, during
which time the oral tradition modified the memories to serve the
purpose of the communities. In addition, Jesus' contemporaries
viewed him through their particular perspective. For example, in
the minds of the first century Jews who were his disciples, he embodied the Jewish idea of the anointed one (messiah, in Hebrew;
christos, in Greek). Others viewed him as a rabbi, a prophet,
a king, or a saviour. Consequently, while the gospels give us a
coherent picture of the kinds of things that Jesus said and did,
very few today argue that they are actual verbatim records.

In viewing the figure of Jesus Christ it is helpful to distinguish
between 'the historical Jesus' and 'the biblical Christ'. The 'historical Jesus' is a reconstruction on the basis of the gospels, using
sayings, parables, teachings, and remembered deeds and actions.
The 'biblical Christ' is the mythological and theological interpretation of Jesus by the early Christian community that thought of him
as divine. The biblical Christ includes the nativity, the miracles,
the pre-existent Logos, the resurrection, the ascension, the eschaton and the incarnation, most of which are well illustrated in the
Fourth Gospel. The biblical Christ contains some elements of the
historical Jesus, but it is an alteration and transformation – a
mythicization.

All too little is known about the historical Jesus of Nazareth. It
has been calculated that, apart from the forty days and nights in
the wilderness (of which we are told almost nothing) everything
reported to have been said and done by Jesus in all four gospels
could have been accomplished in three weeks. Father Jacques
Guillet's study of the gospels concludes

> that Jesus never attributed to himself the quality of Son of God,
> that he did not present himself as the Messiah, and that,
> although he spoke of the coming of the Son of Man in the style of
> the apocalypses, he had no intention of identifying himself with
> the Son of Man, but only of announcing the imminent coming of
> the Kingdom of God.[57]

Of course we can never really know what Jesus thought and
knew about himself. He may have used the mysterious title 'Son of

Man' with reference to himself, and this could have encouraged his disciples to think of him as messiah, the anointed son of David, but he never identified himself as 'Son of God'. It is difficult to imagine that Jesus, being a Jew and a monotheist, thought of himself as God (Yahweh), but more likely as God's agent or servant. It is also extremely unlikely that he thought of himself, or that his first disciples thought of him, as God incarnate. It is more likely that in their relationships with Jesus, the earliest disciples came to the new conviction of the presence and activity of God in their midst, and thus became convinced that God was somehow present and working in and through this man.

The doctrine of the Incarnation was not revealed by Jesus, but emerged in the early church as a way of expressing Jesus' significance. The context of the doctrine was one in which it was not uncommon to refer to an extraordinary human figure as a son of God. The early church saw Jesus as the man whom God had raised and given the Holy Spirit to pour out upon the church (Acts 2:33). Some of the earliest Christians found that they encountered God through Jesus in a manner that entirely filled their lives. As the community grew, more and more men and women experienced the excitement and peace of the 'new way', until before one generation had passed after his crucifixion, they came to think of Jesus as virtually divine. Accordingly, we find in Pliny's report to the Emperor Trajan written about A.D. 112, that the Christians were accustomed to meet before daybreak and recite hymns to Christ as to a god. It was with the writings of Paul, followed by the synoptic Gospels and the Gospel of John, that an incarnational image began to encompass the figure of Jesus. A metaphorical image became a metaphysical doctrine, and although objective in reference and taken to be 'true', the claim that Jesus is God was not an item of empirical knowledge among Jesus' contemporaries and did not emerge in any writings that we know of before A.D. 55 at the earliest.[58]

Scholars and theologians have argued vehemently over the years as to whether Jesus is called 'God' in the New Testament. Jesus is called many names and titles in the New Testament, among which are Lord (Kyrios), King, Priest, Prophet, Son of Man, Son of God, the Word, Christos, Christ, Messiah, suffering Messiah, Messiah designate (Acts 3:20), suffering servant, the lamb of God, Immanuel, High Priest, mediator, Saviour, and God. There are a number of passages therein which imply that Jesus is divine, but few in which the word God (*theos*) explicitly refers to Jesus. The calling of Jesus 'Lord' (Kyrios), is not the same as saying that he is God (Theos), but rather places him on a level approximating God. 'Lord' suggests and may even assert divinity but it is not equated with God. There is no evidence that Jesus was called God in the earliest layers of New Testament tradition. If we date New Testament times from 30 to 110, quite clearly the use of 'God' for Jesus belongs to the second half of that period and becomes frequent only toward the end of the period. Jesus is never called 'God' in the synoptic gospels and even the fourth gospel does not portray Jesus as saying specifically that he is God. The sermons that the book of Acts attributes to the beginning of the Christian mission do not speak of Jesus as God. The suggestion that Jesus is God ('Theos') begins to surface between A.D. 55 and 85, and becomes explicit in The Letter to the Hebrews. Paul does not use the title 'God' for Jesus in any epistle written before A.D. 58.[59] Paul may be calling Jesus 'God' in Romans 9:5, but this is debatable and depends upon how this passage was punctuated.[60]

Paul's varied christological expressions include elements that are incarnational. Of these, one of the most important is his use of the phrase 'Son of God' (Huios Theou) occurring fifteen times in the Pauline epistles. Jesus stands in the closest possible relationship to God, for Paul's favourite phrase, 'his Son', points to the similarity between God and Jesus. For Paul, God's sending of his Son is a unique and decisive act; it is thoroughly new, yet in continuity with God's relationship with Israel and marks its fulfilment. In the letter to the Galatians, Paul writes, 'God sent forth his Son . . . in order that he might redeem those who were under the law' (Gal. 4:4). Very similar in structure is the Johannine passage 'God sent the Son into the world . . . in order that the world might be saved through him' (John 3:17). In Galatians the sending of the Son is not a timeless statement but a unique and definitive act that takes place 'in the fullness of time'. There is no exact parallel in Hellenistic Judaism, for even in the Wisdom of Solomon there is not found the eschatology and soteriology that is implicit in Paul. For Paul, the heart of incarnational christology lies in the sending of the Son to save mankind in the fullness of time. All mankind, according to Paul, is under the dominion of sin and death. Only God can be the rescuer; only God can save man. And yet, even God could not do so without entering, in some sense, into our human condition, for man's enemy is not external to him, but internal. Thus, God's saving action had to take place in and through a man. As through one man had come sin and death (Adam), so through another man must come deliverance and life (Christ). The humanity as well as the divinity of Jesus Christ are essential, for Paul. H. J. Schoeps comments that 'it was Paul who for the first time, reflecting on the messianic figure (of Jesus), made out of a title of dignity an ontological affirmation and raised it to a mythical level of thought'.[61] And Martin Hengel indicates that Paul's conception of Jesus is that he is identical with a divine being, before all time, mediator between God and his creatures, and thus the Son of God.[62]

The Gospel of John written approximately A.D. 90–95 embraces incarnationism and goes full distance, stopping just short of Docetism. The purpose of this gospel is boldly declared, 'These (things) are written that you may believe that Jesus is the Christ, the Son of God' (John 20:31). In John's gospel we have a highly developed explicit christology that even asserts that he is God (Theos). John 1:1 states that 'the Word was God'. This is not 'with God' or 'divine', but *God*. Furthermore, in John 20:28 Thomas is quoted as saying 'My Lord and my God'. The explicit affirmation of John's gospel is that the Incarnation *is* God. 'We have beheld his glory' writes John, 'glory as of the only Son from the Father' (1:14). Here there is no transfiguration scene, for the constant glory of the earthly Jesus leaves no room for it. There are indications that Jesus is omniscient and that there are not limits to his latent, but available, power. It is even suggested that he was not really susceptible to weariness, hunger, or thirst. He is seen as always in complete control, both of what he does and what happens to him. Even his dying is a deliberate act and he knows that he 'had come from God and was going to God' (13:3). The unification of the Father and the Son belongs to the Fourth Gospel and is found in such sayings as 'I and the Father are one' (John 10:30), and 'Anyone who has seen me has seen the Father' (John 14:9). In Jesus is incarnated the 'medium' through which God is seen, his purpose revealed and his fore-ordained will accomplished. The Fourth Gospel portrays a glorified Jesus who is fully deified.

In the synoptic gospels, Jesus is seen within the limits of his earthly life and ministry. The synoptic gospels express what Jesus said and did, while the Johannine gospel is an interpretation of what Jesus represents. John's gospel expresses the understanding of the divine significance of Jesus, which was developing in

Christian circles toward the end of the first century. What seems to have happened during the sixty years following Jesus' death was that the language of divine sonship was transplanted from the soil of Jewish thought and developed a new meaning as it took root again in the Greco-Roman world. Thus the meaning given to Jesus was first expressed by saying that he was the messiah, to whom the Old Testament God had said, 'Thou art my beloved Son'; and this divine sonship became understood in the Christian community as his being God's only begotten son and subsequently of one substance with God. The acclamation of Jesus as God was a response of a believing community to the God who was thought to reveal Himself to men. John 1:18 speaks of the only Son who has revealed the Father, and John 16:28 tells that the son 'came from the Father . . . into the world'. In the late New Testament period can be observed a progression from regarding Jesus as the *Logos* of God to regarding him as the very 'Godness of God'. For many Christians Jesus ceased to be identified merely with the *Logos*, and came to be regarded as God Himself. The confession of Jesus as God is a recognition of the sovereignty and lordship of divine rule in, through, and by Jesus. It is explicitly found in the epistle to the Hebrews, written around A.D. 95–105. All of this incarnational imagery reflected the belief that Jesus was God incarnate, later made doctrinally explicit in such phrases as 'begotten not made, of one substance with the Father, through whom all things were made' as declared in the Nicene Creed. The image of God's descent and incarnation was applied to the historical figure of Jesus transforming the view of him into the biblical and divine Christ.

If perchance the image of the 'son of God' is taken literally it can easily be misleading. When it is linked with the idea of the virgin birth it appears to be interpreting the relation of Jesus to God as almost the same as that of a human son to a father in a genetic and physiological sense, and as a biological fact about Jesus' physical being. But the image of the 'son of God' is not so much an explanation of *how*, as an expression of *what* the significance of Jesus is. When 'son of God' is taken literally it reinforces a mythological structure, turning Jesus into a half-human, half-divine creature, such as the Avatars of Hinduism or the mythological demigods of ancient Greece. The Chalcedonian doctrine of the two natures of Jesus leads to the image of a kind of pasted-together being,[63] and tends to promote mythological, superman-like powers for Jesus, especially his miracles and his descent to earth. The prevailing view of the Christian Church for the past fifteen centuries has been that Jesus Christ is one person with two natures. Arminius described Jesus as 'the Son of God and the son of man, consisting of two natures'.[64] Luther declared 'We merge the two distinct natures into one single person, and say: God is man and man is God.'[65] Calvin said of Christ that 'the divinity was so conjoined and united with the humanity, that the entire properties of each nature remain entire, and yet the two natures constitute only one Christ'.[66] However, the New Testament never explicitly states that Jesus has two natures. The idea of the two natures of Jesus is a product of Greek philosophical thought based on categories of 'substance' and 'essence', and may well be an outgrowth of a two-fold description of Jesus, one as human and the other as divine. As early as 381, Gregory, Archbishop of Constantinople, wrote that Jesus was 'in the body circumscribed, uncircumscribed in Spirit; at once earthly and heavenly, tangible and intangible, comprehensible and incomprehensible'.[67] Loraine Boettner states that 'in view of the fact that Christ has two natures, and depending on which nature we have in mind, it is proper to say that He is infinite or that He is finite, that He existed from eternity or that He was born in Bethlehem, that He was omniscient or that He was limited in knowledge'.[68] And Augustus Strong asserts that 'the union of the two natures in Christ's person is necessarily inscrutable, because there are no analogies to it in our experience'.[69] Could it be that the doctrine of the Incarnation within Christianity has been a mystery because what was transformed into ecclesiastical dogma was originally an historical and a mythical image?

The next issue to be raised is whether it is possible in Christianity for there to be more than one incarnation, as there certainly is in Hinduism. In the gospel of John, Jesus promises that 'I will pray the Father, and he shall give you another comforter, that he may abide with you forever' (14:16), and 'I will see you again, and your heart shall rejoice' (16:22). Let us acknowledge that the 'scandal' of Christianity was not the incarnation but the crucifixion and resurrection (I Cor. 1:23). Incarnation was not as unbelievable as a crucified messiah and his resurrection. Yet the Christian belief in the uniqueness of Jesus, and the Church's stance on the exclusivity of the Incarnation has been the insuperable obstacle to ecumenism between a Christian church like the Roman Catholic and any

non-Christian religion. In light of this it is extremely interesting
that the outstanding theologian of the Catholic Church, St.
Thomas Aquinas, should have devoted considerable attention in
his *Summa Theologiae* to an inquiry into the possibility of other
incarnations of God. It is even more interesting, because so
unexpected, that Thomas held other incarnations of God to be
possible.

In the *Summa* (part 3, question 3, articles 5–8 and question 4,
articles 4–6), Thomas points out that either the Father or the
Holy Spirit could have incarnated just as the Son did. They could
have become human in place of, or in addition to, the Son.
Thomas speculates on the possibility of incarnations stemming
from each of the triune deity and concludes that it is possible. He
also theorizes on the ability of the Father and the Son to be capable
of multiple incarnations, and again arrives at a positive conclusion. Thomas concludes that

> the Son, the eternal Word, is perfectly capable of becoming
> again incarnate in another, a different individual human body
> and soul, born of another mother, or born of another mother and
> father, of a different sex, a different race, in a different country
> at a different time, speaking a different language, using a
> completely different set of human imagery to preach his mes-
> sage and to explain God's relation to the human family.[70]

Thomas discusses how the Son did not choose his human nature
because of the specific characteristics that Jesus possessed. 'God
did not become man in order to be Jewish, male, first-century, of
such and such a height and weight and skin-colour.'[71] Rather, God
chose man for the sake of having universal human nature. For
Thomas Aquinas, Father, Son, and Holy Spirit could all become
incarnate in one human being simultaneously, or in several individuals.

With this in mind, we need only point out that there have been
other incarnational claims in Christianity, in addition to Christ.
One example is Ann Lee (1736–84), founder of the United Society
of Believers in Christ's Second Appearing, commonly known as
the Shakers. Ann Lee claimed to be the second appearance of
Christ, and the incarnation of the Heavenly Father and the Divine
Mother. In the 1930s, Father Divine (born George Baker) claimed
to be God, and was so regarded by members of the Divine Peace

Mission movement.[72] In the 1970s, the founder of the Holy Spirit Association for the Unification of World Christianity, Reverend Sun Myung Moon, was regarded by Unification Church members as the Lord of the Second Coming. While Christianity has always held that Jesus Christ is the unique incarnation, the anticipation of his second coming has given rise to additional claims of incarnation.

The next sub-heading elucidates the various ways in which the Avatars are similar to Jesus, as well as clarifies how Jesus is distinctly different from the Hindu God-men.

CONCLUSION

Similarities Between Avatars and Christ

I pity the Christian who does not reverence the Hindu Christ.

I pity the Hindu who does not see the beauty in Jesus Christ's Character.

(Swami Vivekananda)

Whether the God-man is born in India or in Judea he is regarded with awe, devotion, and love. The devotees and disciples of Avatars willingly surrender their egos to the charismatic God-man bathed in golden glory. At the core of devotion to the God-man is the conviction that he is the embodiment of love, that he is the great *Bhakta*. His teaching is grounded in love, and it demonstrates God's unconditional love for man. As God graciously loves man, so man is to take counsel from this love and learn to love one another, and especially to love the God-man. Love is the essential lesson.

The God-man chooses an inner coterie of disciples and attracts an outer group of admirers. Jesus had his circle of twelve disciples and a larger group of admirers who regarded him as a prophet and a miracle-worker. Likewise, the Avatars often have a coterie with whom they reveal esoteric knowledge and special signs. Ramakrishna and Krishnamurti, like Jesus, had twelve disciples, and Chaitanya and Meher Baba had a close circle of disciples.

If for a moment we imagine Jesus born within an eastern context instead of a western one, in Bengal instead of Bethlehem, we could expect him to be hailed as an Avatar, for this would have been the appropriate expression within India for the same spiritual phenomenon that occurred in ancient Palestine. Evidence can be found within the New Testament, from the writings in Mark and Acts to Paul and John, for a transformation of the portrait of Jesus from what Hindus would term a man-God (Jivanmukti) to a God-man (Avatar).

Professor Parrinder's full-scale study of God-men lists twelve characteristics of Avatars, which are: (1) The Avatar is real; (2) The human Avatars take worldly birth; (3) The lives of Avatars mingle divine and human; (4) The Avatars finally die; (5) There may be historicity in some Avatars; (6) Avatars are repeated; (7) The example and character of the Avatars is important; (8) The Avatar comes with work to do; (9) The Avatars show some reality in the world; (10) The Avatar is a guarantee of divine revelation; (11) Avatars reveal a personal God; (12) Avatars reveal a God of grace.[73] These principal implications of Avatars share many features with Jesus Christ as a God-man. For the Christian, all of these characteristics can be applied to Jesus with the exception of number six. The similarities that exist between the Avatars and Jesus Christ rest upon certain common features of their birth, life, death, and expected return. The Avatars are Christ-like in that their births are frequently foretold, i.e., Vishnu announces to one or both of the parents of the Avatar that he is going to be reborn. Indian religions do not have a doctrine of virgin birth as does Roman Catholicism, but the Avatars are 'conceived' in heaven and 'implanted' in an earthly mother much as Jesus was. All God-men participate in the general notion that they originate in heaven, just as the New Testament says of Jesus, 'The first man was of the earth, a man of dust; the second man is from heaven' (1 Cor. 15:47).

Concerning the accomplishments of the God-men during their lifetimes, the Avatars demonstrate their omnipotence by producing miracles, entering states of superconsciousness, and resurrecting people from the dead. Jesus' healings, exorcisms, resurrections, and miracles are a paradigm for what a God-man does during his ministry here on earth. The Avatars receive a spiritual name, such as Baba, Sai, Divine Mother, World Teacher, much as Jesus received a spiritual epithet, the Christ, and these divine names elicit reverence, awe, and devotion.

That Jesus Christ suffered and died upon the cross, that he endured agony and that he accepted it, is taken as the tribulation that a God-man must endure on earth in order to reveal the human side of his nature. The model of Jesus and his crucifixion has entered the general consciousness of mankind. Meher Baba suffered one mishap after another and viewed it as the divine plan that Avatars must suffer. Ramakrishna was afflicted with cancer of the throat, which was his 'cross to bear'. Concerning Ramakrishna's death, Romain Rolland had this to report:

> Those who knew how terrible was the disease from which he died (cancer of the throat) marvelled at the loving and kindly smile that never left him. If the glorious death upon the Cross was denied to this man, who is the Christ to his Indian followers, his bed of agony was no less a Cross. And yet he could say, 'Only the body suffers. When the mind is united to God it can feel no pain.'[74]

As in Christianity where Jesus' suffering is understood as an atonement for human sins, so the dying Ramakrishna was addressed by a devotee who said, 'Sir, your illness is for the sake of others. You take upon yourself the sins of those who come to you. You fall ill because you accept their sins.'[75]

God-men tend to inspire the belief that the end of the age is near and the eschaton is rapidly approaching. The suspicion arises that the advent of God to earth as evidenced in the God-man may be a sign that an apocalypse is about to occur. That is why many Avatars have been thought to be Kalki in disguise, the apocalyptic Avatar, and why many Christians await the second coming of Christ at the supposed end of the age. God-men seem to inspire eschatological expectations in the minds of their followers, especially with the hope that they shall inaugurate a kingdom inhabited by devoted and righteous individuals.

For these reasons millions of Hindus believe that Jesus Christ is an Avatar and see no distinction between the Christian God-man and their own God-men. This is largely due to their mystical view of Christ. Ramakrishna's disciple, Swami Vivekananda, voiced this attitude years ago when he called upon people to 'become Christ' and to delve into the 'Christ within'. Gandhi expressed a similar attitude when he asked,

> What, then, does Jesus mean to me? To me, He was one of the greatest teachers humanity has ever had. To his believers, He

was God's only begotten son. Could the fact that I do or do not accept this belief make Jesus have any more or less influence in my life? Is all the grandeur of His teaching and of His doctrine to be forbidden to me? I cannot believe so. To me it implies a spiritual birth. My interpretation, in other words, is that in Jesus' own life is the key to His nearness to God; that He expressed, as no other could, the spirit and will of God. It is in this sense that I see Him and recognise Him as the son of God.[76]

Nevertheless, many Christians feel uneasy about the comparison between the Avatars and Christ but are simply at a loss as to how to make a critical differentiation. Numerous people, Hindus, Westerners, even Christians, when they are in the presence of Satya Sai Baba, feel that they are witnessing the glory of God, and tend to associate their own experience with those who witnessed the life of Jesus two thousand years ago. The many similarities that God-men share give the grand impression that these similarities extend beyond coincidence, and that they all possess divinity.

Distinctions between Avatars and Christ

Priest: It is our faith that if we seek such a one, in meekness and innocence, it is *only* in Jesus of Nazareth that we can 'dare to believe' such a thing has happened – and is happening without cease. We other human beings image ourselves to be the only ones to understand ourselves. Jesus Christ *knew* that 'only the Father knows his mystery' – and so knew that only he knows the 'Father.'
Swami: Yes, we have those, too, that in 'meekness and inno-cence' believe that only *their* Savior is completely given over to the mystery. But would you agree, at least hypothetically, that any human being who knows that only the Father – or Mother – knows his mystery *is* Christ?[77]

(John Moffitt, 'Incarnation and Avatars:
an Imaginary Conversation')

Soul and Sole
Having discussed the most prominent similarities between Avatars and Christ, let us now turn to the differences. First, the Avatars possess a 'yogic consciousness'. The general Hindu attitude contends that yoga assists in the spiritualization of man so

that something God-like may be uncovered in the deepest reaches of the soul, which connects man with the divine. The various types of yoga afford man a means by which to attain transcendent consciousness (*samadhi*) and become united with God. Hinduism suggests that the individual soul (*jivatman*) becomes one with the Supreme soul (*Paratman*) as it rediscovers its true identity. In Hinduism, where the individual enshrines the eternal soul of the universe (*Brahman-atman*), there are numerous instances where the divine shines forth in a conspicuous manner in Avatars. In Christianity a sole incarnation highlights the divinity enshrined in Jesus.

Unlike the Hindu Avatars, Jesus does not possess a yogic consciousness but rather a theocentric consciousness. Jesus' life was centered entirely upon the being, grace, and demands of God. His entire life was dominated by a total and overwhelming passion for God. 'It is in Jesus, and Jesus alone, that there is nothing of self to be seen, but solely the ultimate, unconditional love of God.'[78] His message, grounded in love, is concerned with the attitudes that people are to have toward God and then toward one another. His teaching is to do the will of God, to follow the way of God, not to become God. In Christianity, God's becoming human neither implies that each man and woman can become God, nor does God come to earth for the purpose of divinizing human nature. Rather, in Christianity, Jesus is the unique 'son of God', revealed once and for all as the sole locus in human existence where God's revelation and presence are to be found. Hinduism denies the exclusive belief in a sole incarnation, placing its faith in ascending and descending souls that occasionally manifest as Avatars.

The Serpent – Good and Evil

The epilogue to book one pointed out the supernatural relationship between the Avatars and the cobra. The spiritual relationship between Avatar and royal serpent has its basis in the myths dealing with Vishnu and Sesha, Vishna and Vasuki, and Krishna and Kaliya. The multi-headed cobra Sesha protects and shields Vishnu, and the cobra Vasuki aids the Kurma (Tortoise) Avatar in retrieving the elixir of immortality from the Ocean of Milk. The cobra serves as Vishnu's bed and canopy while he sleeps between the world's ages, and is homologous with Vishnu himself.

The cobra is both the source of life as the cosmic ocean, and the agent of death as producer of the cosmic poison. The residue of the cosmogony is both poison and elixir, a potion of death and a medicine of life, depending upon the state of being of whoever partakes of it. Krishna frees mankind from the threat and peril of the serpent Kaliya, yet he recognizes the rights of the destructive power, for the venomous serpent is as much a manifestation of the Supreme Lord as are the good forces. Therefore Krishna banishes Kaliya to a remote region rather than annihilate him altogether. Kaliya is allowed to remain unchanged both in power and in nature.

The mythical serpent is conceived of as both poisonous and health-giving. In tribal folklore, various parts of the snake are believed to cure ailments and the serpent itself is the guarantee of health and wholeness. It is the homeopathic treatment that uses poison to cure poison and that views the snake as the one creature capable of overcoming venom. Asclepius, the Greek god of healing, possessed a staff with a serpent coiled around it, and this evolved into the caduceus, a staff with two entwined snakes, the symbol associated with medicine. Likewise, the serpent that was raised by Moses in the desert, was to cure the Hebrews of snake-bite, for the Lord said unto Moses, 'Make a fiery serpent, and set it on a pole; and every one who is bitten, when he sees it, shall live' (Numbers 21:8–9).

A reflection of this harmonious inter-relation is found today on a popular level in the village of Shirala in Southwestern India, where the cobra is worshipped and celebrated at a serpent festival. The people of Shirala live in perfect harmony with the cobras. They view cobras as symbols of Shiva and his generative power; therefore, the women feed and worship the cobras in the hope that they will be fertile. The villagers believe that Shiva offered one of their ancient sages a boon. The sage asked that his people be protected for all time against the cobras so common in their fields. The boon was granted, and ever since the people of Shirala have believed that they have nothing to fear from the cobra, emblem of the god himself. The cobra has received the epithet *Nulla Pambu*, the 'good snake', and nobody is ever bitten there.[79] A similar attitude is found on the fictitious island of Pala, where an Oriental child says, 'snakes are your brothers; snakes have a right to your compassion and your respect; snakes, in a word, are good, good, good'. When the Western visitor insists that 'snakes are also poisonous, poisonous, poisonous', the child replies, 'but if you remember that they're just as good as they're poisonous, and act accordingly, they won't use their poison'.[80]

In the Western tradition the serpent stands for chaos, evil, death, and the forces of destruction, and it must be conquered and cut to pieces in order that the cosmos may survive. The basis of serpent lore in the Judeo-Christian tradition has its origin in the Garden of Eden. This serpent has become associated in the Western mind with disobedience, evil, sin, Eve, woman, etc. A legend from the Jewish Midrash explains that menstruation is a punishment for Eve's sin, and folklore further connects the cause of menstruation with the bite of the snake.[81]

Mythologist Joseph Campbell explains that goddesses and their serpents were strongly associated with early agricultural civilizations. When the Semitic people invaded the neighbouring farming tribes, they initiated a struggle between their masculine deity and the various goddesses whose symbol of life and rebirth was the serpent. In many traditions there occurred a merging of the two, e.g. Zeus married the goddesses of some of the neighbouring civilizations and cohabited with numerous nymphs and wives. But in the Hebraic tradition there was no such marriage. The goddess was viewed as an abomination, and associated with her was her symbol of life, the serpent. The patriarchal accent of the Bible includes a degradation of the imagery associated with the goddess and the serpent. According to Campbell, 'the Bible is the only tradition where the serpent is condemned and regarded as absolutely evil'.[82]

The serpent as an image of evil appears in both Old and New Testaments. The Israelites began to worship the fiery bronze serpent that Moses had made, calling it Nehushtan. It is likely that Nehushtan was the name of a snake deity associated with a form of Canaan's Baal religion. Hezekiah, king of Judea, called it 'a thing of brass', and destroyed it (II Kings 18:4). Later the prophet Isaiah asked God, 'was it not thou that didst cut Rahab in pieces, that didst pierce the dragon?' (Isaiah 51:9–11). And Jesus called the Pharisees serpents and vipers destined for hell (Matt. 23:33). In the book of Revelation, 'that ancient serpent, who is called the Devil and Satan, the deceiver of the whole world – he was thrown down to the earth, and his angels were thrown down with him . . . and when the dragon saw that he had been thrown down to the earth, he pursued the woman who had borne the male child' (Rev. 12:9, 13). The serpent imagery in the Bible culminates in the cross on Golgotha which pins the serpent's head and holds chaos and sin in check. Mary, the mother of Jesus, is often portrayed standing upon the serpent, symbolizing how she and her son have conquered sin.

The New Testament also contains an ambivalent image of the serpent, regarding it as wise as well as evil. Jesus tells his twelve apostles to be 'wise as serpents' (Matt. 10:16). A sect of Gnostics, known as Ophites, took this statement by Jesus quite literally and worshipped the serpent as a bestower of wisdom and a divine creature. They celebrated the eucharist by setting loaves of bread on a table and having a venerated snake crawl among the loaves.

In the Christian tradition the savior generally acts to destroy the serpent who represents polytheistic religions and chaos, while in the Hindu tradition the Avatar interacts harmoniously with the serpent who is part of the cosmos. In India the serpent and the God-man are two basic manifestations of the one divine substance. This substance cannot be at variance with either of its polarized aspects, for within it the two are reconciled and subsumed.[83] D. H. Lawrence seems to have gleaned an ancient truth when he said:

> . . . man can have the serpent with him or against him. When the serpent is with him, he is almost divine. When his serpent is against him, he is stung and envenomed and defeated from within. The great problem, in the past, was the Conquest of the *inimical* serpent and the liberation within the self of the gleaming bright serpent of gold, golden fluid life within the body, the rousing of the splendid divine dragon within a man, or within a woman.[84]

Reincarnation and Resurrection

The traditions of Hinduism and Christianity differ in their conception of life after death. Avatars conceive of life after death in terms of reincarnation while Jesus thought of it as resurrection. The Indian idea of reincarnation implies that a soul comes back to earth in one of 8 million possible reincarnations and chooses a human body either because it hasn't fully learned the lessons it was supposed to or because, in the case of a highly spiritual person, it has a special task to perform in helping others. In the *Bhagavad Gita*, God makes his appearance in the context of reincarnation, for it is stated:

For Me have passed many
Births, and for thee, Arjuna;
These I know all;
Thou knowest not, scorcher of the foe.

For protection of the good,
And for destruction of evil-doers,
To make a firm footing for the right,
I come into being in age after age.
(*Bhagavad Gita*, IV. 5,8)

The modern Indian Avatars proclaim that the soul reincarnates in accordance with the divine will, entering into a mortal body and transcending karma. Meher Baba and Satya Sai Baba claimed that they had been Jesus Christ in a previous life, and Ramakrishna informed two of his disciples that they had been apostles of Jesus, all this in accordance with a belief in reincarnation.

The notion of reincarnation is foreign to the New Testament and to Jesus. The Jews of Jesus' day and the early Christians were concerned with the resurrection of the dead and not with reincarnation. The early Christians expected the imminent end of the world, probably within their own lifetimes, and they believed that Jesus would soon return to raise the dead and establish his kingdom on earth. They believed that they were living in the final moment of the present age, and for this reason they were more concerned with living their lives so that they would be ready for Jesus' second coming and with the repentence of their sins than they were with what happened to the soul after death. They also believed there would be a general resurrection of the dead at the second coming of Jesus.

The goal in Hinduism is to be released from reincarnation, and a negative value is placed on preserving individuality after death. Westerners, on the other hand, generally wish to survive after death as individuals, and resurrection entails a revivification with the same body and soul that the person formerly possessed. According to Christian belief the resurrection of Jesus Christ demonstrates his victory over death and the New Testament reports that during his lifetime Jesus raised three people from the dead: Lazarus (John 11:1–44), a widow's son (Luke 7:11–17), and Jarius' daughter (Mark 5:35–43 and Luke 8:49–56). Matthew records that at the time of Jesus' crucifixion 'the tombs also were opened, and many bodies of the saints who had fallen asleep were raised, and coming out of the tombs after his resurrection they went into the holy city and appeared to many' (Matthew 27:52–3). The New Testament also records that between his resurrection and his ascension Jesus made eleven appearances within 40 days to more than 525 people, but in no sense is this a case of reincarnation as with the Avatars.

On occasion, the association of Jesus with reincarnation has been based upon the statement in the Fourth Gospel that he who believes in Christ 'hast everlasting life' (John 3:36). Everlasting life is an idea to which the author of the Fourth Gospel loves to allude and it permeates his gospel. However, everlasting life is not synonymous with reincarnation, and Jesus never refers to the reincarnation of his, or any other individual's soul. Reincarnation of a soul falls within the tradition of Hinduism, while resurrection of the body and soul is clearly in the province of Judeo-Christianity. Satya Sai Baba, in claiming to reincarnate and resurrect, combines life-transcending elements from both the Eastern and the Western traditions.

Baba and Abba
Beginning with Ramakrishna in the late 19th century, the Avatars have proclaimed their divinity. Avatar Meher Baba was adamant, insisting that he was 'the Highest of the High' and the 'Avatar of the Age'. For the Avatars, Lord Krishna looms in the background as the divine progenitor, and beyond Krishna, in the primordial past is Vishnu. Modern Avatars emphasize their divinity through a wealth of mythic themes such as a divine colour, the royal serpent, a miraculous birth and suffering death, disciples, powers, omnipotence and apocalyptic expectation. As an actual manifestation of the deity they encourage mankind to love them as Baba, the Father.

We have encountered three Babas among Hindu Avatars, Meher Baba, Satya Sai Baba, and Babaji (alias Hariakhan Baba). The word Baba means father and so the Avatar stands for paternity in some sense. The names Meher Baba and Satya Sai Baba are theophoric names and not birthnames and point to the Avatar's paternal role. The Avatar Babaji, who is the original Kriya Avatar according to Yogananda, strikes one as mythic, comparable to the Rama Avatar. His miraculous nature – immortal, doesn't need food, speaks all languages, astral travel, invisibility, and non-material body – gives an overwhelming impression that he is a mythic embodiment, and his name Babaji represents his fathering of the Kriya Avatar lineage. Thus the use of the name Baba among Hindu Avatars describes a function, i.e., serving in the role of father, rather than a thing.

With Jesus Christ it is different. He used the Aramaic word 'Abba', meaning father, to refer to God the father rather than to himself. The gospels record the word 'Abba' upon the lips of Jesus at least 170 times. Jesus calls upon, and points to, Abba, the father in heaven, in the tender way that a child addresses its father, similar perhaps to our word 'Daddy'. Among his most famous words were 'Our Father (Abba) who art in heaven hallowed be thy name' (Luke 11:2), and his last words, 'Father (Abba), into thy hands I commit my spirit' (Luke 23:46). Even the statement in the Gospel of John 'He who has seen me has seen the Father', does not obfuscate the distinction between Jesus and the heavenly Father. Jesus' use of 'Abba' establishes a filial relationship between the Father in heaven and the son here on earth. Baba, on the other hand, points to the role of father that the Avatar himself assumes. The letters 'a' and 'b' can be combined to spell either the Hindu word Baba or the Aramaic word Abba, but between the two conceptions of father there is a world of difference.

Hindu Love and Christian Love

The God-men of India are beacons of love, inspiring humanity with the signal and radiance of blissful love. The love which the Avatars profess is known in India as *bhakti*, and Krishna revealed its importance in the *Gita* two thousand years ago. *Bhakti* is at the heart of Hindu theistic religion. The emotion that *bhakti* elicits is a mixture of awe, fascination, love, and dependence. *Bhakti*, more than any other term, expresses the Hindu attitude toward a deity, and an accurate translation of *bhakti* is 'devotional faith'. *Bhakti* implies the taking of refuge in God for protection, for assistance, or for special benefits, with confidence that God is approachable and that He will reciprocate with at least as much love as the devotee has for Him.

Bhakti can be interpreted as 'love', but it is a type of love that is based upon devotion to a beloved deity and in which there is a separation between the devotee and his God. There is in *bhakti* an emphasis on the relationship between lover and beloved, and the various aspects of *bhakti* are viewed as stages of spiritual progress. Hindu *bhakti* also involves a separation between God's surrogate, the Avatar, and man. The intimacy of love between the two never erases the distinction even though they may become united through their love. It is an emotion that separates the subject and the object, man and his God. Both are personal; one is the finite *bhakta* (lover), the other is the infinite *Bhagavan* (Loved One, God).

Bhakti may be translated as 'love', but it is understood to be the loving attitude of the devotee for God or the Avatar. *Bhakti* is always seen from the side of the devotee, therefore it is somewhat inaccurate to equate this with the Christian concept of love which is primarily the attitude that God takes toward the creation. Christian love corresponds more appropriately to the Hindu concepts of *prasada* (grace), *karuna* (mercy), or *vatsalya* (protecting and forgiving love), than to *bhakti*.[85] The direction of the love is essentially toward God or Baba in Hinduism and from God or Abba in Christianity.

The scholar Claude Montefiore pointed out some years ago that Christianity presents a picture of God who not only receives those who turn to Him, but who takes the initiative in seeking those who have not yet turned to Him. This is the image of the divine shepherd going into the wilderness to seek a lost sheep, and this differs from the Hindu image of a flock of sheep seeking guidance from the shepherd. Abba, the Christian God, loves to save; Baba, the Hindu Avatar, saves who love.

Epilogue: Mythicization
Avatarization
Incarnationism

> The unconscious naturally does not produce its images from conscious reflections, but from the worldwide propensity of the human system to form such conceptions as the . . . avatars of Hinduism . . .[1]
>
> (C. G. Jung)

Certain events lend themselves to immortalization. These events so capture the human imagination that they alter a people's way of looking at the totality of its experience, illuminate all other events, and bring about new orientations of thought. These events have a paradigmatic quality for they fuse the unique with the ultimate and the universal. The community preserves the event in legend or song and utilizes it as a vehicle for expressing its own self-understanding and for inculcating its youth in its values and ethos.

Among these major events are theophanies, epiphanies, and divine incarnations, that is, the appearance of a God. Blending the unique with the universal and the ultimate, they cast up 'archetypes'. 'Wherever known reality stops, where we touch the unknown, there we project an archetypal image.'[2] The more fundamental these events the more they are capable of being transformed into myth. And the distinctive characteristic of religious paradigmatic events is that they are believed to focus some insight into the human quest for liberation and fulfilment and into the nature of reality itself. A pattern is abstracted from the event and forms a mythic gestalt into which men and events can be inserted.

Religion may be regarded as a perspective from which certain dominant images from the past are used by its adherents to orient themselves to the present and future. The man of antiquity, before taking action, searched the past for a pattern into which to fit his life. His life was in a sense a reanimation, including an archaizing attitude, and this is precisely the mythic life. For example, Alexander the Great walked in the footsteps of Miltiades; Julius Caesar probably took Alexander as his prototype, and even Napoleon mythically confounded himself with Alexander. Mythic existence is the reconstitution of the myth in flesh and blood. Only by reference to the past can the mythic life approve itself as genuine and significant, for myth assists in the legitimization of life by adding self-awareness, sanction, and consecration. John McKenzie observed that 'the purpose of myth is not to explain reality but to enable man to live with it'.[3]

Myth is at the foundation of life, a timeless schema, a formula into which life flows when it emerges out of the unconscious. Like the evolution of consciousness, the process of mythicization has evolved out of the dream-like world of symbols and myths. Myth is primary, and the enveloping of a person within it, i.e. the process of mythicization, is secondary. Myth is a controlling image that gives meaning to the experiences of life. It has organizing value for experience and is capable of numerous configurations upon which opinions and attitudes rest. It can be said that the ontogeny of dream recapitulates and phylogeny of myth, for myth is the primary awareness of man in the universe. Myth expresses a 'haunting awareness of transcendental forces peering through the cracks of the visible universe'.[4] A mythology is a vaguely articulated body of such images without which experiences would be chaotic and fragmentary. 'Myth embodies the nearest approach to absolute truth that can be stated in words. To the extent that we form any positive mental conception of God, that conception must be a myth'.[5]

The great poet and myth-maker, William Blake, would have us see a vision of the Almighty, a form of God. Visions enable man to see beyond the immediately sensed world, thus situating man *vis-à-vis* an ultimate reality. Visions impel man out of the ordinary and enable him to participate in a transcendent realm of otherness. Blake wrote:

> We are led to believe a lie
> When we see *with* not *through* the eye,
> Which was born in a night to perish in a night
> When the soul slept in beams of light.
> God appears and God is light
> To those poor souls who dwell in night;

But doth a human form display
To those who dwell in realms of day.[6]

But how are we to see through the eye and not mistakenly with it? One way in which God's form appears to us is through the eye of the myth-making faculty. In this mythic sense Avatars are like Superman recognised here as Clark Kent.[7] As Superman comes from the planet Krypton, his 'secret' place, so Avatars descend from heaven, their hiding place. Avatars play a type of 'theological striptease',[8] hinting that there is more beyond what is actually seen and tantalizing the viewer with what is beyond the veil. We humans take delight in the idea of a divine visitation, a divine descent, whether it be Superman, an Avatar, or an Incarnation, because we would really like to see something of God.

The process of avatarization has developed over many centuries and is still evolving. Avatarization and incarnation are both aspects of the mythicization process and are rooted in that matrix. We saw in the first chapter how the seed of avatarology was planted millennia ago in the soil of India. The waters of the Ganges nurtured the seed and it grew in a free-flowing form in which images germinated easily into a variety of animal and human Avatars. The early mythic imagination did not concern itself with discrepancies but saw all things as part of the whole, i.e. all Avatars were really Vishnu in disguise and Vishnu was omnipotent.

The second chapter revealed how the Avatar plant burst into the light of an expanding consciousness as Vishnu-Krishna manifested as God-men who are born, live, suffer, and die as mortals do. The six modern Avatars witness to the evolving manifestation of the phenomenon of the Avatar. From Chaitanya to Satya Sai Baba the growth of divine awareness and realization of a cosmic purpose is observed. Three of these historical God-men, Ramakrishna, Meher Baba, and Satya Sai Baba claimed to have merged with or incarnated from Jesus Christ. In acknowledging Jesus as a God-man, a point of contact between East and West was begun. The concept of the Avatar took on universal proportions and the Avatar plant formed branches that spread to other parts of the world.

Chapter three witnesses the transplanting of the Avatar to European and American soil. Here the Avatar blooms in eight spiritual movements and less and less of Indian soil clings to the

plant as it sprouts from Theosophy to science fiction. The Western-
ization of the Avatar tradition demonstrates that when the link
with the mother tradition grows thin the mythic process takes on
some very novel forms. God-men such as Krishna, Buddha, and
Christ, become mythicized in both East and West where factions
of both cultures want them within their camp. Krishna becomes
Krishna consciousness, Buddha comes to represent divine light,
and Christ comes to symbolize divine love. Christ as God-man is
perceived in a multitude of ways, for it is said that he is 'all things
to all men' (I Cor. 9:22). Christ becomes a God-man for all seasons
and all reasons, a superstar Avatar, and the multiplicity of
interpretation may be due to His archetypal image.

In chapter four we see that the mythological soil of the Near East
and its development of Christology provides what is needed to
nourish the plant of Incarnation in the West. The Avatar plant and
the Incarnation plant are both fertilized by the myth-making
faculty. From *Krishna* to Rama*krishna* to *Krishna*murti to the Hare
Krishna Avatar to *Christ*, the mythicization process continues to
grow and grow.

The eminent psychologist Carl Gustav Jung has suggested that
the primordial archetype of the Anthropos (primal man) was
condensed in Jesus, was a part of the collective mentality of his
time, and took possession of the people at the beginning of the
Christian era as the Zeitgeist.[9] Jung said, 'the fact that the life of
Christ is largely myth does absolutely nothing to disprove its
factual truth – quite the contrary. I would even go so far as to say
that the mythical character of a life is just what expresses its
universal human validity. . . . The life of Christ is just what it had
to be if it is the life of a god and a man at the same time'.[10]
According to Jung, God's intention to become man was fulfilled in
Jesus' life and suffering,[11] and 'Christ is the archetype of the hero,
representing man's highest aspiration.'[12]

The content of faith can be mediated through history and/or
myth. The form and structure of the myth are vital, and what one
age can accept another age cannot. A modern way of viewing Jesus
Christ was heralded by the German New Testament scholar Rudolf
Bultmann thirty years ago in his attempt to 'demythologize' the
New Testament. He wished to purge the Christian scripture of the
mythology by which its faith was first expressed. Bultmann would
argue that the mythology of the only-begotten Son who existed
before all worlds, came to earth as the Incarnation, was raised from

the dead and was exalted to heaven, is difficult to accept in this age. We may understand now why that mythology took the form it did, we can seek to interpret it and demythologize it, but perhaps a greater truth can be mediated through the historical Jesus, the man who went about doing good, healing the sick, teaching and spreading love with a concern for humanity. From the Christian perspective Jesus can viably be taken as a point in history in which this very man expresses the presence and love of God, and offers a genuine clue for human understanding about the ultimates of our existence. Herein lies a real meaning of the orthodox formula which proclaims the Son of the same substance as the Father (*homoousios*). Jesus is God incarnate in the sense that Jesus reveals God and is love incarnate. In Jesus' actions, God's love was enacting itself and God's Kingdom was being actualized. From an orthodox perspective of Christian theology, Dr. Rashdall espouses this view,

> In Jesus Christ there is the completest, fullest, most central revelation of God that has ever been made, both because of the unique perfection of the moral and religious ideals which disclose themselves in His words, His character, and His life, and because from Him proceeds the fullest stream of further self-revelation which God has bestowed upon the world since that typical life of Sonship was lived.[13]

In other words, in Bultmann's de-mythologizing, Christ is not the Word made flesh, but flesh made Word. Today, however, the trend has been to reverse this, to re-mythologize, i.e. to reveal the unity between the historical Jesus and the Christ of faith, for in spite of the four interpretive and confessional gospels the figure of Jesus filters through. The historical concreteness and the specificity of Jesus shine through in spite of all the interpretations made by the early Christian communities. It was precisely the greatness of the historical man, Jesus, that motivated the Christological process and the multiple interpretations. They called Jesus by numerous titles such as Messiah, Son of God, and Lord, to decipher the greatness, the godliness, and the claims that emerged from his special mode of being. What is being called for here is a 'Jesusology' to replace Christology, that is, a focusing upon the immediacy of God that emerged in Jesus, and a learning from the example that he set.[14]

The situation is, then, that both Christians and Hindus are graced with a mythic image of divine descent in the person of the God-man, but regarding it from different traditions each interprets it according to his own perspective, as Avatar or as Incarnation. In attempting to explain his position a Catholic priest could say to a Hindu swami,

> it might indeed be imagined that God becomes human as often as men come into existence, that the Incarnation is in no way a unique miracle. If that were so, the historicity and personality in question – which through revelation we *know* to be unique and to fulfil God's own prophecy through the prophets – these would be reduced to the level of our human nature, pure and simple, which is everywhere and always the same. This would be, so to speak, a 'mythologizing' of divine truth.

And the swami might respond to the priest, saying, 'to me, not convinced that the Christian scripture is God's sole revelation for humanity, it would seem almost the opposite – that to say there *must* be a unique Incarnation at one unique point of history is itself a "mythologizing" of truth'.[15] Each of these religious men accuse the other of mythologizing the truth, yet both would do well to acknowledge the mythic nature of incarnation itself. And professor Raymond Panikkar offers an insightful suggestion, that if Christianity and Hinduism are to be brought into a fruitful relationship, then a process of 'transmythologization' must take place.[16] He explains that

> the differences between the two religions, [Hinduism and Christianity] are very often complementary. To put it succinctly, if Hinduism claims to be the *religion of truth*, Christianity claims to be the *truth of religion*. Hinduism is ready to absorb any authentic religious truth; Christianity is ready to embrace any authentic religious value. The genuinely Christian attitude is to call forth that 'truth' of Hinduism without destroying the latter's identity. To Christianity, Hinduism in turn offers the authentically Hindu gift of a new experience and interpretation – a new dimension, in fact – of the Mystery. The 'catholicity' of Hinduism calls forth the true 'catholicity' of Christianity, while the truth of Christianity calls forth the truth of Hinduism. The passage from a narrow catholicity and an exclusive 'truth' to a

full catholicity and to recognition of the fact that Truth can be neither limited nor monopolized is the Paschal adventure of every religion.[17]

Incarnation and avatarization are complementary 'truths', for it has now been demonstrated that the reality of the God-man is based upon the myth of the divine descent.

Notes

INTRODUCTION: RELIGIONS AND THEIR GOD-MEN

1. Wilfred Cantwell Smith, 'The Role of Asian Studies in the American University', Plenary Address of the New York State Conference for Asian Studies, Colgate University, 10 Oct. 1975, p. 12.
2. Friedrich Nietzsche, *Thus Spake Zarathustra*, trans. Thomas Common, II, XXIV. (New York: Boni & Liveright, n.d.) p. 98.
3. Bertrand Russell, *Power: a New Social Analysis* (London: Allen & Unwin, 1938).
4. Franklin Edgerton, trans. *The Bhagavad Gita* (Cambridge, Mass.: Harvard University Press, 1944) p. 23.
5. S. Radharishnan, *The Bhagavadgita* (New York: Harper & Row, 1948) pp. 153–4.
6. Juan Mascaro, *The Bhagavad Gita* (Baltimore, Md: Penguin Books, 1962) pp. 61–2.
7. Swami Jagadiswarananda, *Kalki Comes in 1985* (Belur, India: Sri Ramakrishna Charmachakra, 1965) p. 114.
8. Swami Prabhavananda, *The Spiritual Heritage of India* (Hollywood, Calif.: Vedanta Press, 1963) p. 120.
9. Ibid., p. 120.
10. Ibid., p. 121.
11. Emil Brunner, *The Mediator* (London: Lutterworth, 1934).
12. Aldous Huxley, *The Perennial Philosophy* (New York: Harper & Row, 1944) pp. 49, 56.
13. Murry Titus, *Islam in India and Pakistan* (Calcutta: YMCA Publishing House, 1959), p. 107.
14. Frithjof Schuon, *Understanding Islam* (Baltimore, Md: Penguin Books, 1963) p. 91. However, Schuon acknowledges that this is to view Muhammad through Hindu, not Muslim eyes (p. 90).
15. Kirpal Singh, *Godman*. (Tilton, NH: The Sant Bani Press, 1974) pp. 150–1.
16. Rabindranath Tagore, 'Crisis in Civilization' in S. Ghose (ed.), *Faith of a Poet: Selections from Rabindranath Tagore* (Bombay: Bhavan's Book University, 1964) p. 56.

CHAPTER 1: CLASSICAL AVATARS OF INDIA

1. Mircea Eliade, *The Sacred and the Profane* (New York: Harcourt, Brace, Jovanovich, 1959) p. 76.
2. Erich Neumann, *The Origins and History of Consciousness*, part II (New York: Harper & Brothers, 1962) p. 275.

3. Louis Dupre, *The Other Dimension* (New York: Doubleday and Co., 1972) pp. 252–3.
4. Mircea Eliade in Norbert Schedler, 'Archaic Myth and Historical Man', in *Philosophy of Religion* (New York: Macmillan, 1974) p. 61.
5. Ibid., p. 61.
6. Rig Veda, x. 129.3.
7. Heinrich Zimmer, *Myths and Symbols in Indian Art and Civilization* (Princeton University Press, 1974) p. 34.
8. Ibid., p. 38.
9. Rene Guenon, 'The Heart and the World Egg', in *Studies in Comparative Religion*, vol. 7 (1973) p. 200.
10. Jan Gonda, *Aspects of Early Vishnuism* (Uitgevers MiJ-utrecht, 1954) p. 23.
11. Wendy Doniger O'Flaherty, *Women, Androgynes and Other Mythical Beasts* (University of Chicago Press, 1980) p. 323.
12. *Linga Purana*, 1.41.7–12.
13. Zimmer, *Myths and Symbols*, op. cit., pp. 27–8.
14. J. Michael McKnight, Jr., 'Kingship and Religion in India's Gupta Age: an Analysis of the Role of Vaisnavism in the Lives and Ideology of the Gupta Kings', in *Journal of the American Academy of Religion*, vol. 45, no. 2 (June 1977) p. 692.
15. Ibid., pp. 696–7.
16. Heinrich Zimmer, *Myths and Symbols in Indian Art and Civilization* (Princeton University Press, 1946). Zimmer describes the Sage Agastya on pp. 113–4.
17. David Kinsley, *The Sword and the Flute* (University of California Press, 1975) p. 22.
18. Ibid., p. 42.
19. Ibid., p. 32.
20. Ibid., p. 39.
21. Ibid., p. 39.
22. Carl G. Jung, *Collected Works*, vol. 10 (New York, Pantheon Books, 1958) p. 520.
23. Wendy Doniger O'Flaherty, *The Origins of Evil in Hindu Mythology* (The University of California Press, 1976) p. 188.
24. Vishnu Purana, 3.17.9–45; 3.18.1–34, from O'Flaherty, op. cit., p. 189.
25. The demons were explained on p. 15.
26. Bhagavata Purana 1.3.24; 2.7.37; 11.4.22; 10.40.22, from O'Flaherty, op. cit., p. 188.
27. Agni Purana 16.1–14, from O'Flaherty, p. 188.
28. O'Flaherty, op. cit., p. 200.
29. Varaha Purana 48:22 from O'Flaherty, p. 204.
30. Matsya Purana 47:24, 54:19, from O'Flaherty, p. 204.
31. Kshmendra converted from Shaivism to Vaishnavism. See V. E. V. V. Raghavacharya and D. G. Padhye (eds), *Minor Works of Kshemendra*, The Sanskrit Academy, Osmania University, Hyderabad, 1961, p. 3. I cannot agree with O'Flaherty, op. cit., p. 204 that Kshemendra was a Jain.

32. Jayadeva, *Gita Govinda*, 1.1.9.
33. Devibhagavata Purana, 10.5.13, from O'Flaherty, p. 204.
34. Swami Jagadiswarananda, *Kalki Comes in 1985* (Behur, India: Sri Ramakrishna Dharmachakra, 1965) preface, p. 12.
35. Julia Day Howell, 'Vehicles for the Kalki Avatar: the Experiments of a Javanese Guru in Rationalizing Ecstatic Religion' Stanford University, Ph.D. Dissertation, 1977.
36. Gore Vidal, *Kalki* (New York: Random House, 1978).
37. Norman Cohn, *The Pursuit of the Millenium* (New York: Harper & Brothers, 1961) pp. 115–116.
38. Rudolf Otto, *India's Religion of Grace and Christianity Compared and Contrasted* (London: SCM Press, 1930) p. 109.
39. Dr Norvin Hein, 'Early Protestant Views of Hinduism, 1600–1825', Unpublished paper, Yale Divinity School, n.d., no pagination.
40. P. J. Marshall, *The British Discovery of Hinduism in the Eighteenth Century* (London: Cambridge University Press, 1970) p. 28.
41. Ibid., pp. 28–9.
42. Ibid., p. 243.
43. Ibid., p. 244.
44. Ibid., p. 33.
45. Ibid., p. 33.
46. Louis Jaccoliot, *Christna et Le Christ* (Paris, 1877) p. 8.
47. William H. McNeill and M. Iriye, *Modern Asia and Africa* (New York: Oxford University Press, 1971) p. 93.
48. Ibid., pp. 99 and 101.
49. Kersey Graves, *The World's Sixteen Crucified Saviors*, 6th edn (New Hyde Park, New York, University Books, 1971) pp. 256–73.
50. M. K. Gandhi, *Christian Missions* (Ahmadabad: Navajivan Publishing House, 1941) p. 113.
51. M. K. Gandhi, *The Message of Jesus Christ* (Bombay, 1940) p. 35.
52. Geoffrey Parrinder, *Avatar and Incarnation* (New York: Barnes & Noble, 1970) p. 277.
53. Rabindranath R. Maharaj, *Death of a Guru* (Philadelphia: A. J. Holman Co., 1977) pp. 148–9.

CHAPTER 2: MODERN AVATARS OF INDIA

1. Charles S. J. White, 'The Sai Baba Movement: Approaches to the Study of Indian Saints', in *The Journal of Asian Studies*, vol. 31, no. 4 (Aug. 1972) pp. 862, 878.
2. Swami Sivananda Radha, 'Kundalini: an Overview', in John White (ed.), *Kundalini, Evolution and Enlightenment* (New York: Doubleday, 1979) p. 52.
3. Norvin J. Hein, 'Caitanya's Ecstasies and the Theology of the Name', in Bardwell L. Smith (ed.) *Hinduism, New Essays in the History of Religions* (E. J. Brill, Leiden, 1976) p. 29.

4. Christopher Isherwood, *Vedanta for the Western World* (The Viking Press, New York, 1945) p. 225.
5. S. K. De, *Early History of the Vaishnava Faith and Movement in Bengal* (General Printers and Publishers Ltd., Calcutta, 1942) p. 333.
6. Romain Rolland, *The Life of Ramakrishna* (Advaita Ashrama, Calcutta, 1965) p. 297.
7. Ibid., p. 13.
8. Swami Prabhavananda, *The Spiritual Heritage of India* (Vedanta Press, Hollywood, California, 1963) p. 336.
9. Arvind Sharma, 'Ramakrsna Paramhamsa: a Study in a Mystic's Attitude Towards Women', unpublished paper, on p. 9 Sharma suggests that during Ramakrishna's six months of worship as Radha, that Ramakrishna began to menstruate, and his source is Saradananda, p. 238.
10. Swami Saradananda, *Sri Ramakrishna, The Great Master* (Sri Ramakrishna Math, Mylapore, India, 1952) p. 188.
11. Ibid., p. 189.
12. Ibid., p. 189.
13. Ibid., pp. 189–90.
14. Christopher Isherwood, *Ramakrishna and His Disciples* (Simon & Schuster, New York, 1970) p. 96.
15. Swami Saradananda, op. cit., p. 169.
16. Ibid., p. 250, n. 1.
17. Prabhavananda, op. cit., p. 340.
18. Isherwood, op. cit., p. 148.
19. Harold W. French, *The Swan's Wide Waters, Ramakrishna and Western Culture* (Port Washington, N.Y.: National University Publications, Kennikat Press, 1974) p. 33.
20. Prabhavananda, op. cit., pp. 120–1.
21. *Teachings of Sri Ramakrishna* (Calcutta, 1975) pp. 47–9.
22. Swami Akhilananda, *Hindu View of Christ* (Branden Press, Boston, Mass., 1949) ch. one, pp. 15–44.
23. C. Isherwood, op. cit., p. 300.
24. Ibid., p. 299.
25. Sri Aurobindo, *Speeches and Writings* p. 90.
26. Dilip K. Roy and Indira Devi, *Pilgrims of the Stars* (New York: Macmillan, 1973) p. 299.
27. H. Zimmer, *Myths and Symbols*, p. 142.
28. Aurobindo, *Savitri*, XI, I.
29. Beatrice Bruteau, *Worthy is the World – the Hindu Philosophy of Sri Aurobindo* (Fairleigh Dickinson University Press, Teaneck, N.J., 1972) pp. 39–40.
30. Sri Aurobindo, *Essays on the Gita* (New York: Sri Aurobindo Library, 1959) p. 15.
31. V. Madhusudan Reddy, *Avatarhood and Human Evolution* (Institute of Human Study, Hyderabad, India, 1972) p. iii.
32. Ibid., p. ii.
33. Ibid., p. ii.
34. Pagal Baba, *The Temple of the Phallic King* (New York: Simon & Schuster, 1973) p. 184.

35. Vijay, *Sri Aurobindo and the Mother on Avatarhood* (Pondicherry, India: Sri Aurobindo Society, 1972) p. 24.
36. Sri Aurobindo, *The Mother* (Pondicherry, India: Sri Aurobindo Ashram Press, 1928) pp. 31, 33.
37. *Sri Aurobindo and His Ashram*, p. 65.
38. The Mother, *The Mother on Sri Aurobindo* (Pondicherry, India: Sri Aurobindo Ashram Press, 1972), not numbered.
39. Ashram Bulletin (Nov., 1970).
40. Narayan Prasad, *Life of Sri Aurobindo Ashram* (Pondicherry, India: Sri Aurobindo Press, 1965) p. 331.
41. Ibid., p. 332.
42. Marvin H. Harper, *Gurus, Swamis and Avatars* (Philadelphia: The Westminster Press, 1972) p. 196.
43. Pasupati, *On the Mother Divine* (West Bengal: Sri Phanibhusan Nath, 1968) p. 11.
44. Ibid., pp. 11–12.
45. Prema Nandakumar, *The Mother (of Sri Aurobindo Ashram)*, (New Delhi: National Book Trust) p. 114.
46. Pasupati, op. cit., p. 4.
47. Ibid., p. 53.
48. Ibid., p. 66.
49. Ibid., p. 52.
50. Wendy D. O'Flaherty, *Women, Androgynes and Other Mythical Beasts* (University of Chicago Press, 1980) p. 118.
51. Aurobindo, *The Mother*, op. cit., p. 62.
52. Aurobindo, *Savitri*, Book VII, Canto 5.
53. Pasupati, op. cit., pp. 51, 56.
54. Ibid., pp. 73–4.
55. Ibid., p. 47.
56. Miguel Serrano, *The Serpent of Paradise* (New York: Harper & Row, 1972) p. 129.
57. John White, *Kundalini*, op. cit., p. 88.
58. Meher Baba, *Compassionate Father* (Berkeley, Calif.: Meher Baba Information, 1971).
59. Charles B. Purdom, *The God-Man* (Sheriar Press, Crescent Beach, S.C., 1964) p. 24.
60. Meher Baba, *God Speaks* (Dodd, Mead & Co., New York, 1970) p. 243.
61. Ibid., p. 231.
62. Purdom, op. cit., pp. 210, 247.
63. Ibid., p. 99.
64. Ibid., p. 291.
65. Ibid., p. 254.
66. Meher Baba, *Listen Humanity*, narrated and edited by D. E. Stevens (New York: Harper & Row, 1971) p. 227.
67. Robert Ellwood, Jr., *Religious and Spiritual Groups in Modern America* (Englewood Cliffs, N.J.: Prentice-Hall, 1973) p. 283.
68. Purdom, op. cit., p. 393.
69. Ibid., p. 390.
70. Ibid., p. 315.

71. Raymond Panikkar, *Salvation in Christ: the Problem and the Promise* (Santa Barbara, Calif., 1972) p. 51.
72. Samuel H. Sandweiss, M.D., *Sai Baba the Holy Man and the Psychiatrist* (San Diego, Calif.: Birth Day Publishing Co., 1975) p. 229.
73. Five biographies and two films made by Richard Bock, 'The Advent of the Avatar', and 'My Life is my Message'.
74. Robert Ellwood, Jr., op. cit., p. 248.
75. Vinayak Krishna Gokak, *Bhagavan Sri Satya Sai Baba* (New Delhi, Abhinav Publications, 1975) p. 28.
76. Howard Murphet, *Sai Baba, Man of Miracles* (Madras, The Macmillan Company of India, 1971) p. 72.
77. Eruch Fanibunda, *Vision of the Divine* (Bombay: E. B. Fanibunda, 1976) p. 13.
78. Gokak, op. cit., p. 39.
79. Ibid., p. 302.
80. Ibid., pp. 36–7, and Sandweiss, p. 185, and Murphet, p. 188.
81. Gokak, p. 6, and Sandweiss, p. 150.
82. Gokak, p. 24.
83. Gokak, p. 207.
84. Gokak, p. 54.
85. Howard Murphet, *Sai Baba, Man of Miracles* (Madras: The Macmillan Co. of India, Ltd., 1971).
86. *The Encyclopedia of Occultism and Parapsychology*, vol. 1, pp. 46–50.
87. Murphet, p. 168, and Sandweiss, p. 22.
88. Murphet, p. 68.
89. Murphet, pp. 88–9, 180.
90. Murphet, p. 84.
91. Erlendur Haraldsson and Karlis Osis, 'The Appearance and Disappearance of Objects in the Presence of Sri Satya Sai Baba', in *The Journal of the American Society of Psychical Research*, vol. 71 (Jan. 1977) p. 36.
92. Murphet, p. 48.
93. Sandweiss, p. 46.
94. Murphet, p. 185.
95. Murphet, p. 83.
96. Sandweiss, p. 97.
97. Murphet, p. 157, and Sandweiss, p. 224.
98. Murphet, p. 179.
99. Haraldsson and Osis, op. cit., pp. 33–43.
100. Ibid., pp. 40–1.
101. Ibid., p. 42.
102. Sandweiss, p. 86.
103. Gokak, pp. 14–15.
104. Gokak, p. 13.
105. Sandweiss, p. 178, and Fanibunda, p. 48.
106. Sandweiss, p. 175.
107. Sandweiss, p. 175, and Fanibunda, p. 46.
108. Sandweiss, p. 175.
109. Murphet, p. 180.

110. Murphet, p. 207.
111. Sandweiss, p. 212.
112. Murphet, p. 155.
113. Murphet, p. 119.
114. Murphet, pp. 131–4.
115. Sandweiss, pp. 101–3.
116. Murphet, p. 120.
117. Murphet, p. 120.
118. Murphet, pp. 128–9.
119. Murphet, p. 120.
120. Murphet, p. 160.
121. Gokak, p. 67.
122. Sandweiss, pp. 99–100.
123. Gokak, p. 276.
124. Gokak, p. 292.
125. Arnold Schulman, *Baba* (New York: Simon & Schuster, Pocket Books, 1973) pp. 141–2.
126. Agehananda Bharati, 'The Hindu Renaissance and its Apologetic Patterns', in *Journal of Asian Studies*, vol. 29 (Feb. 1970) pp. 282–3.
127. Romain Rolland, *The Life of Ramakrishna*, op. cit., p. 77.
128. Ibid., p. 278, n. 1.
129. *The Life of Swami Vivekananda by his Eastern and Western Disciples*, p. 448.

EPILOGUE: CRITERIA FOR AVATARHOOD BASED ON MYTHEMES

1. Lawrence A. Babb, *The Divine Hierarchy: Popular Hinduism in Central India* (New York: Columbia University Press, 1975) p. 16.
2. Eugene N. Trubetskoi, *Icons: Theology in Color* (New York, St. Vladimir's Seminary Press, 1973) p. 48.
3. Heinrich Zimmer, *Myths and Symbols in Indian Art and Civilization* (Princeton University Press, 1974) p. 87.
4. Charlotte Vaudeville, 'The Govardhan Myth in Northern India', in *Indo-Iranian Journal*, vol. 22, no. 1 (Jan. 1980) p. 13.
5. J. P. Vogel, *Indian Serpent Lore* (London: Arthur Probstain, 1926).
6. A. K. Majumdar, *Chaitanya: His Life and Doctrine*, p. 109.
7. Charles Purdom, *The God-Man, the Life, Journeys, and Work of Meher Baba with an Interpretation of his Silence and Spiritual Teaching* (South Carolina, Sheriar Press, 1964) pp. 336–7.
8. Howard Murphet says this of Satya Sai Baba, 'He seemed to be not only a father and mother but the very essence of parenthood itself, the archetype of all fathers and mothers', p. 49.
9. Jan Gonda, *Aspects of Early Vishnuism*, pp. 66–7.
10. Aurobindo, *Essays on the Gita*, pp. 333–4.

CHAPTER 3: THE AVATAR INCARNATES IN THE WEST

1. Henry David Thoreau, *Walden* (New York: New American Library, 1942) p. 199.
2. Walt Whitman, *Passage to India* (New York: The Viking Press, 1973) p. 283.
3. Abraham Roger, *De Open-Deure tot het Verborgen Heydendom* (Leyden: Francoys Hackes, 1651). Abridged English Version in Bernard Picart, *The Religious Ceremonies and Customs of the Several Nations of the Known World*, III (London, Nicholas Prevost, 1731) pp. 309–64.
4. Philip Baldaeus, *Naauwkeurige Beschrijvinge van Malabar en Choromandel en het Eylandt Ceylon, nevens de Afgoderije der Oost-Indische Heydenen* (Amsterdam: J. J. van Waesberge, 1672). Slightly abridged English translation in Awnsham and John Churchill, *A Collection of Voyages and Travels*, II (London, 1704) pp. 562–901. On the plagiarism of Baldaeus, see Stephen Neill, *A History of Christianity in India* (Cambridge University Press, 1984) pp. 382–3.
5. Bartholomaeus Ziegenbalg, *Propagation of the Gospel in the East*, tr. Joseph Downing, 3rd edn (London, 1718) pp. 19–25.
6. Sir William Jones, *In Asiatic Res.*, I, p. 234.
7. Arthur Christy, *The Orient in American Transcendentalism* (New York: Columbia University Press, 1932) p. 23.
8. Ibid., p. 23.
9. *The Journals of R. W. Emerson*, III, pp. 510–11.
10. George Hendrick, *Facsimile Reproduction of Bhagvat-Geeta, trans. by Charles Wilkins, 1785* (Gainesville, Fla, 1959) p. xi.
11. Ibid., p. xi.
12. Thoreau, *Walden*, ch. 16.
13. Regarded as a misspelling of Sankara.
14. *Leaves of Grass*, 'Salut Au Monde!', section 6, ll. 1–3.
15. Ibid., 'So Long!', v. 64–8.
16. E. A. Poe, *The Masque of the Red Death*.
17. Theophile Gautier, *Avatar*. The Works of Theophile Gautier, vol. 15.
18. Ibid., p. 69.
19. Charles Marion, *Les Avataries* (Paris, 1906).
20. Omer Chevalier, *L'Avatar d'Yvan Orel* (Paris, 1919).
21. Gaston Cherpillod, *Les Avatars de Juste Palinod* (Lausanne, 1973).
22. Robert S. Ellwood, Jr., *Alternative Alters, Unconventional and Eastern Spirituality in America* (University of Chicago Press, 1979) p. 105.
23. H. S. Olcott, *Old Diary Leaves*, Second Series (Adyar, Theosophical Publishing House, 1900) pp. 13–14.
24. Marion Meade, *Madame Blavatsky: the Woman Behind the Myth* (New York: G. P. Putnam's Sons, 1980) pp. 379–80.
25. H. P. Blavatsky, *The Secret Doctrine*, vol. 5, p. 350.
26. Ibid., p. 351.
27. Robert Ellwood, op. cit., p. 123.
28. A. Nethercot, *The Last Five Lives of Annie Besant*, p. 46.
29. Annie Besant, *Avataras*, pp. 28–9.

30. Ibid., pp. 80–1.
31. Nethercot, *The Last Five Lives of Annie Besant*, p. 133.
32. Ibid., p. 145.
33. Ibid., p. 148.
34. Ibid., p. 149.
35. Mary Lutyens, *Krishnamurti: the Years of Awakening* (New York, Farrar, Straus & Giroux, 1975) p. 46.
36. Ibid., p. 55.
37. Ibid., p. 56.
38. Ibid., p. 81.
39. Ibid., p. 192.
40. Ibid., pp. 159, 166, 186.
41. Ibid., p. 206.
42. Nethercot, *The Last Five Lives of Annie Besant*, p. 349.
43. Lutyens, op. cit., p. 224.
44. Ibid., p. 241, and Nethercot, *Five*, p. 390.
45. Nethercot, op. cit., pp. 377–8.
46. Lutyens, op. cit., p. 246.
47. Ibid., p. 251, and Nethercot, *Five*, p. 397.
48. Lutyens, p. 252.
49. Ibid., p. 262, and Nethercot, *Five*, p. 409.
50. Lutyens, pp. 262–3.
51. Nethercot, *Five*, p. 425.
52. Ibid., p. 449.
53. Henry Summerfield, *That Myriad-Minded Man* (Gerrards Cross: Colin Smythe, 1975) p. 74.
54. C. C. Coates, *Some Less Known Chapters in the Life of AE* (Dublin, Privately Printed, 1939) p. 8.
55. George Russell, (AE), *The Living Torch* (1937) pp. 167–8.
56. Summerfield, op. cit., p. 76.
57. Ibid., pp. 74–5.
58. Ibid., p. 77.
59. George Russell, (AE), *The Avatars: a Futuristic Fantasy* (London: Macmillan, 1933).
60. *The Mythology of all Races*, vol. 3. 'Aodh is Morna's son. Aoife is the wife of Ler, and is transformed into the shape of a crane by the jealous Iuchra.'
61. Alice Bailey, *The Externalisation of the Hierarchy* (New York: Lucis Publishing Co., 1970) pp. 285–6.
62. Marion Meade, *Madame Blavatsky: the Woman Behind the Myth* (New York: G. P. Putnam's Sons, 1980) p. 468.
63. Ibid., p. 468.
64. Alice Bailey, *Esoteric Healing* (New York: Lucis Publishing Co.) p. 616.
65. Alice Bailey, *The Externalisation of the Hierarchy* (New York: Lucis Publishing Co.) pp. 297–301.
66. Alice Bailey, *The Reappearance of the Christ* (New York: Lucis Publishing Co.) p. 66.
67. Ibid., p. 67.

68. Ibid., p. 77.
69. Ibid., p. 77.
70. Ibid., pp. 98–9.
71. Paramahansa Yogananda, *Autobiography of a Yogi*, pp. 345, 350.
72. Robert Ellwood, Jr., *Religious and Spiritual Groups in Modern America* (Englewood Cliffs, N.J.: Prentice Hall, 1973) p. 229.
73. Yogananda, *Autobiography of a Yogi*, pp. 279, 573.
74. Ibid., p. 385.
75. Ibid., p. 346.
76. T. M. D. Mahadevan, 'Saiva and Sakta Schools, in S. Radhakrishnan's *History of Philosophy Eastern and Western* (London, 1952) p. 373.
77. S. L. Katre, 'Avatars of God', in *Allahabad University Studies*, vol. 10 (1933) p. 128.
78. Yogananda, *Autobiography*, p. 348.
79. Ibid., p. 347.
80. Ibid., p. 354.
81. Ibid., p. 348.
82. Ibid., pp. 345, 355.
83. Ibid., p. 348.
84. Ibid., p. 352.
85. Baba Hari Dass, *Hariakhan Baba, Known, Unknown* (Davis, Calif.: Sri Rama Foundation, 1975).
86. Ibid., p. 25.
87. Ibid., pp. 50, 63.
88. Ibid., p. 74.
89. Ibid., p. 56.
90. Ibid., p. 62
91. Ibid., p. 20.
92. Dio Neff, *Yoga Journal* (May–June, 1980) pp. 42–57.
93. Ibid., p. 45.
94. Ibid., p. 51.
95. Ibid., p. 54.
96. Yogananda, *Autobiography*, p. 362.
97. *Baba Hari Dass*, pp. 65–7.
98. Yogananda, *Autobiography*, pp. 380, 385.
99. Ibid., p. 343.
100. Ibid., p. 396.
101. Ibid., p. 137.
102. Ibid., p. 121.
103. Ibid., p. 121.
104. Ibid., p. 218.
105. Ibid., p. 131.
106. Ibid., p. 125.
107. Ibid., p. 460.
108. Ibid., p. 477.
109. Ibid., p. 476.
110. Ibid., p. 479.
111. Ibid., p. 10.

112. Ibid., p. 276.

113. Ibid., p. 275.

114. Ibid., p. 362.

115. Ibid., p. 350.

116. Ibid., pp. 350–1.

117. Ibid., p. 347.

118. Ibid., p. 575.

119. Ibid., p. 385, footnote.

120. Francine J. Daner, *The American Children of Krsna – a Study of the Hare Krisna Movement* (New York: Holt, Rinehart & Winston, 1976) p. 23.

121. *Back to Godhead* (magazine), vol. 10, no. 1, pp. 9–10.

122. *Back to Godhead*, no. 29, p. 14.

123. *The Krshna Consciousness Handbook* (Boston, Mass.: ISKCON Press, 1970) p. 37.

124. *Back to Godhead*, no. 29, p. 14.

125. *The Krshna Consciousness Handbook*, op. cit., p. 10.

126. A. C. Bhaktivedanta, *The Spiritual Master and the Disciple* (Los Angeles: The Bhaktivedanta Book Trust, 1978), p. 112.

127. For a list of the complete disciplic succession see Francine Daner, op. cit., p. 107.

128. *Back to Godhead*, vol. 63, p. 6.

129. Ibid., vol. 10, no. 8, p. 6.

130. Ibid., vol. 63, p. 5.

131. A. C. Bhaktivedanta Swami Prabhupada, *The Science of Self Realization* (Los Angeles, Bhaktivedanta Book Trust, 1977) p. 125.

132. *Back to Godhead*, vol. 63, p. 4.

133. Ibid., vol. 16, no. 7, p. 11.

134. Ibid., vol. 16, no. 7, p. 6.

135. Ibid., p. 7.

136. *Gleanings from the Writings of Baha'u'llah*, p. 5.

137. Jacques Chouleur, 'The Baha'i Faith: World Religion of the Future?' in *World Order* (vol. 12, no. 1 (autumn, 1977) p. 12.

138. 'One Universal Faith', no author (Ill.: Baha'i Publishing Trust, Wilmette), n.d.

139. Abdul-Baha, *Star of the West*, vol. VI, no. 15 (12 Dec. 1915) pp. 114, 117.

140. S. P. Raman, 'My Quest for the Fulfillment of Hinduism', in *World Order*, vol. 3, no. 2 (Spring 1969) pp. 2–28.

141. Jamshed Fozdar, *Buddha Maitrya-Amitabha Has Appeared* (New Delhi: Baha'i Publishing Trust, 1976).

142. William N. Garlington, 'Baha'i Bhajans', in *World Order* (winter 1982) pp. 46–8.

143. *The Life of John van Ryswyk*, printed by Avatar Imperium Internum, p. 3.

144. *Whom Say Men That I Am?* by Hero Elder, published by author (London, 1980) p. 7.

145. The Avatar School of Philosophy by John van Ryswyk, lecture 23.

146. Hero Elder, op. cit., p. 11.

147. The Avatar School of Philosophy by John van Ryswyk, lecture 42, p. 9.
148. Ibid., lecture 42.
149. Hero Elder, op. cit., p. 32.
150. Geof Gray-Cobb, *The Miracle of New Avatar Power* (New York: Parker Publishing Co., 1974) p. 42.
151. Ibid., p. 17.
152. Ibid., p. 73.
153. Ibid., p. 15.
154. Ibid., p. 52.
155. Ibid., p. 50.
156. Ibid., p. 74.
157. Ibid., p. 199.
158. Ibid., p. 35.
159. Michael Moorcock, *Behold The Man* (New York: Avon Books, 1966) Introduction.
160. Frederick A. Kreuziger, *Apocalypse and Science Fiction* (Chico, Calif.: Scholars Press, 1982) pp. 133–4.
161. Frank Herbert and Bill Ransom, *The Jesus Incident* (New York: Berkley Books, 1979) p. 318.
162. Ibid., pp. 63, 12.
163. Poul Anderson, *The Avatar* (New York: Berkley Publishing Co., 1976).
164. Roger Zelazny, *Lord of Light* (New York: Avon Books, 1969).
165. Ibid., p. 9.
166. Op. cit.
167. Kenneth Rexroth, 'The Bhagavadgita', *Saturday Review* (2 Nov. 1968) p. 28.

CHAPTER 4: AVATARS AND CHRIST

1. Harvey Cox, *Turning East* (New York: Simon & Schuster) p. 124.
2. V. Chakkarai, *Jesus the Avatar* (Madras: Christian Literature Society for India, 1930).
3. Ibid., p. 153.
4. Hazrat Mirza Ghulam Ahmad, *Jesus in India* (Rabwah, Pakistan: The Ahmadiyya Muslim Foreign Missions Department, 1962).
5. Ibid., pp. 78–9.
6. Miguel Serrano, *The Serpent of Paradise* (New York: Harper & Row, 1972).
7. Ibid., p. 63.
8. Ibid., pp. 78–9.
9. Levi Dowling, *The Aquarian Gospel of Jesus Christ* (Santa Monica, Calif.: De Vorss & Co., 1972) pp. 13–14.
10. Clifford Owens (ed.), *A Story of Jesus* (Virginia Beach: ARE Press, 1963), p. 28, reading #5749-2.

11. Noel Langley, *Edgar Cayce on Reincarnation* (New York: Warner Books, 1976) p. 158.
12. Ibid., p. 159.
13. I. C. Sharma, *Cayce, Karma and Reincarnation* (New York: Harper & Row, 1975) pp. 137, 138.
14. H. Spencer Lewis, *The Mystical Life of Jesus* (San Jose, Calif.: Supreme Grand Lodge of AMORC, 1929).
15. Ibid., p. 179.
16. Ibid., pp. 186–7.
17. Ibid., p. 291.
18. Ernst von der Planitz (ed.), *Der Benan-Brief* (Berlin, 1910).
19. George Hunt Williamson, *Secret Places of the Lion* (New York: Warner Destiny Book, 1958, 1977).
20. From the cover of Williamson's book, op. cit.
21. Ibid., p. 181.
22. Ibid., pp. 163, 170, 253.
23. Ibid., p. 175.
24. Justin Martyr, *Apology*, 54ff.
25. Diogenes, *Lives of the Philosophers* (Loeb Classical Library), viii, 1.11.
26. Ibid., viii. 2.66.
27. Ibid., viii. 2.59 and 60.
28. Plutarch, *Table Talk*, viii. 1.2.
29. Lucian, *Alexander the false-prophet*, 2.
30. Ibid., 2–3.
31. Francis Legge, *Forerunners and Rivals of Christianity*, pp. 17–18.
32. Adolf Deismann, *Light from the Ancient East* (Hodder & Stoughton, 1927) pp. 342ff.
33. Ibid., pp. 342ff.
34. Seneca, 'The Pumpkinification of Claudius', in Robert Graves, *Claudius the God* (New York: Smith & Haas, 1935) pp. 566–82.
35. Cicero, *Ad Quintum fratrem*, I, i.7.
36. Virgil, *Eclogue*, iv.
37. Horace, *Odes*, I.2.
38. Ovid, *Metamorphoses*, VIII. 626–721.
39. Origen, *Contra Celsum*, vii.9.
40. Lucian, *The Passing of Peregrinus*, 11–16.
41. John Hick, *The Myth of God Incarnate*, p. 91.
42. *Encyclopedia Britannica*, 15th edn, *Micropaedia*, vol. 1, p. 449 and *Macropaedia*, vol. 2, p. 949.
43. Sigmund Mowinckel, *He That Cometh*, trans. G. W. Anderson (Oxford: Basil Blackwell, 1959) p. 67.
44. *Tobit*, ch. 12, vv. 14, 15, 19, 20.
45. Justin Martyr, *Apology*, 26.
46. John Hick, *The Myth of God Incarnate*, p. 79.
47. Martin Hengel, *The Son of God* (Philadelphia, Fortress Press, 1976) pp. 25–30.
48. Walter Nigg, *The Heretics* (New York: Alfred A. Knopf, 1962) pp. 32, 34.

49. Pheme Perkins, *The Gnostic Dialogue* (New York: Paulist Press, 1980) p. 209.
50. A. D. Nock in Zeph Stewart (ed.), *Essays on Religion and the Ancient World*, vol. I (Oxford University Press, 1972) p. 35.
51. Alan Dundes, *The Hero Pattern and the Life of Jesus* (Berkeley, Calif.: The Center for Hermeneutical Studies in Hellenistic and Modern Culture, Protocol of the 25th Colloquy, 1977) p. 10.
52. Mircea Eliade, 'Archaic Myth and Historical Man' in *McCormick Quarterly* (1965) p. 31.
53. This image belongs to Norman Perrin, *The New Testament: an Introduction* (New York: Harcourt, Brace Jovanovich, Inc., 1974) p. 23.
54. J. K. Mozley, *The Doctrine of the Incarnation* (London: Geoffrey Bles, 1949) pp. 53–4.
55. Amos Wilder, *Early Christian Rhetoric* (Cambridge: Harvard University Press, 1971) p. 121.
56. Norman Perrin, op. cit., pp. 29–33.
57. Jacques Guillet, S. J., *The Consciousness of Jesus* (New York: Newman Press, 1972) p. 7.
58. Gordon Kaufman, *Systematic Theology*, p. 189.
59. Raymond Brown, *Jesus God and Man* (Milwaukee: Bruce Publishing Co., 1967) p. 30.
60. Joseph A. Fitzmyer, S. J., 19th Annual Scripture Institute Address, Georgetown University, Washington, D.C., 21–25 June 1982.
61. H. J. Schoeps, *Paul: the Theology of the Apostle in the Light of Jewish History* (1961) p. 150.
62. Martin Hengel, *The Son of God* (Philadelphia: Fortress Press, 1976) p. 15.
63. Gordon Kaufmann, op. cit., p. 203.
64. *The Writings of James Arminius*, trans. Nichols & Bagnall (Grand Rapids Michigan: Baker, 1956). Disputation 34, 2, 84.
65. Martin Luther, *Word and Sacrament*, vol. III in Helmut Lehman (ed.), *Luther's Works*, vol. 37 (Philadelphia: Fortress Press, 1961) p. 212.
66. John Calvin, *Institutes of the Christian Religion*, trans. Henry Beveridge (Grand Rapids, Michigan: Eerdman, 1957) II, 14, 1.
67. Henry Bettenson, *Documents of the Christian Church*, 2nd edn (London: Oxford University Press, 1963) p. 64.
68. Loraine Boettner, *Studies in Theology* (Philadelphia: Presbyterian and Reformed, 1947) p. 197.
69. Augustus Strong, *Systematic Theology* (Westwood, N.J.: Revell, 1907) p. 693.
70. Dr Quentin Quesnell, 'Aquinas on Avatars' paper delivered at New ERA Conference, Ft. Lauderdale, Fla 3 Jan. 1983, p. 8.
71. Ibid., p. 15.
72. Sara Hall, *Father Divine: Holy Husband* (New York: Doubleday & Co., 1953) ch. 1, 'John Doe, Alias God', pp. 9–23.
73. Geoffrey Parrinder, *Avatar and Incarnation* (New York: Barnes & Noble, 1970) pp. 120–6.
74. Romain Rolland, *The Life of Ramakrishna* (Advaita Ashrama, Calcutta, 1965) pp. 272–3.

75. M. (Gupta, Mahendranath), *The Gospel of Sri Ramakrishna*, p. 832.
76. M. K. Gandhi, *What Jesus Means to Me*, compiled by R. K. Prabhu (Ahmadabad: Navajivan Publishing House, 1959) pp. 9–10.
77. John Moffitt, 'Incarnation and Avatara: an Imaginary Conversation', in *Journal of Ecumenical Studies*, vol. 14, Spring (1977) p. 273.
78. John A. T. Robinson, *Honest to God* (SCM Press, 1963) p. 74.
79. Harry Miller, 'The Cobra, India's "Good Snake"', *National Geographic*, vol. 138, no. 3 (Sept. 1970).
80. Aldous Huxley, *Island* (New York: Harper & Row, 1962) p. 199.
81. *Midrash Rabbah*, vol. I (Genesis) p. 139.
82. Joseph Campbell, 'Myths to Live By', Part 2, *Bill Moyer's Journal* (24 Apr. 1981) p. 3.
83. Heinrich Zimmer, *Myths and Symbols in Indian Art and Civilization* (Princeton University Press, 1946) p. 90.
84. D. H. Lawrence, *Apocalypse* (Florence: G. Orioli, 1931) p. 223.
85. John Carman, 'Is Christian Faith a Form of Bhakti?' in the *Visva-Bharati Journal of Philosophy*, p. 4.

EPILOGUE:
MYTHICIZATION/AVATARIZATION/INCARNATIONISM

1. C. G. Jung, *Collected Works*, vol. 9, Pt. 1, p. 310.
2. M.-L. von Franz, 'Patterns of Creativity Mirrored in Creation Myths' (Zurich: *Spring* Publications, 1972) p. 5.
3. John McKenzie, *The Old Testament Without Illusion* (New York: Doubleday, 1980) p. 34.
4. This is attributed to Philip Wheelwright in 'The Necessity of Myth' by Mark Schorer as found in Henry A. Murray, *Myth and Myth-making* (New York: George Braziller, 1960) p. 355.
5. Ken Wilber, *The Spectrum of Consciousness* (Wheaton, Ill.: Theosophical Publishing House, 1977) p. 113.
6. William Blake from 'Auguries of Innocence'.
7. Wendy D. O'Flaherty, *Women, Androgynes and Other Mythical Beasts* (University of Chicago Press, 1980) p. 69.
8. Ibid., p. 68.
9. C. G. Jung, *Memories, Dreams, Reflections* (New York: Vintage Books, 1965) pp. 211–12.
10. C. G. Jung, *Collected Works*, vol. 11, p. 409.
11. Ibid., p. 409.
12. 'Talks with Miguel Serrano: 1959' in William McGuire and R. F. C. Hull (eds), *C. G. Jung Speaking, Interviews and Encounters*, p. 401.
13. From Dr Rashdall, in his *The Idea of Atonement in Christian Theology*, as quoted in J. K. Mozley's *The Doctrine of the Incarnation*, p. 96.
14. Leonardo Boff, O. F. M. deserves the credit for this idea, see his *Jesus Christ Liberator: a Critical Christology for Our Time* (Maryknoll, N.Y.: Orbis Books, 1978).

15. John Moffitt, 'Incarnation and Avatara: an Imaginary Conversation', in *Journal of Ecumenical Studies*, vol. 14 (Spring 1977) pp. 273–4.
16. Raymond Panikkar, *Kultmysterium in Hinduismus und Christentum* (Freiburg and Munchen: Karl Alber, 1964), which is trans. and revised in French as *Le mystere du culte dans l'hindouisme et le christianisme* (Paris: Les Editions du Cerf, 1970).
17. Raymond Panikkar, *The Unknown Christ of Hinduism* (London: Darton, Longman & Todd, 1968) p. 4.

Bibliography

Books:

Adriel, Jean, *Avatar: the Life Story of Avatar Meher Baba* (Berkeley, Calif.: John F. Kennedy University Press, 1947).

Ahmad, Hazrat Mirza Ghulam, *Jesus in India* (Rabwah, Pakistan: The Ahmadiyya Muslim Foreign Missions Department, 1962).

Akhilananda, Swami, *Hindu View of Christ* (Boston: Branden Press, 1949).

Anderson, Poul, *The Avatar* (New York: Berkley Publishing Co., 1978).

Archer, William, *The Loves of Krishna in Indian Painting and Poetry* (New York: Macmillan, 1957).

Aurobindo, Sri, *Essays on the Gita* (New York: The Sri Aurobindo Library, 1950).

—— in Robert McDermott (ed.), *Six Pillars, Introductions to the Major Works of Sri Aurobindo* (Chambersburg, PA: Wilson Books, 1974).

——, *Savitri* (Pondicherry, India: Sri Aurobindo Ashram, 1950).

Avalon, Arthur (Sir John Woodroffe), *The Serpent Power* (London: Luzac, 1919).

Babb, Lawrence, *The Divine Hierarchy: Popular Hinduism in Central India* (New York: Columbia University Press, 1975).

Bailey, Alice A., *The Reappearance of the Christ* (New York: Lucis Publishing Co., 1948).

——, *Esoteric Healing* (New York: Lucis Publishing Co.)

——, *The Externisation of the Hierarchy* (New York: Lucis Publishing Co., 1970).

Basham, A. L., *The Wonder That Was India* (New York: Grove Press, 1954).

Besant, Annie, *The Bhagavad Gita* (trans.) (Adyar: The Theosophical Publishing House, 1914).

——, *Avataras* (Chicago: The Theosophical Press, 1923).

Bhaktivedanta, A. C., *Bhagavad-Gita as It Is* (New York: The Bhaktivedanta Book Trust, 1975).

——, *Teachings of Lord Chaitanya* (New York: The Bhaktivedanta Book Trust, 1972).

——, *The Spiritual Master and the Disciple* (New York: The Bhaktivedanta Book Trust, 1978).

Bhandarkar, R. G., *Vaisnavism, Saivism and Minor Religious Systems* (Varanasi: Indological Book House, 1966).

Bhattacharji, Sukumari, *The Indian Theogony: a Comparative Study of Indian Mythology from the Vedas to the Puranas* (Cambridge University Press, 1970).

Boff, Leonardo, O. F. M., *Jesus Christ Liberator: a Critical Christology for Our Time* (Maryknoll, N.Y.: Orbis Books, 1978).

Bouquet, A. C., *Hinduism* (London: Hutchinson's University Library, 1948).

215

Brandes, Georg, *Jesus – a Myth* (New York: Albert & Charles Boni, 1926).

Brent, Peter, *Godmen of India* (Quadrangle Books, Chicago, 1972).

Brown, Raymond E., *Jesus God and Man* (Milwaukee: The Bruce Publishing Co., 1967).

Brunner, Emil, *The Mediator* (London: Lutterworth, 1934).

Bruteau, Beatrice, *Worthy is the World: the Hindu Philosophy of Sri Aurobindo* (Rutherford, N.J.: Fairleigh Dickinson University Press, 1971).

Bultmann, Rudolf, *Jesus Christ and Mythology* (New York: Charles Scribner's Sons, 1958).

Campbell, Joseph, *The Masks of God: Oriental Mythology* (New York: Penguin Books, 1962).

Carey, George L., *God Incarnate* (Leicester: Inter-Varsity Press, 1977).

Cave, Sidney, *Redemption, Hindu and Christian* (London: Oxford University Press, 1919).

Chakkarai, V., *Jesus the Avatar* (Madras: Christian Literature Society for India, 1930).

Chakravarti, K. C., *Ancient Indian Culture and Civilization* (London: Luzac & Co., 1942).

Chaudhuir, Nirad C., *Hinduism, A Religion to Live By* (Oxford University Press, 1979).

Christy, Arthur, *The Orient in American Transcendentalism* (New York: Columbia University Press, 1932).

Cohn, Norman, *The Pursuit of the Millenium* (New York: Harper & Brothers, 1961).

Coomaraswamy, Ananda K., *The Dance of Shiva* (Bombay: Asia Publishing House, 1948).

Cox, Harvey, *Turning East* (New York: Simon & Schuster, 1977).

Craig, Clarence T., *The Beginning of Christianity* (New York: Abingdon-Cokesbury Press, 1943).

Daner, Francine J., *The American Children of Krsna: a Study of the Hare Krisna Movement* (New York: Holt, Rinehart & Winston, 1976).

Dasgupta, S. B., *Aspects of Indian Religious Thought* (Calcutta: A. Mukherjee & Co., 1957).

Dass, Baba Hari, *Hariakhan Baba, Known, Unknown* (Davis, Calif.: Sri Rama Foundation, 1975).

De, S. K., *Early History of the Vaishnava Faith and Movement in Bengal* (Calcutta: General Printers & Publishers Ltd., 1942).

deNicholas, Antonio, T., *Avatara: the Humanization of Philosophy Through the Bhagavad Gita* (Nicolas Hays Ltd., 1976).

Dimmitt, Cornelia and van Buitenen, J. A. B. (eds and trans.), *Classical Hindu Mythology: a Reader in the Sanskrit Puranas* (Philadelphia: Temple University Press, 1978).

Dimock, Edward, *Bengali Tales from Court and Village* (University of Chicago Press, 1963).

——, *In Praise of Krishna, Songs from the Bengali* (trans. with Denise Levertov) (New York: Doubleday & Co., 1967).

Dowling, Levi, *The Aquarian Gospel of Jesus the Christ* (Santa Monica, Calif.: De Vorss & Co., 1972).

Dunne, John S., *The Way of All the Earth* (New York: Macmillan, 1972).

Dupre, Louis, *The Other Dimension* (New York: Doubleday & Co., 1972).

Edgerton, Franklin, *The Bhagavad Gita* (trans. and interpreted), (Cambridge: Harvard University Press, 1972).

Eliade, Mircea, *Yoga: Immortality and Freedom* (New York: Pantheon Books, 1958).

——, *The Sacred and the Profane* (trans. by Willard R. Trask), (New York: Harcourt, Brace, Jovanovich, 1959).

——, *Images and Symbols: Studies in Religious Symbolism* (Kansas City: Sheed Andrews & McMeel, Inc., 1961).

Ellwood, Robert S. Jr., *Alternative Altars, Unconventional and Eastern Spirituality in America* (University of Chicago Press, 1979).

——, *Religious and Spiritual Groups in Modern America* (Englewood Cliffs, N.J.: Prentice Hall, 1973).

Enslin, Morton, *Christian Beginnings* (New York: Harper & Brothers, 1938).

Fakirbhai, Dhanjibhai, *Khristopanishad (Christ-Upanishad)* (Bangalore: The Christian Institute for the Study of Religion and Society, 1965).

Fanibunda, Eruch, *Vision of the Divine* (Bombay: E. B. Fanibunda, 1976).

Farquhar, J. N., *An Outline of the Religious Literature of India* (Delhi: Motilal Banarsidass, 1967).

Fozdar, Jamshed, *Buddha Maitrya-Amitabha Has Appeared* (New Delhi: Baha'i Publishing Trust, 1976).

French, Harold W., *The Swan's Wide Waters: Ramakrishna and Western Culture* (Port Washington, N.Y.: Kennikat Press, 1974).

Furst, Jeffrey (ed.), *Edgar Cayce's Story of Jesus* (New York: Berkeley Publishing Co., 1970).

Gandhi, M. K., *Christian Missions* (Ahadabad: Navajivan Publishing House, 1941).

——, *The Message of Jesus Christ* (Bombay: 1940).

——, *What Jesus Means to Me*, compiled by R. K. Prabhu (Ahmadabad: Navajivan Publishing House, 1959).

Gautier, Theophile, *Avatar: the Works of Theophile Gautier*, vol. 15 (Cambridge, Mass.: The Jenson Society, 1902).

Ghurye, G. S., *Gods and Men* (Bombay: Popular Book Depot, 1962).

Gokak, Vinayak Krishna, *Bhagavan Sri Sathya Sai Baba* (New Delhi: Abhinav Publications, 1975).

Gokhale, B. G., *Ancient India, History and Culture* (Bombay: Asia Publishing House, 1952).

Gonda, Jan, *Ancient Indian Kingship from the Religious Point of View* (Leiden, Netherlands: E. J. Brill, 1966).

——, *Aspects of Early Vishnuism* (Utrecht: N. V. A. Oosthoek's Uitgevers Mij, 1954).

——, *Visnuism and Sivaism: a Comparison* (University of London, Athlone Press, 1970).

Goulder, Michael (ed.), *Incarnation and Myth: the Debate Continued* (Grand Rapids, Mich.: William B. Eerdman's Publishing Co., 1979).

Grant, Frederick C., *An Introduction to New Testament Thought* (New York: Abingdon Press, 1950).

Graves, Kersey, *The World's Sixteen Crucified Saviors* (New Hyde Park, N.Y., University Books Inc., 1971; orig. pub. 1875).

Graves, Robert, *Claudius the God* (New York: Harrison Smith and Robert Haas, 1935).

Gray-Cobb, Geof., *The Miracle of New Avatar Power* (West Nyack, N.Y.: Parker Publishing Co., 1974).

Grousset, Rene, *The Civilization of India*, trans. by Catherine Phillips (New York: Tudor, 1939).

Guenon, Rene, *Introduction to the Study of the Hindu Doctrines*, trans. by Marco Pallio (London: Luzac, 1945).

Guillet, Jacques, S. J., *The Consciousness of Jesus* (New York: Newman Press, 1972).

Hackin, J., *Asiatic Mythology* (New York: Crescent Books, n.d.).

Hall, Sara, *Father Divine: Holy Husband* (New York: Doubleday & Co., 1953).

Harper, Marvin H., *Gurus, Swamis and Avataras* (Philadelphia: The Westminster Press, 1972).

Harvey, Van A., *The Historian and the Believer* (New York: Macmillan, 1969).

Hein, Norvin, J., 'Hinduism', in Charles J. Adams (ed.), *A Reader's Guide to the Great Religions* (New York: The Free Press, 1977).

Hendrick, George, a facsimile reproduction of *The Bhagavat-Geeta* (1785) by Charles Wilkins (Gainesville, Fla: Scholars' Facsimiles and Reprints, 1959).

Hengel, Martin, *The Son of God* (Philadelphia: Fortress Press, 1976).

Herbert, Frank, *The Jesus Incident* (New York: Berkeley Publishing Co., 1979).

Hick, John (ed.), *The Myth of God Incarnate* (Philadelphia, The Westminster Press, 1977).

——, *God and the Universe of Faiths* (New York: St. Martin's Press, 1973).

Hixon, Lex, *Coming Home: the Experience of Enlightenment in Sacred Traditions* (New York: Anchor Books, 1978).

Hopkins, Thomas, *The Hindu Religious Tradition* (Encino, Dickenson Publishing Co., 1971).

Huxley, Aldous, *The Perennial Philosophy* (New York: Harper & Row, 1944).

Isherwood, Christopher, *Ramakrishna and His Disciples* (New York: Simon & Schuster, 1965.

——, *Vedanta for the Western World* (New York: The Viking Press, 1945).

Ions, Veronica, *Indian Mythology* (London: Paul Hamlyn, 1975).

Jaccoliot, Louis, *Christna et Le Christ* (Paris: 1877).

Jagadiswarananda, Swami, *Kalki Comes in 1985* (Belur: Sri Ramakrishna Dharmachakra, 1965).

Jung, C. G., *The Collected Works*, vols. 9 and 11 (New York: Pantheon Books, 1958).

——, *Memories, Dreams, Reflections* (New York: Vintage Books, 1965).

Kaufman, Gordon D., *Systematic Theology: a Historicist Perspective* (New York: Charles Scribner's Sons, 1968).

Kerenyi, C., *Asklepios* (New York: Pantheon Books, 1959).

Kinsley, David R., *The Sword and the Flute* (Berkeley, Calif.: University of California Press, 1977).

Kirk, James A., *Stories of the Hindus* (New York: Macmillan, 1972).

Knox, John, *The Humanity and Divinity of Christ* (London: Cambridge University Press, 1967).

——, *Myth and Truth* (The University Press of Virginia, 1964).

Kosambi, D. D., *The Culture and Civilization of Ancient India* (London: Routledge & Kegan Paul, 1965).

Kreuziger, Frederick A., *Apocalypse and Science Fiction, A Dialectic of Religious and Secular Soteriologies* (Chico, Calif.: Scholars Press, 1982).

Langley, Noel, *Edgar Cayce on Reincarnation* (New York: Warner Books, 1976).

Lawrence, D. H., *Apocalypse* (Florence: G. Orioli, 1931).

Legge, Francis, *Forerunners and Rivals of Christianity* (New York: University Books, 1964).

LeMaitre, Solange, *Ramakrishna and the Vitality of Hinduism*, trans. by Charles L. Markmann (New York: Funk & Wagnalls, 1969).

Lewis, H. Spencer, *Mystical Life of Jesus* (San Jose, Calif.: Supreme Grand Lodge of AMORC, 1929).

Lutyens, Mary, *Krishnamurti, The Years of Awakening* (New York: Farrar, Straus & Giroux, 1975).

M-Gupta, Mahendranath, *The Gospel of Sri Ramakrishna* (New York: Ramakrishna–Vivekenanda Center, 1942).

Macnicol, Nicol, *Hindu Scriptures* (London: J. M. Dent and Sons, 1938).

——, *The Making of Modern India* (London: Oxford University Press, 1924).

Maharaj, Rabindranath R., *Death of a Guru* (Philadelphia: A. J. Holman Co., 1977).

Majumdar, A. K., *Caitanya, His Life and Doctrine: a Study in Vaisnavism* (Chowpatty, India: Bharatiya Vidya Bhavan, 1969).

Marshall, P. J., *The British Discovery of Hinduism in the Eighteenth Century* (London: Cambridge University Press, 1970).

Mascaro, Juan (trans.), *The Bhagavad Gita* (Baltimore: Penguin Books, 1962).

Maury, Curt, *Folk Origins of Indian Art* (New York: Columbia University Press, 1969).

McCain, David (ed.), *Christianity – Some Non-Christian Appraisals* (New York: McGraw-Hill, 1964).

McKenzie, John, *The Old Testament Without Illusion* (New York: Doubleday, 1980).

McNeill, William H. and M. Iriye, *Modern Asia and Africa* (New York: Oxford University Press, 1971).

Meade, Marion, *Madame Blavatsky, The Woman Behind the Myth* (New York: G. P. Putnam's Sons, 1980).

Meher Baba, *God Speaks* (New York: Dodd, Mead & Co., 1970).

—— in Ivy O. Duce (ed.), *Life at its Best* (New York: Harper & Row, 1972).

——, *Sparks from Meher Baba* (Crescent Beach, S.C.: Sheriar Press, 1971).

——, *The Everything and the Nothing* (Berkeley, Calif.: The Beguine Library, 1963).

——, *Listen, Humanity*, narrated and edited by D. E. Stevens (New York: Harper & Row, 1971).

Mookerji, Radha, K., *Men and Thought in Ancient India* (London: Macmillan, 1924).

Moorcock, Michael, *Behold The Man* (New York: Avon Books, 1966).

Moore, Charles A. (ed.), *The Indian Mind* (Honolulu: East–West Center Press, 1967).

Morgan, Kenneth W., *The Religion of the Hindus* (New York: Ronald Press, 1953).

Mozley, J. K., *The Doctrine of The Incarnation* (London: Geoffrey Bles, 1949).

Mozoomdar, P. C., *The Oriental Christ* (Boston: George H. Ellis, 1894).

Nandakumar, Prema, *The Mother (of Sri Aurobindo Ashram)* (New Delhi: National Book Trust, 1977).

Needleman, Jacob, *The New Religions* (New York: Doubleday Pocket Books, 1972).

Nethercot, Arthur H., *The First Five Lives of Annie Besant* (University of Chicago Press, 1960).

——, *The Last Four Lives of Annie Besant* (University of Chicago Press, 1963).

Neumann, Erich, *The Origins and History of Consciousness* (New York: Harper & Brothers, 1954).

Nichols, Aidan, O. P., *The Art of God Incarnate* (New York: Paulist Press, 1980).

Nietzsche, Friedrich, *Thus Spake Zarathustra* (trans. Thomas Common), (New York: Boni & Liveright, n.d.).

Nikhilananada, Swami, *The Essence of Hinduism* (New York: Ramakrishna–Vivekananada Center, 1946).

——, *Hinduism: Its Meaning for the Liberation of the Spirit* (New York: Harper & Brothers, 1958).

Noble, Margaret and Coomaraswamy, Ananda, *Myths of Hinduism* (London: Harrap, 1920).

Northrop, F. S. C., *The Meeting of East and West* (New York: Macmillan, 1946).

O'Flaherty, Wendy (trans.), *Hindu Myths* (Harmondsworth, Middx: Penguin Classics, 1975).

——, *The Origins of Evil in Hindu Mythology* (University of California Press, 1976).

——, *Women, Androgynes and Other Mythical Beasts* (University of Chicago Press, 1980).

Ogden, Schubert M., *Christ Without Myth* (Dallas: SMU Press, 1961).

Organ, Troy Wilson, *The Hindu Quest for the Perfection of Man* (Athens: Ohio University Press, 1970).

Otto, Rudolf, *India's Religion of Grace and Christianity Compared and Contrasted* (London: Student Christian Movement, 1930).

——, *Mysticism East and West*, trans. by Bertha Bracey and R. Payne, (New York: Macmillan, 1932).

Owens, Clifford (ed.), *A Story of Jesus* (Virginia Beach, VA: ARE Press, 1963).

Pagal Baba, *The Temple of the Phallic King* (New York: Simon & Schuster, 1973).

Panikkar, Raymond, *Kultmysterium in Hinduismus und Christentum* (Freiburg and Munchen: Karl Alber, 1964), which is trans. and rev. in French as *Le mystere du culte dans l'hindouisme et le christianisme* (Paris: Les Editions du Cerf, 1970).

——, *Salvation in Christ: the Problem and the Promise* (Santa Barbara, Calif.: (no publisher), 1972).

——, *The Unknown Christ of Hinduism* (London: Darton, Longman & Todd, 1968).

Parekh, Manilal, C., *A Hindu's Portrait of Jesus Christ* (Rajkot, 1953).

Parrinder, Geoffrey, *Avatar and Incarnation* (New York: Barnes & Noble, 1970).

Pasupati, *On the Mother Divine* (Pondicherry, India: Sri Aurobindo Ashram, 1968).

Perrin, Norman, *The New Testament – an Introduction* (Harcourt, Brace, Jovanovich, Inc., New York, 1974).

Pope, Harrison, Jr., *The Road East: America's New Discovery of Eastern Wisdon* (Boston: Beacon Press, 1974).

Prabhavananda, Swami and Christopher Isherwood, *The Song of God: Bhagavad-Gita* (New York: New American Library, 1954).

——, with Frederick Manchester, *The Spiritual Heritage of India* (Hollywood, Vedanta Press, 1969).

Prasad, Naragyan, *Life of Sri Aurobindo Ashram* (Pondicherry, India: Sri Aurobindo Press, 1965).

Purdom, C. B., *The God-Man. The Life, journeys and work of Meher Baba with an interpretation of his silence and spiritual teaching* (Crescent Beach, S.C.: Sheriar Press, Inc., 1964).

Radhakrishnan, S., *The Bhagavadgita* (New York: Harper & Row, 1973).

——, *The Hindu View of Life* (London: Allen & Unwin, 1927).

Ramacharaka, Yogi, *The Philosophies and Religions of India* (Chicago: The Yogi Publication Society, 1908).

Ramakrishnananda, Swami, *God and Divine Incarnations* (Mylapore: Sri Ramakrishna Math, 1970).

Rao, T. A. G., *Elements of Hindu Iconography* (New York: Paragon Book Corp., 1968).

Reddy, V. Madhusudan, *Avatarhood and Human Evolution* (Hyderabad: Institute of Human Study, 1972).

Reed, Elizabeth, *Hinduism in Europe and America* (New York: G. P. Putnam's Sons, 1914).

Renou, Louis, *The Nature of Hinduism* (trans. by Patrick Evans), (New York: Walker & Co., 1962).

Richard, Mira (The Mother), *The Mother on Aurobindo* (Pondicherry, India: Sri Aurobindo Ashram Press, 1972).

Riepe, Dale, *Indian Philosophy and Its Impact on American Thought* (Springfield, Ill.: Charles Thomas, 1970).

Robinson, John A. T., *Honest to God* (London: SCM Press, 1963).

Rolland, Romain, *The Life of Ramakrishna* (Calcutta: Advaita Ashrama, 1965).

Roy, Dilip Kumar, and Indira Devi, *Pilgrims of the Stars* (New York: Macmillan, 1973).

Russell, George William (A.E.), *The Avatars: a Futuristic Fantasy* (New York: Macmillan, 1933).

Sandmel, Samuel, *We Jews and Jesus* (New York: Oxford University Press, 1965).

Sandweiss, Samuel, *Sai Baba: the Holy Man and the Psychiatrist* (San Diego: Birth Day Publication Company, 1975).

Saradananda, Swami, *Sri Ramakrishna, The Great Master* (trans. by Swami Jagadananda), (Mylapore: Sri Ramakrishna Math, 1952).

Sastry, T. V. Kapali, *Men of God* (Pondicherry, India: Sri Aurobindo Ashram, 1960).

Satprem, *Sri Aurobindo or the Adventure of Consciousness* (New York: Harper & Row, 1968).

Schoeps, H. J., *Paul: The Theology of the Apostle in the Light of Jewish History* (1961).

Schulman, Arnold, *Baba* (New York: Simon & Schuster Pocket Books, 1973).

Schuon, Frithjof, *Understanding Islam* (Baltimore: Penguin Books, 1972).

Serrano, Miguel, *The Serpent of Paradise* (New York: Harper & Row, 1972).

Sharma, I. C., *Cayce, Karma and Reincarnation* (New York: Harper & Row, 1975).

Shridharani, Krishnalal, *My India, My America* (New York: Duell, Sloan & Pearce, 1941).

Singer, Milton (ed.), *Krishna: Myths, Rites, and Attitudes* (University of Chicago Press, 1966).

Smith, Bardwell, L. (ed.), *Hinduism – New Essays* (Leiden, Netherlands: E. J. Brill, 1976).

Summerfield, Henry, *That Myriad-Minded Man* (Bucks: Colin Smythe, 1975).

Thomas, M. M., *The Acknowledged Christ of the Indian Renaissance* (London: SCM Press, 1969).

Thomas, P., *Epics, Myths and Legends of India* (Bombay: D. B. Taraporevala Sons & Co., 1973).

Thomas, Wendell Marshall, *Hinduism invades America* (New York: The Beacon Press, 1930).

Titus, Murray, *Islam in India and Pakistan* (Calcutta: YMCA Publishing House, 1959).

Trubetskoi, Eugene N., *Icons: Theology in Color* (New York: St. Vladimir's Seminary Press, 1973).

Vidal, Gore, *Kalki* (New York: Random House, 1978).

Vijay, *Avatarhood*, compiled from the writings of Aurobindo and the Mother (Pondicherry, India: Sri Aurobindo Society, 1973).

Vitsaxis, Vassilis G., *Hindu Epics, Myths and Legends in Popular Illustrations* (Delhi: Oxford University Press, 1977).

Vivekananda, Swami, *My Master* (New York: The Baker & Taylor Co., 1901).

Vivekananda, *The Life of Vivekananda by his Eastern and Western Disciples* (Calcutta: Advaita Ashrama, 1965).

Vogel, J. P., *Indian Serpent Lore* (London: Arthur Probsthain, 1926).

Warburton, Stanley, *An Avatar in Vishnu Land* (New York: Charles Scribner's Sons, 1928).

White, John (ed.), *Kundalini, Evolution and Enlightenment* (Garden City, N.Y.: Doubleday, 1979).

Wilber, Ken, *The Spectrum of Consciousness* (Wheaton, Ill.: The Theosophical Publishing House, 1977).

Wilder, Amos, *Early Christian Rhetoric* (Cambridge, Mass.: Harvard University Press, 1971).

Williams, Howard, *Down to Earth, An Interpretation of Christ* (London: SCM Press Ltd., 1964).

Williamson, George Hunt, *Secret Places of the Lion* (New York: Warner Destiny Book, 1958).

Wilson, H. H., *The Vishnu Purana*, 3rd edn (Calcutta: Punthi Pustak, 1961).

Yogananda, Paramahansa, *Autobiography of a Yogi* (Los Angeles: Self-Realization Fellowship Publishers, 1972).

Zelazny, Roger, *Lord of Light* (New York: Avon Books, 1967).

Zimmer, Heinrich, *Myths and Symbols in Indian Art and Civilization* (Princeton University Press, 1974).

—— in Joseph Campbell (ed.), *Philosophies of India* (Cleveland: World Publishing Co., Meridian Books, 1956).

Zouboff, Peter P., *Vladimir Solovyev's Lectures on Godmanhood* (Poughkeepsie, N.Y.: International University Press, 1944).

Dissertations, Articles, Lectures, etc.

Bharati, Agehananda, 'The Hindu Renaissance and Its Apologetic Patterns', in *Journal of Asian Studies*, vol. 29 (Feb. 1970).

Carman, John B., 'Is Christian Faith a Form of Bhakti?' in *The Visva-Bharati Journal of Philosophy*, (vol. and no. unknown) pp. 2–15.

Chatterkee, Chinmayi, 'A Note on the Vaisnavic Concept of Avatara and Lila of God', in *Anviska*, vol. 6 (Calcutta: Jadavpur University, Mar. 1972).

Chouleur, Jacques, 'The Baha'i Faith: World Religion of the Future?' in *World Order*, vol. 12, no. 1 (autumn 1977).

Dundes, Alan, 'The Hero Pattern and the Life of Jesus', Protocol of the 25th Colloquy, Berkeley, Calif., The Center for Hermeneutical Studies in Hellenistic and Modern Culture, 1977.

Elder, Hero, *Whom Say Men That I Am?* (London: Charles Garner & Co., 1980).

Eliade, Mircea, 'Archaic Myth and Historical Man', in *Philosophy of Religion* by Norbert Schedler (New York: Macmillan, 1974).

Ellwood, Robert, 'Harvest and Renewal at the Grand Shrine of Ise', in *Numen*, vol. xv, no. 3 (Nov. 1968).

Garlington, William N., 'Baha'i Bhajans', in *World Order* (winter, 1982).

Guenon, Rene, 'The Heart and the World Egg', in *Studies in Comparative Religion*, vol. 7 (1973).

Hacker, Paul, 'Zur Entwicklung der Avataralehre', in Wiener Zeitschrift fur die Kunde Sud und Ostasiens, vol. IV (1960) pp. 47–70.

Hawley, John S., 'Krishna's Cosmic Victories', in *Journal of the American Academy of Religion*, vol. 47, no. 2 (June 1979).

Hein, Norvin J., 'Early Protestant Views of Hinduism, 1600–1825', unpublished paper, Yale Divinity School, n.d.

Howell, Julia Day, 'Vehicles for the Kalki Avatar: the Experiments of A Javanese Guru in Rationalizing Ecstatic Religion', unpublished doctoral dissertation, Stanford University, 1977.

Huntington, Ronald M., 'Avataras and Yugas: an Essay in Puranic Cosmology', in *Purana*, vol. VI, no. 1 (Jan. 1964).

Katre, S. L., 'Avataras of God', in *Allahabad University Studies*, vol. 10, no. 10 (1933).

Larson, Gerald J., 'The Bhagavad Gita as Cross-Cultural Process: Toward an Analysis of the Social Locations of a Religious Text', in *Journal of the American Academy of Religion*, vol. 43, no. 4 (Dec. 1975).

Leigh, Ronald W., 'Jesus: the One-Natured God-Man', *Christian Scholar's Review*, vol. 11, no. 2 (1982).

McDermott, Robert A., 'Indian Spirituality in the West: a Bibliographical Mapping', in *Philosophy East and West*, vol. 25, no. 2, pp. 213–39.

McKnight, J. Michael, 'Kingship and Religion in India's Gupta Age: an Analysis of the Role of Vaisnavism in the Lives and Ideology of the Gupta Kings', in *Journal of the American Academy of Religion*, vol. 45, no. 2 (June 1977).

Miller, Harry, 'The Cobra, India's "Good Snake"', *National Geographic*, vol. 138, no. 3 (Sept. 1970).

Moffitt, John, 'Incarnation and Avatara: an Imaginary Conversation', *Journal of Ecumenical Studies*, vol. 14 (Spring 1977).

Neff, Dio Urmilla, 'The Legend of Herakhan Baba', in *Yoga Journal* (May–June, 1980).

Parrinder, E. G., 'Sri Aurobindo on Incarnation and the Love of God', in *Numen* (June 1964).

Quesnell, Quentin, 'Aquinas on Avatars', printed for New ERA Conference, Ft. Lauderdale, Fla, Jan. 1983.

Rexroth, Kenneth, 'The Bhagavadgita', in *Saturday Review* (2 Nov. 1968), p. 28.

Sharma, Arvind, 'Ramakrsna Paramhamsa: A study in a Mystic's Attitudes Towards Women', unpublished paper.

Smith, Wilfred Cantwell, 'The Role of Asian Studies in the American University', Plenary Address of the New York State Conference for Asian Studies, Colgate University, 10 Oct. 1975.

Sundararajan, K. R., 'The Doctrine of Incarnation According to Hinduism and Christianity', unpublished doctoral dissertation, University of Madras, Center for Advanced Study in Philosophy, 1966.

Talbert, Charles H., 'The Myth of a Descending–Ascending Redeemer in Mediterranean Antiquity', in *New Testament Studies*, vol. 22.

van Ryswyk, John, Avatar School of Philosophy, 116 Lectures (London, 1942–47).

Vaudeville, Charlotte, 'The Govardhan Myth in Northern India', in *Indo-Iranian Journal*, vol. 22, no. 1 (Jan. 1980).

Wiles, M. F., 'Does Christianity Rest on a Mistake?' in *Journal of Religious Studies*, vol. 6 (1970) pp. 69–76.

Index

225